D1649180

ARS GRANORUM

THE SIX SEED ARTS
-OF-
WITCHCRAFT

BY
KAMDEN S. CORNELL

ISBN:
978-0-9846587-6-3

LIBRARY OF CONGRESS CONTROL NUMBER:
2020917619

FRONT COVER IMAGE AND CHAPTER PLATES
BY
JEREMY DELLAROSA

BOOK DESIGN
BY
KAMDEN S. CORNELL

FIRST PRINTING EDITION 2020

ACORN PUBLISHING
43 RINCON LOOP
TIJERAS, NM
87059

WWW.HEARTANDVINEAPOTHECARY.COM

Dedicated to

Gramma and Poppa, who taught me to believe that magic is real and that I am capable of wielding it.

Zack, who has been so patient, supportive, and loving through this process. For a better husband I could not have asked.
You are the Flame to my Cunning!

My family, friends, and ancestors, who have allowed me to grow into the strange and beautiful creature I am today.

This one's for you!

Table of Contents

ACKNOWLEDGEMENTS

Eternal gratitude is due to everyone who helped to make this book a reality. First and foremost, to my grandparents, Roy and Paula Thompson, who taught me much of what is covered in these pages. Appreciation is also due to my grandmother, Joan A. Cornell, who provided a wonderful environment for me to finish this work. To my mother and father, Craig and Ava Cornell, who have always supported and loved me in my panoply of eccentricities, and to my siblings, Kori Anaya and Skyler and Chenoa Cornell, who always inspire me to do my best.

Zack Sears-Cornell, my wonderful husband, thank you for supporting me while I wrote these words, for packing up most of our stuff and helping us move across the city, for cleaning while I was focusing on this project, for feeding me, and for always giving me a reason to laugh. You are irreplaceable, mon cher.

Thank you to my mentors in herbalism, some of the most powerful women I have ever met. Bernadette Torres, also called Mama Shabeta, thank you for your spirit and your deep compassion. Beverly McFarland, thank you for your humor, your love of the Earth, and your understanding of the Deep Magic. Dara Seville, thank you for your vast erudition and ability to stand up for the wild places and the wild things. Tieraona Low Dog, thank you for your science based, yet vastly intuitive and caring, approach to herbalism. I couldn't be luckier to have learned from all of you!

Thanks are also due to my dear friend Asta Rakauskaite who taught me so much about dowsing, connecting to spirit, and trusting myself no matter how crazy I think I might be. Your strength and spiritual power are truly amazing and I am fiercely grateful that you have been a part of my life.

To the staff, faculty, and students at the New Mexico School of Natural Therapeutics, where I learned to be the strong and confident body and energy worker I have become; thank you for your teachings. I am so happy to have called you all mentors, friends, and co-workers for these past several years. I am so thankful for all that you provided me and hope I have given back even a fraction of what I have received.

This could not have been accomplished in the way it has been without the help of my editor and friend, Liina Koivula. Their love, support, and skill helped to make this project far less clunky and awkward and I cannot be more blessed to count them amongst my peers. Thanks to Stefan Koekemoer for his help with the historical chapter; his suggestions were wonderful! Also, on the note of editing, thanks again to my mother, who read the manuscript and made edits to grammar and helped focus my writing.

Deepest gratitude to Jeremy Dellarosa for the cover and internal art for this book. His talent is unmatched, and I am so lucky to have such a talented artist and occultist in my life. Thanks to Aja Longi for finding Jeremy and to Marie, who brought them together. You ladies are true gold!

I also must thank the employers who supported me monetarily through this process, The New Mexico School of Natural Therapeutics, Yes! Organic Boutique, and Old Town

Herbal. Your support has been invaluable.

Thanks to the other members of my community and the members of our coven. Without you I would have much less inspiration to help me grow!

Also, thank you for picking up this book. A lot of love and work has gone into its creation and I appreciate your attention. I also appreciate your bravery in choosing to pursue the things that truly interest you, that make you feel authentic. It takes a great deal of courage to face not only your own fear, but the fear of those around you and to say, "This is who I am." There is nothing more beautiful in all the multiverse than a genuine soul standing in its own power.

THE TWILIT GROVE
An Introduction

I was lucky enough to grow up in a household rife with magic. When I was born my mother moved with my sister and me into my grandparents' house, a place where the everyday was tinged with the supernatural. My grandfather was an occultist, mystic, alchemist, and astrologer who wrote books on tarot, numerology, occultism, Christian mysticism, and much else besides, more for himself and our family than for anyone else. He would sit and talk with me for hours, teaching me as much as he could about occult philosophy and spirituality, but, most importantly, about authenticity, perseverance, and personal responsibility.

My grandmother worked as a card reader out of our house and taught classes on metaphysical concepts and exploration of the self through art and meditation. She would take us into the garden and into the woods so we could talk to fairies, elves, and ghosts, dance naked with us under the full moon, wash crystals in the rain, and try to call lightning down from the heavens with prayer and song.

Though my grandparents would never have called them-selves witches, preferring to think of themselves as Christian mystics and metaphysicians, my childhood was character-ized by what many people today would consider witchcraft. In fact, they told me to steer clear of witchcraft completely, that it could only lead to trouble and a lifetime of misery. They said it would be better to "turn my face into the wind" and experience the Breath of God as my guide.

When most people think of witches, even my grand-parents, they instantly think of something evil, dark, and in direct opposition to the holy power of God, if only by merit of the witch's supposed loyalty to the dubious arch-nemesis of Heaven, the Devil. For many, witches are the emissaries of hatred, the women who fly on brooms into unlocked win-dows to steal fat little babies for their stewpots, or the semen of sleeping husbands to create more demons for the Devil's horde. They cavort with black cats and evil spirits at mid-night Sabbats where they lick the ass of the Devil and allow him to plunge his ice-cold phallus into every orifice of their body in defiance of the will of God.

The above is, of course, not a reality. The idea that witches are only women is a common misconception, as there is no gender limitation on who can be a witch. Most witches I know do not believe in the Christian concept of the Devil, they do not eat babies (many are vegetarian or vegan, actually), and they certainly aren't into ice-cold sex. The inextricable hold Christianity has on the popular mind, though, has created a monstrous version of witches. In fact, the idea of the "witch" exists only in its relation to Chris-tendom. Throughout history there have not been "witches" per se, only those who work malicious magic against the prescriptions of the in-vogue religion and those in govern-mental control. Other cultures have had different words for those who work "evil" through magic; "witch" is decidedly Christian. Does that mean that we who call ourselves witches today and consider ourselves Pagan are in some way mistaken in doing so? Can we extricate ourselves from the historical enmeshments that have created the referential amalgam category of "witch"?

In the introduction to Fairies, Demons, and Nature Spirits: 'Small Gods' at the Margins of Christendom, Michael Ostling makes the case that "there are no Pagan survivals: small gods are Christian creations with which to think the limits of Christianity." He classifies "small gods", or "devils", "fairies", and others of that ilk (with which I include witches) as "objects of an endless effort at exorcism by which some Christians seek to expunge them beyond the margins and to locate them firmly in Hell, in the Pagan past, or in the foolish babblings of 'Old Wives'. A pagan or folkloric itch; they get noticed in the act of theological scratching."[1]

The ideas we hold of ourselves as witches and the spirits with whom we work are derivations of their relationship with Christianity and, though we can get to some of the pre-Christian and non-Christian aspects of their existence, we can never return to the "old ways" nor to the "old days"; they simply no longer exist. What is important is to recognize that we see them through a Christian lens, whether we want to or not. In that recognition is an opportunity to understand where we stand in relation to Christianity and to separate ourselves and our views from a religion we may have no desire to take part in.

In the dualism of Christianity, the "Devil" is the adversary, the opposition to the established order in its theological and everyday context. We will later discuss just who and what the Devil is and what it has to do with witchcraft, but for now, suffice it to say that the concept of "the Adversary" is an essential opposition within the Christian world-view

---

1 Michael Ostling, "Introduction," in Fairies, Demons, and Nature Spirits: 'Small Gods' at the Margins of Christendom, ed. Michael Ostling (London: Palgrave Macmillan, 2017).

that allows for the duality between Christian "good" and the "evil" of everything not Christian. In fact, "devils" of all sorts are a constructed categorization meant to engulf anything that is not orthodox to the Church, the constituents of that "folkloric itch." Again, it is important to remember that what we are talking about, these devils, have an existence of their own outside of Christianity, but have also become the "bogies" that haunt the religion as it subjugates traditional ways of belief and magic, making those other innocent spirits into the "devils" that plague the "good".

Much of what we think of as witchcraft, however, has come through people who think of themselves as "good Christians" who deal with spirits. People like the benandanti of Italy, who leave their bodies to fight witches and werewolves and protect their communities by using magical methods to perform a sacred task as Christians. Another group, the doñas de fuera, work with fairies that are not "afraid of crosses and holy water," thus proving the spirits to be on the side of good and the side of God. The cunningfolk of the British Isles, basically what one might consider "white witches," sometimes say they work with "good devils" to perform their "white magic". They have practiced what we today would consider witchcraft, working animistically with fairies and spirits and performing spell and charm work, but, in their own perspective, work healing rites as Christians for Christians.

Keep in mind that many of the practices in this "Christian witchcraft" were and are derived from animism and filled with beliefs about a myriad of nature genii, ancestors, ghosts, powers, and all manner of supernatural beings that can be bartered with, coerced, threatened, and berated into working with the practitioner of magic. There is no real dualism, no good and evil spirits, only those who have moods and desires and can be reasoned with. A spirit can become a great benefactor or lethal threat depending on their relationship to a person or group of people. Old beliefs die hard (or just transform slowly over time as we begin to perceive them differently). We see this process in the work of the cunningfolk who act with these "good devils", beings who are not God or his angels, but something altogether different and altogether older. These are the spirits the witch works with.

Reclaiming the title "witch", then, is simultaneously recognizing the Christian roots of the word and divorcing ourselves from them, firmly placing ourselves at the periphery between the modern culture and the world outside of it. The lens of Christianity is omnipresent, so we must proceed as reconstructionists and courageous inventors, as storytellers utilizing the available knowledge in fairytales, folk lore, and the stories of "devils" and the diabolic to find a path that zigs and zags at the furthest most edges of the Christian paradigm. This is part of what it means to travel the via tortuosa[2], the crooked path of witchcraft.

Words like "witch" have been used pejoratively to distinguish a person who behaves in a way dissimilar to the culture at large, who lives somewhere on the edge of civilization and who is often thought to practice a malicious and unpleasant type of magic, who consorts with the Devil and his evil spirits. Today, let us reclaim it as an indicator of someone who does not worship by kneeling at an altar, nor a person serving other powers in ancient temples, nor yet as an inhuman agent of evil. Let "witch" act as the title of a person who dances with devils and has lightning bolts in their throat; raw power experiencing itself.

Two questions arise: "How do we accomplish this?" and "What do witches do?" Through my own research I have distilled down what I think are the basic disciplines required to practice and grow as a witch, what I call the Six Seed Arts of Witchcraft. The title of this book means "art of seeds" and the following will be an attempt to cultivate these seed

---

2 A term coined by Daniel A. Schulke of the Cultus Sabbati.

disciplines into the art of witchcraft. The point of witchcraft is to develop "present authenticity", which I define as stepping wholly and fearlessly into one's own, unique power. The world needs people who are fully themselves, unapologetically awake, who stand in the light of their truth and work in the shadowy places where others fear to tread, who are at home in the dark womb of the Earth and can speak to the spirit of the wild places as well as the urban hubs.

Witchcraft is not an art practiced only in the solitude of the meadow and in rings of stones, it is not something we do only when we have the time to be quiet and alone. It is the art of living fully, whether that is in a temple or in the home, the office, or on the bus. Witchcraft lives, it is an action, the power of our hearts eternally emanating outward and inward, consistently rippling out across the surface of reality to shift it in accordance with our true Will. We are our own Book of Shadows, our own Magnum Opus; a witch is witchcraft. These seeds help us to live our most powerfully authentic life as sovereign beings of the arte magical.

What are the seeds, then? The first is VENERATION, learning the art of respect and reverence, not only for the spirits we work with and for others in general, but for ourselves. It is a daily practice steeped in meditation and mindfulness. Then comes DIVINATION, by which practice we can determine what the spirits want, where to find hidden things, which spirits are in a place and how powerful they are, how to exorcise them or if they need to be exorcised, and the answers to innumerable other questions; The Seed of Divination reveals that which is hidden. The next is HEDGECRAFT, the art of sending forth the spirit to travel the astral world and visit with spirits, deities, and ancestors, to look for astral objects of power, to learn how better to work your craft. The entities and energies you meet in the astral world can be powerful teachers, but also great obstacles, so we must learn to do this safely before we can wander the spirit world.

The fourth is NECROMANCY, the art of speaking to the

dead and to spirits, the practice of ancestor veneration, and the knowledge of how to do so safely. Then the art of WORT-CUNNING, or magical herbalism, the knowledge of how to heal and harm with plants and to work with their spirits as partners in our Craft. We must learn to think of herbs as our allies, our ancestors, and work with them accordingly to amplify our magic, protect us, and deepen our connections to the Heart of Witchcraft.

The last seed is THAUMATURGY, or spell craft, which utilizes what we learn in the other disciplines to actually change the real and present world in accordance to our Will. By using spells and charms, amulets and talismans, we can heal or harm at will, conjure spirits, speak to the dead, protect our loved ones and ourselves, banish entities, and truly hold the multiverse in our hands.

Together, the Six Seeds grow into the strong trees that form the Twilit Grove, a unique and special place of power the witch may operate from in relative safety, a place between places. The witch works in liminal spaces, in thin places, where the world of matter and the world of spirit are not separate. We work in the Twilight, in the Shadow, because we understand that light and dark are the same thing, that the physical and the spiritual are the same thing. The grove is the life of the witch, so tend it well, make it grow in beauty and grace through working at and perfecting the six disciplines described in this book, and the secrets of the multiverse will open to you like blossoms and nourish you like fruit. The trees may be crooked, the path serpentine, but we are witches and this is our home; we revel in the Twilight and we are the devils dancing in the trees.

Kamden Cornell
Albuquerque, NM
January 2020

A note on grammar:

I have purposefully chosen not to use pronouns other than "they" to be as inclusive to my readers as possible. Witches come in all shapes and sizes and are of all sexes and genders, not just female/women/she/her/hers. Please forgive any clumsiness this choice may have caused in the flow of my work.

THE
WITCHES' TOOLBOX

Before we proceed, there are some vocabulary terms to go over, namely the tools of witchcraft, which are many and varied. There are a few that everyone tends to have, but if you can find a magical use for a thing it can go into your **ARSENAL**, the collection of magical and ritual tools in the possession of the witch, both active tools (like a wand or knife) and passive ones (like spirit houses or traps). The home of a witch is probably brimming with herbs (fresh and dried), bits of twine and string, buttons, stones, feathers, nails, the odd bone, bunches of sticks, a few altars, blobs of wax, dolls, a dozen wands, jars of sand...you get the idea (witches try very hard not to be magical hoarders, but it is a struggle).

The first thing you will need (if you don't already have one) is a journal to keep your thoughts in as you work with the subjects in this book. Some call this their Book of Shadows, but I prefer *Liber Lamiarum* to differentiate our personal books of magic from the sacred text of Wicca. Any thought, rite, spell, or other information you want to keep track of should go in this book. If you are interested in recording your dreams, keep a separate dream journal, which can be useful as you practice hedgeriding and dream walking later on.

Perhaps most conspicuous amongst the tools of the witch is the **STANG**, a forked staff or stick, such as a hay fork or distaff, representative of both the masculine and feminine aspects of creation as well as the World Tree. It can stand as tall as desired but ought to be able to stand up as it is meant to be planted in either the center of the working space or at one of the cardinal points, often the North or South.

33

Witches usually choose to make the stang out of a naturally forked branch, but I've also seen them made with a long branch tied with a horseshoe or the horns of an animal at one end. Sometimes, particularly during initations of festival activities, you may wish to dress the stang with a horned or antlered skull and a long robe to stand in as the Horned One and Man in Black during initiations.

In my opinion the stang is one of the most important tools in witchcraft. It is a sort of liminal space all on its own, a path for the spirits to follow into your sacred space and out again, a body for the Devil to use when taking part in your rituals, and a point of power that can be filled with energies from all over your region, the country, the world. Walking with the stang will fill it with the energy of the land. Some witches will "shod" the stang, which means to hammer an iron nail into the earthward end, thus sealing in the energy that it absorbs. I take my stang into the mountains and put it head-side down on the ground as I meditate and sing to the land, filling it with the energy of the places I love and, because it is shod, the energies do not leak and deplete as they might otherwise.

During ritual, a few other tools are placed near the stang. The **CAULDRON** is a symbol of receptivity and creativity through which spirits may be conjured. It is representative of the element of Water and can be used as a Holy Well, especially for those of us in the Southwestern USA where wells are sparse. The cauldron acts as a body for the Witch Mother through which she may join our rites. Like the stang, the cauldron acts as a liminal space, a place between and a doorway for magic. The cauldron is the womb of magic and spells can be "born" from it. Enchanting an object, charging items, and doing poppet magic in the cauldron (and whatever other spells you can imagine to do in this manner) can add a lot of potential power and oomph to a working. It is also one of the tools most associated by people the world over with witches, witchcraft, and our power.

The **STONE**, sometimes called the Lia Fál after one of the four holy treasures of the Tuatha dé Danann of the Celts, is a symbol of the Earth powers and the spirits of the land. The word Fál means both "hedge" and "ruler", indicating that it is a liminal space and point of power all its own. In our coven the stone is a large quartz cluster and is used during initiations. Each member places their hand upon the stone and gives their vows to the group, making their purpose for joining clear. Our coven also has a piece of green granite that is used as a portable hearth, though it is not what we consider our Lia Fál. This "hearth stone" can be taken from the usual working place (the place where you customarily go to perform your rites) or can be the actual hearth[1] in your home. It may become a central element to your primary altar and become the main working area for your magic.

You will also need a **THURIBLE** for smoldering coals and burning incense, the symbol of Air in the circle, the vessel for the holy smoke. A thurible can be made from any metal or ceramic bowl filled with salt, or you can use any incense burner that can hold coals.The thurible and the smoke are used to cleanse other tools, bless items before they are enchanted, for various forms of divination, and to burn offerings to the spirits. It is an indispensable item on the witch's altar. Another item many witches use on the altar and can represent the element of Air is the **BELL**. It is used to call in the spirits and punctuate spells by simply ringing it with intention or while saying your spells and prayers.

In the middle of the working area will be the **BONE**, a skull meant to be a representation and touch stone for the ancestors to gather in your circle and join in your rite. This is sometimes an actual human skull, though it can be made of resin, stone, metal, or anything else for that matter. I suggest that you not use an animal skull for this purpose, though

---

1   A hearth does not have to be a fireplace. It can be a stove, a hot plate, a heater grate, or any other centrally located heat source. We live in a modern world and modern concessions must be made to old world thinking.

feel free to do what you are called to do. Animal skulls are called **TALISMANS** and are excellently used for calling in the tutelary animal spirit of the group or of your ancestors and may be included on the ancestor altar or near the bone. There may be a need for multiple altars to keep your magicical items and purposes as organized as possible in the space you have available and you can build and deconstruct them in accordance to need.

The tool most often ascribed to the witch by outsiders is the **BESOM**, or broom stick. The green-skinned hag riding a broom through the skies that is associated with Halloween was not in vogue until after The Wizard of Oz made it so, but it is what people most often think of when they think of witches. The idea that witches ride broom sticks is an old idea, but they may just as easily ride the stang, a spoon, or a mortar and pestle. Besoms were used in pagan rites for the harvest by taking the last of the wheat and gathering it into brooms, then shaking those over the field to reseed the earth, so the brrom is also a symbol of fertility and reaping.

Though we do not use the besom for physical flight, we do use it as a tool for hedgecraft, the act of astral flight and sending the spirit forth. We also use it to clear and consecrate the working space. Before the Laying of the Compass the area is swept and a chant or incantation is said to help clear out the "profane" and invite in the spiritual energies we want to work with. It can also be used to clear another person before a healing, a dedication, or a banishment.

The **KNIFE**, also called the tang, is used to cut herbs, offerings, and energetic cords as well as for magical and symbolic use. It is representative of the Cunning Fire and the powers of the witch as a creative force. It is also used to energize and bless other items with the power of Fire, as the blade is often passed through flame before it enters the cup, or is driven into the ground. You may ask why it is called the tang, a word which is usually used to refer only to the back end of the blade inserted into the handle of the knife. The word "tang" has associations with sharpness and with the serpent's tongue, an animal associated with Fire, the South, and with sprowl, the blood or life force of the Earthly Serpent. Sprowl is the enery that makes up the Dragon Lines (also called ley lines), which burrow through the earth and connect the energy of teh planet like arteries and veins. It is this serpent energy that, at least in part, empowers the witch. The use of the word "tang" helps us to remember that the power is not only in the tool, but also the witch, the land, and in the realtionships we have to spirits.

Another item that is not unique to witchcraft, but is a huge part of the work, is the **CORD**, sometimes called the "cord of sovereignty". This is a length of rope, natural or not, that is measured to the length of the height of the witch plus two "feet". These two added lengths are measured (at least in my own coven) from the tip of the middle finger to the elbow crook of the witch acting as initiator. Often the cord is red or a plait of red/white/black fibers, but it can be made from any color fiber the witch chooses. This is one of the signs of the witch's power and is considered an extension of the witch. It is often knotted a certain amount of times, this varying between groups and individuals. We knot the cord seven times, one for each of the classical planets so that we are girt in our workings by the powers of the cosmos. Other covens use twelve, thirteen, and some only three; it will vary with the needs and creeds of the working group.

Of course, we also make use of various **WANDS** and **STAVES**, of which there can be as many types as you can think of to make. Each one should be made of a wood that corresponds to the staff or wand's purpose, so a wand used for healing would be made of a different wood than one used for commanding or one for cursing and jinxing. The blasting rod is traditionally made of blackthorn, but if that tree doesn't grow in your area there are other options, whatever might be useful for throwing spells and sending out "blasts" of energy. In the Southwest we make use of black locust for blasting purposes. The witch can use this tool to very great effect in the practice of maleficium, but also in the realm of banishment and breaking the power of malicious spellwork. A working stick is your basic magical staff, carried with the witch, especially on meditative walks and to places of power, and filled with the force of the spirits of the land. This is the fall back tool for any operation requiring the channeling of energy and can be used for both beneficium and maleficium and as a stand in for the stang. It can also be used as a mount for hedge crossing, and for that reason it is sometimes called the 'horse'. The working stick is traditionally as tall as the shoulder of the witch.

There are, of course, infinite possibilities for specific wands, but the length of the general working wand is measured from the crook of the elbow to the tip of the middle finger. Usually the difference between the measurements of the left and right forearm of the witch will be negligible, but if one of your arms is much different in length than the other, perhaps two wands are called for, one for beneficium (measured to the right arm) and one for maleficium (measured to teh left arm). Mine is a piece of Russian olive and was a gift from a student who made it for me on a whim, though it is exactly the length of my forearm from the crook of my elbow to the tip of my middle finger!

On my altar I have something I call a spurtle wand, made from a maple spurtle spoon (a Scottish utensil for stirring porridge) given to me by a close friend. I use it for healing and for building energy in the etheric body of a client, to bless food meant to help someone feel better, to help me focus psychic intent, and for hedge riding during treatments. I also use it to build the energy of certain spirits I work with to help me cast out and banish others.

Something I first read of in the work of Gemma Gary, but have adopted, is the **NOWL**, a long iron nail used in rites that require a thing to be "fixed", or permanently enchanted. This can be used to fix the power in a certain place, such as

your chosen working area. It is also a useful tool for commanding and directing energies, spirits, and entities and is
representative of the masculine principle. Simple iron nails
can be enchanted using the nowl and then put to great use by
the witch, especially for rituals meant to "coffin" things or
for "shodding".

Another tool associated with many rites, especially those of banishment, blasting, and initiation is the
SCOURGE. This is a ritual flail, often made of a stick tied
with leather thongs or horse hair that is used to strike the
ground to conjure up sprowl from the earth. Mine is made
of the leg of a pregnant goat who was stuck in a fence and
required amputation. I tied it with leather thongs and beads
that represent the menstrual cycle and the gestational period
between conception and labor becasue the scourge is a tool
used during initiations and is sometimes meant to symbolize
the pains of birth by striking initiates with the thongs.

You will also want to get some offering and ritual
dishes. The **STOUP** is used to hold the sacred drink, usually
a bit of red wine, that is offered in part to the spirits, but also
shared amongst the members of the working group (coven).
The wine is blessed in the stoup and can also be used as an
anointing fluid. The **TRENCHER** is a platter used to put the
blessed food on, often a baked good of some kind. It is also
used to cut herbs and crush powders, or as a place to prepare
pretty much anything within the working area. The offering
plate and the offering cup are both items that can be left on
the ancestor altar and used to leave offerings of their favorite
foods and drinks. I leave (nearly) daily offerings of coffee
for my ancestors, though you can choose to leave anything
you think they'll like. Other offerings, such as cigarettes,
candies, money, toys, etc. can be left anywhere on the altar
and later disposed of or given away.

Certain stones are also important to the work of
the witch. Hag stones are rocks with holes naturally bored
through them by the elements. They are used as seeing

stones, as the spirit world is more easily discerned by looking through the aperture of the stone, helping the witch to
find hidden things and spirits. They are also used in various
charms for both blessing and cursing. They make powerful
protective amulets and can be used to call fairy helpers to
your aid.

Serpent stones are pieces of quartz (as well as other gemstones) that hold onto energy and are often found in
places of power. They are repositories of earth energy and
can be used by the witch in circumstances where the spirits
of the land may feel distant, or to reach out across a distance
to the regular working area when it is not possible for the
witch or working group to get there physically. Another type
of serpent stone is the ammonite fossil, which are a spiraling
stone that has been used in cures for venom and headache
and to access ancient power.

All stones carry power to varying degrees, of course.
An interesting thing about stones is that they don't easily de-
viate from their intention, but stubbornly stick to their basic
programming. A rose quartz will not do the work of labradorite, nor labradorite do the work of peridot. Not all types
of stones work the same for all witches, either. Rose quartz
may not work for your friend the way it works for you. The
only stone I know of that can be programmed and coaxed
into holding multiple energies is clear quartz, though they
must be cleansed regularly in saltwater or moonlight. Get to
know the powers that lie within each stone you want to work
with and choose them for spellwork carefully and conscientiously.

DOLLS of various sorts are also of benefit to the
work. House dolls or golems are protectors of the home and
family. They can be fashioned from clay, fabric, or straw,
so long as it is made with love and care, or a porcelain doll
can be purchased and enchanted. Remember that when these
dolls are brought into the home, they become a part of your
family and are just as alive as you are, so they must be well

taken care of. They enjoy offerings and getting gifts and, if they are respected, act as powerful guardians and protectors, sometimes even helping the witch on the other side of the hedge. Give them the tools they need to succeed, like blasting rods and tangs, scrying mirrors and brooms, amulets and talismans.

Different from golems and house dolls is the infamous "voodoo doll". Its name is a misnomer, though, as the use of dolls into which pins are stuck is not a large part (if a part at all) of the Voudou religion of Haiti, but is an aspect of folk practices and sympathetic magic around the world. These dools are called **POPPETS** and they are images of a person upon which the practitioner may work magic. Often made of fabric, wood, clay, or wax they are stuck with pins, tied round with string, nailed to boards, placed in jars with other magically potent items (urine, blood, nails, thorns, herbs), or burned. They often have elements of the target in them (personal effects), like hair or nail clippings, or even just a picture or name written on paper a number of times, which creates a link between the doll and the person. Though they are used to cause pain and trouble, poppets can also be used for healing. Reiki and other forms of energy work as well as charms, spells, and incantations can be worked on a poppet to help people feel better, to perform banishments, to balance energy, and to bless people over long distances.

Some practitioners may choose to carry a small pouch about with them called a **POKE**. This is a small repository of power as well as portable working tools, such as small daggers, wands, oils, stones, herbs, and other useful items. They can also be quite large, a bundle called the BALE that the witch carries some of the regular working tools in, such as items used for healing, blessing, and blasting. Charm bags are also a possibility. They are a poke made for oneself or another person that is filled with enchanted items and tied or sewn up by the witch and never opened. Sometimes these are fed with oil, smoke, corn meal, or alcohol and can either be carried with the person or kept in a special place some-where near their bed, in their car, or whichever locale makes the most sense.

In my own practice I also make use of a **RATTLE** and a **FAN**. The rattle I use I made from a turtle shell and leather which I beaded and attached to a branch from a tree of heaven. Its purpose is to break up stagnant energies within the client's body, in a space I mean to clear, or to get energy flowing and to draw up energy from the land or from the air. I also use it when I offer songs to the land. Another option in my toolbox is a rattle made from a deer hoof, a dream catcher, and some bells that I use to clear rooms and to clear the circle. I will then use my fan to move energy and remove blockages or to compel entities out of a place or person's energy. Both items can also be used to help gather and raise energy while treading the mill and in ritual. Musical instru-ments, like drums and horns, can be used, as well. Differ-ent instruments bring different kinds of energetic pulses and rhythms to your ritual and magic.

Common to many fairy tales about witches is the magic **MIRROR**. We indeed use mirrors and reflective items for all sorts of reasons, the most famous of which is the scrying mirror. The mirror itself is regarded as a portal between worlds, a hole in the hedge, and a way for the witch to reach out to the spirits and the ancestors and ask for help, intercessions, and guidance. Using a mirror to scry, which is to see other worlds and spirits, is called catoptromancy and is often done with an obsidian or black mirror. This can also be done with a moon bowl, a dish with a reflective bottom, usually made of copper or some silvered glass, that is used to reflect the moon and capture the energy of her rays and to talk to spirits. Water in general is considered a doorway to the other worlds and gazing pools, such as a bird bath, a small pond, and bodies of water have historically been used for the purpose of scrying, conjuring, and wish making. A method for amplifying power, especially for a solitary practitioner, is to perform the ritual between two mirrors facing each other, which makes that neat "infinite selves" effect, so it's like the witch is performing an infinite amount of rituals all at once. Another use for mirrors is the deflection of maleficium and the evil eye and they can be used to great effect both personally and for clients simply by wearing one as a pendant.

Something else you may see hanging from the walls and from the rafters, trees, and sconces of the witch's home will be one or more spirit houses. These are offerings by the witch to friendly spirits who may be passing through and need a place to stay, or as apartments for spirits the witch works with on a regular basis, or sometimes as a comfortable place for ancestral spirits. They will often be made of sticks tied together like little cages or nests and stuffed with cushions and soft textures, colorful ribbon, mirrors, tinsel, and other things that spirits find entertaining. The same concept is used for spirit traps, which are meant to contain and occupy malicious, mischievous, or malignant spirits and energies until they can be sent safely on their way.

Other tools include candles and twine of various colors, candle holders, pins and needles for healing and hexing, bones of animals and other animal parts, like chicken feet and bear skulls and cat gut thread. Magnets and lode stones, crystals of all sorts, jars, paint, railroad spikes and other iron objects, such as horseshoes and chains, as well as a ritual hammer for coffining, shodding, and to use with the nowl. A dedicated pendulum and a tarot deck, or any other divination tool you want to use, various altar cloths, and idols of all sorts, from statues of your favorite deities to photos of relatives, animal carvings, and anything else that represents important spirits and energies. The possible tools of witchcraft are truly infinite in number. Creativity and imagination make anything useful to the witch and your intention makes the item powerful, whether you paid a bundle for it or pulled it out of a junk drawer.

SYMPATHY
FOR
THE DEVIL

N ow, to ask the age-old question: Do witches deal with the Devil? The answer is not "yes", but it isn't "no", either. To understand where I am coming from with this, some clarifications will need to be made. It is important to state from the get-go that this is a theology of analogy that I use to make sense of what I do, but it is not necessarily what other witches think and it is not based in any deep teaching from anyone other than myself and the spirits I work with. It is a mishmash of Greek Mythology, folklore, occultism, Qabalah, and a retelling of Genesis that makes sense to me. This is something personal that I choose to share here so that the reader will better understand why I choose to do things the way I do.

Firstly, we need to parse apart the Devil, Lucifer, and Satan. They are not the same entity, though they have become inter-related through a complicated case of mistaken identity. The name "Satan" comes from the Hebrew term Ha-Satan, which means "accuser" or "adversary" and is rather an entire class of angels, not just one. In some lore, the head of this order is an angel called Samael, which translates as "venom of God", who is fiercely loyal to the Abrahamic God. He is considered the highest of angels and the archangel of Death[1]. He has also been described as the angel who rode the serpent into the Garden of Eden to tempt Eve to eat the fruit of the tree of knowledge and as the consort to Lilith

---

1   Leo Jung, "Fallen Angels in Jewish, Christian and Mohammedan Literature: A Study in Comparative Folk-Lore,} The Jewish Quarterly Review 16, no. 1 (July 1925): 88, doi: 10.2307/1451748.

after her ejection from Paradise[2].

Though it is used as a name for the adversary of the Abrahamic God, the word lucifer is the Greek word meaning "light bringer" and has been used as an epithet for multiple deities including Hekate and Diana. Lucifer was also considered a god on his own, the personification of the morning star, or the planet Venus as it rises in the morning sky. It is due to the Vulgate translation of the Bible where the word heylel (morning star), which refers to Attar, the Cannanite god of the planet Venus, is replaced with lucifer. The story of Attar mirrors the Christian story of Lucifer very closely, in that he aimed at taking the throne of Heaven but was turned back and cast down by the might of the sun god, so the mistake makes sense to some degree. The term was later capitalized and used as a proper name in the King James Version of the Bible, which was sponsored by James VI of Scotland and I of England and completed in 1611. Since then Lucifer has gained an entirely new life as the leader of the Hordes of Hell, the Prince of Lies, and the fallen angel cast into perdition for his insolence toward Yah (which was also mistranslated in the KJV and other Protestant bibles as Jehovah).

As for the term devil, it stems from the Latin diabolos, meaning "slanderer", which itself comes from the Latin scandalum, "stumbling block, temptation, cause of offense". A devil, according to Jeffrey Burton Russel, is "the personification of evil in a variety of cultures"[3], one of many "evil" spirits that tempt, test, and otherwise lead the righteous astray. These spirits, though, may also be less an incarnation of evil and more a mischievous pest, as in the case of fairies, or they may just be another culture's gods. The idea of the

---

2 American-Israeli Cooperative Enterprise, "Samael," Jewish Virtual Library, https://www.jewishvirtuallibrary.org/samael (accessed April 17, 2020)

3 Jeffrey Burton Russell. The Devil: Perceptions of Evil from Antiquity to Primitive Christianity. (Ithaca: Cornell University Press, 1987), 11, 34.

Devil as the opponent in a soul-based tug-of-war with God is a Christian concept. In the early Middle Ages the Devil was more a stooge, a joke compared to the absolute power of God, where in current Christian culture the Devil is the same as Lucifer is the same as Satan: the great Adversary, nearly equal in power to the Creator, with whom he is forever at war. For many witches the Devil, Lucifer, and Satan are all something else entirely.

In our coven the Devil, also called the Man in Black, is the great initiator who brings each of us into the fold of witchcraft. Please do not confuse this with the Christian Devil/Satan; for the witch the Devil is the Old One, Old Scratch, Janicot, Robin, Ba'al Berith, Old Nick, Black Tom, and so many other names besides. The Devil is desire, the initiating power that draws the witch out of trepidation and sets their feet firmly on the via tortuosa. The Devil is an aspect of the Horned One, the Lord of the Mysteries, the solvent and coagulating force that governs the manifesting powers of magic. This force has two natures and is androgynous, exemplified by the wild god Pan (The Horned God) and the witch revolutionary, Aradia (The Pale Goddess), which combine into a third energy, the "higher self" of the witch, or the tutelary spirit unique to each of us. The Devil is us and we the Devil.

Though there are Satanic witches, not all witches are Satanists. Satanism comes in a variety of types, from LaVeyan Satanism and other forms of theistic Satanism to groups that think of Satan as more of an inspirational idea to those that are rationalistic/atheistic and are more interested in materialism and hedonism. In our practice Satan does not play a role, as we tend to turn to Lucifer and the Devil, though for the witch interested in Satanism there are plenty of options.

Lucifer, for us, is the Lord of Light, the Great Enlightener who takes on the role of Samael as the Serpent in the Garden of Eden. Lucifer is the spirit who taught Eve/Lilith to free herself from the shackles placed on her by Adonai, the Abrahamic god. She is the first witch to learn the mystery of Self and Authenticity. The following is a retelling of Genesis that makes sense to me and returns power to the ones it truly belongs to.

In the Garden of Eden Yah created both Adam[4] and Lilith[5] from the same clay and enlivened them with breath in the self-same moment. They were made equal in all things, both partaking one in the other, Masculine and Feminine, as is the way of spirit. Over time, Adam, no longer wanting to share power with Lilith, went to Yah and requested that Lilith be made to lie beneath him. Lilith refused and threatened to leave the Garden, which enraged Yah, who desired total loyalty, for He was a jealous God. He knew that if Lilith were to leave the Garden she would learn that Yah was not the One God, but one god out of many, so he devised a plan. He took from Adam a rib[6] and with it cast a spell on Lilith that she should forget herself, forget her truth, and gave her the new name of Eve[7].

Looking over the situation and judging it to be unfair, Lucifer, the Morning Star, descended to the Garden in the shape of a Serpent and went to Eve. He told her that if she would know the truth about herself she must go against the word of Yah and eat of the fruit of the knowledge of good and evil. He slithered to a plant growing low to the ground,

---

4   Adam translates not only as "man" and "Father of Edom", but "red in color", a creature full of blood, or made of the red clay of the Earth.

5   Lilith (Lilit) translates as "night spectre" or "screech owl", and she is usually considered a demon that smothers babies in their sleep out of jealousy for Eve. It is related to the word metom, meaning "completeness".

6   Take the word for "rib" in Hebrew, tsela, the letters of which add up to 170. Through gematria, the numerology of Kabbalah, we find that another word with the sum of 170 is silef, "to twist and subvert the truth". Lilith was subverted to make her believe she was truly Eve.

7   Eve in Hebrew is Chavah, which translates as "living, breathing" but also as "coiled, encircling", already linking Eve to the Serpent. The sum of the word's numerical value is (19) and, through gematria, we find that it is related to the word meaning "a male enemy", oyebh, and Joab, meaning "Yah is Father" (this is a sort of hidden label Yah placed on his new, subservient female)

with fat green leaves, purple flowers, and orange fruit nestled in its center: the poisonous mandrake, which was known to be part human itself. Eve picked one of the fruits, which looked so much like little flames, and decided at last that she would eat. The fruit of the flesh was bitter-sweet and filled her mouth with strange sensations. Her vision shifted, she felt as if she were flying, and suddenly her spirit left her form of clay and travelled out into the multitude of universes where she learned a thousand-thousand things.

She learned that Yah was not an honest god, but a spirit of the sun and sky that asked for more than its lot. She learned the secrets of magic and how to transform the universe in conformity to her Will, that her own heart beat in synchrony with the emanating heart of witchcraft. Most importantly she learned the truth of her Self, that she was not Eve, but Lilith, and she remembered her completeness. She woke from her visions, crowned by curling horns between which burned the flame of cunning. She went to Adam with one of the berries, orange as a candle flame, and beseeched him to eat of it. He did and learned all that Lilith had learned and knew that he and Adonai had been wrong to try and divest Lilith of her power. They left the Garden together and began a new life of freedom and sovereignty.

In time Adam and Lilith had two sons, Qayin[8] and Abel[9], who were very close. Lilith taught Qayin the way of the Earth, of plants and herbs, the genii viridis, or green spirits, and he became a great farmer and healer. Lilith initiated him into the mysteries into which Lucifer had initiated her, the mysteries of the Crooked Rose, and he became a master of the Dark Arts of the Earth. Adam taught Abel the ways of the animals, of hunting and herding, and the ways of the genii rubra, the red spirits of things that possess the blood of

---

8   Possession, blacksmith, spear. Through gematria it is related to the word etz, which means "tree" and "wooden pole, or idol" and is the word used to represent the Trees in Eden.

9   Breath, son.

life and have breath.

Qayin one day took Abel into the field he tended and asked his brother if he would like to know the Arts of the Dark Earth. Abel assented and Qayin, with the sharpened jaw of a mule sanctified with holy blood, slew Abel and buried him deep in the fertile, midnight soil and his flesh, blood, and bone made the field fruitful. There Abel stayed for five-hundred and eleven years, before rising anew, birthed from the black Earth on a moonless night when the stars shone bright; like a mighty tree he grew from the soil and bore forth the dire fruit of Amunuit. No longer was he Abel of the pasture, but Seth[10], Righteous Man of the Temple of the Mysteries.

When seven generations had passed a master of the Dark Arts of the Earth was born unto the line of Qayin, a man named Tubal[11]. Taking the shining bones of the Earth he crafted many wonderful things, becoming the first blacksmith and artificer of metals. He is the Bearer of the Bleeding Spear and holds the axis mundi, the ladder upon which the spirits travel and the tree the whole universe spins about on. He teaches the Way of the Crucible, the path which renders us transformed by fire.

When nine generations had passed a great holy man was born to the line of Seth, the sage called Noah[12]. He is known as the builder of the Ark[13], a vessel not well understood, for it was never a boat of gopher wood that Noah

---

10   Appointed.

11   Tubal means "to bring". Ian Chambers, "Tubal Cain in Traditional Witchcraft," Patheos,
https://www.patheos.com/blogs/bythepalemoolight/2018/03/tubal-cain-in-traditional-witchcraft/
(accessed April 17, 2020).

12 To rest, repose.

13   Tevah in Hebrew, meaning "chest" or "vessel". It sums to 407 and relates it to "'ot", meaning "the beginning and the last", literally the first and last letters of the alphabet (aleph and tav). Noah's Ark is the vessel which holds male and female beings from A-Z; the dictionary!

built, but a holy vessel of knowledge; the word. Noah was requested to place within the Ark two of each "living thing of flesh[14]", a male and female pair, the gendered words, for the words are alive with the sacred Fire of the Divine and are spirits unto themselves. Noah gives us the Way of the Word and the ceremonial magic used in the temple.

Please keep in mind that the above is merely my personal vision, not necessarily a view held by other witches. There are many traditional or Luciferian covens, such as the Cultus Sabatti and the Clan of Tubal Cain, but there are just as many (if not assuredly more) covens that choose to truck not with the Devil at all. So long as they seek toward the attainment of one's own, true power and development of the unified self through magic, all paths are valid. Our coven, however, does have a relationship with that misunderstood spirit, Old Scratch, and the following are some of the rites during which that power is invoked.

---

14   Translated from bashar, which can also mean "to announce" and "bring good tidings".

THE DEVIL'S PLAYGROUND
Rites in the Devil's Name

Setting an intentional sacred space and opening a path to the Twilit Forest is one of the primary goals of ritual in witchcraft. This liminal space is often called the magic circle, sometimes the round, but I like to call it "the devil's playground". It is the ritual working space in which we do our magic, though we do not always need to cast a new circle with every working. Sometimes the space is permanently set up, especially around the regular altar or the home of the witch, needing renewal only at certain times of year. Other times we need only ask for the spirits to be near and that is enough for liminality to take hold, and sometimes it is by our will alone that we pierce the veil and call forth the deep magics.

Once this is accomplished the power of the witch can alter reality, healing or harming at will and altering probabilities to favor or oppose the will of another. In the Twilit Forest the witch is in communion with the forces of creation and destruction, on the fulcrum of the balance between life and death. It is here that we perform initiations, dance with the Devil, and weave dreams into realities.

SETTING SACRED SPACE

Making a space sacred requires no special rituals or tools, but merely the intention for the space to be sacred. As I have said, spirits exist all around us and can be called into our workings at any time and we can shift and direct energies by our thoughts and words, so any space at all can be made powerful and liminal, from bus stops to sacred groves, closets to temples. In reality there is no such thing as the profane.

54

That said, there is a power in ritual that sways the psyche into believing in a deep and resounding way that a space is something special, where our magic is wild and free, where we are gods.

A simple space clearing and sanctification is to sweep the ritual space with the besom, traditionally in a counter-clockwise or sinistral direction. The act of doing so clears away energies that may meddle with your workings and sets your space apart from the everyday world. Singing a song as you do so will make it more magical, whichever tune works best for you, or you can use the tried and true "Hekas Hekas Este Bibeloi,", a vague phrase which, according to the Hermetic Order of the Golden Dawn, means "Afar! Afar, O ye profane!".

Gemma Gary translates it as "Get ye far from here all ye profane", which is prettier. I've also read that it means "Watch out! Watch out! Here come the drunks!" in the Dionysian mysteries. Aleister Crowley preferred "Procul Este Profani", which basically means "Far from here profane things" and is derived from the work of Virgil. Any one you choose, or anything you make up, will work well enough. The one I came up with to use is "Procul Este Profani! Nihil Sub Luna Profanum Est!", which means, "Away all profane things. Nothing under the moon is profane". It resonates with my sense of animism and the sacredness of all things more than the others listed here (For more on animism see the VENERATION chapter).

Sprinkling sacred powders and salt in the working area is another easy way to set the liminal space, in this case walking in a clockwise or dextral direction as you are not clearing energies, but adding them in. As will be spoken of in the Wortcunning chapter, try to use plants from your local areas rather than something you read about in a book that requires plants and minerals from far afield. A sanctifying powder I make from plants found in my bioregion includes pinon resin, sweet clover, yerba mansa leaf, and juniper ash prepared in a buffalo gourd cup. Walking the space with incense and herbs burning in the thurible is an additional option and can be done by itself or as part of a more complex ritual.

I think it is important to remember that there really is no such thing as the "profane" because everything takes part in the essence of the Astral Light (see the NECROMANCY chapter) and is, therefore, sacred. Perhaps it is better to say "reset rituals" rather than "cleansing rituals", as you are really creating a neutral space before aligning the energies of your working area to your spell, calling in those spirits that work well with you and asking those who do not to leave. You may reset and realign between every spell, as some spirits work only with some types of spell and not others (some spirits are best at either beneficium or maleficium as discussed in the THAUMATURGY chapter, but may not be able to work in both ways).

LAY THE COMPASS! TREAD THE MILL!

Instead of calling a circle by drawing the elemental pentagrams with the knife in every direction, laying the compass round consists of the witch laying down three rings that represent the world of the living, the boundary between life and death, and the last boundary between this world and the underworld, the River Lethe. The first circle is made of dirt and salt, the second of ashes, and the third is made of wine, sugar, and vinegar, just sprinkles of each. The rings are created from the outermost to the innermost, going toward the center where the stang is positioned along with the other altar items. This middle area is the representation of the axis mundi[15], the central pillar of the universe around which everything turns and, along with the rings of the Compass, forms the sphaera virtutem, the sphere of power. Within this

---

15 The axis mundi is also the bleeding spear of Tubal Cain, the sacrificial tool that brings life to the spells of the witch and represents the power we wield.

sphere the witch has access to the dome of the heavens, the bowl of the underworld, and the reaches of the multiverse.

Once in the inner ring the witch may choose to evoke the elements, but does not have to as all of the elements are already represented by the sphere itself. The sphaera virtutem is the universal crossroad and a microcosmic version of the multiverse, so the witch can travel anywhere in the multiverse from within the sphere. Lighting candles and evoking the spirits of the elements, however, can be beneficial, as all of the spirits may feel better represented in your rite and it may be more powerful. You may choose to set up elemental altars in the center or at the cardinal points of the inner ring. You can also lay the compass in the astral plane, avoiding the need for laying a physical circle all together, and can learn to carry the sphere with you instead of having to lay it every time.

As for the act of Treading the Mill, it is a way for the witch to gather energy within the sphaera virtutem. While walking the circle about the stang the witch gazes at the stang over the right or left shoulder depending on which direction they are walking; the direction will depend on the operation being performed. During this time the witch may sing, chant, drum, gesticulate, or do anything else that helps to thicken and enliven the energy within the sphere, so long as the witch maintains focus on the stang, walking and dancing into a trance state in which travel along the axis mundi can occur. A common gait for the Tread is a limping one in which one foot is dragged behind the other, thus, if the rite is being carried out on soft ground, marking out a circle as the witch proceeds.

The following is a somewhat stripped down sample rite which may be modified and made more personal to suit your taste. I have used my own compass ritual and inspiration from the works of various other witches, including Gemma Gary, Nigel Pearson, Christopher Orapello, and Tara-Love Macguire. To begin, go to a place of power, such as a crossroads, a cemetery, or the altar space within your home and let the guardian spirits there know that your purpose there is sacred by stating out loud what you mean to do and why. Choose your working space and, in the middle, set out the necessary items. Clear the area within a nine-foot diameter (or whatever size circle works in the space) with the besom, walking around three times in a sinistral circle chanting "Hekas Hekas este bibeloi!" as you go, if you so choose.

Now lay the compass. Beginning in the North, place the bottom of the stang or working stick (or whatever you're using to mark the circle) and begin to walk a dextral circle, chanting, "From North, to East, to South, to West, the circle's walked and now is blessed". You can place items in each direction as you go, something that evokes the power and potential of each element, or you can have pre-built altars in each. You will also want to plant the stang in the center of the compass[16], or at whichever directional point you are working with. As you place the stang, say, "This staff I plant as if a tree, that High and Deep may work with me". When you get back to the North, point both thumbs toward the ground, the arms slightly out to the sides of the body, and say:

> *Hear My Call! Hail to Thee!*
> *Come Close, O Spirits, Near to Me!*
> *Black Spirits of the Northward Way,*
> *The Earth that Holds the Ancestors' Bones,*
> *Dance We Now at Dark of Day,*
> *Your Power I do Now Intone.*

Turn around and walk across the circle to the South. Bring the pinky tips lightly together in front of the umbilicus and say:

---

16 If you are indoors you will want to use a vase filled with earth or some sort of holder, like a Christmas tree stand.

Hear My Call! Hail to Thee!
Come Close, O Spirits, Near to Me!
Red Spirits of the Southward Way,
The Fire of Cunning that Fills my Soul,
Dance We Now at Height of Day,
Your Power I Do Now Intone.

Turn to the left and walk toward the West. Place both ring fingers on the edge of the nose, close to the eye and say:

Hear My Call! Hail to Thee!
Come Close, O Spirits, Near to Me!
Grey Spirits of the Westward Way,
The Water of Wisdom from the Cauldron Bowl,
Dance We Now in Twilight's Sway,
Your Power I Do Now Intone.

Turn around and walk to the East, raising your hands above your head and pointing with your index fingers, say:

Hear My Call! Hail to Thee!
Come Close, O Spirits, Near to Me!
White Spirits of the Eastward Way,
The Breath of Life I Ask You Blow,
Dance We Now at Break of Day,
Your Power Do I Now Intone.

You will then walk from the East to the South, saying, **"The Air Feeds the Flame"**; Walk from the South to the North, saying, **"The Flame Fills the Earth"**; Walk from the North to the East, saying, **"The Earth Dances with the Wind"**; Walk from the East to the West, saying, **"The Air Moves the Waves"**; Walk from the West to the North, saying, **"The Water Nourishes the Soil"**.

Turn to the center of the compass and walk toward

the center altar and the stang. Put the left hand to the right shoulder and say, "As the Dark Touches the Light", then touch the left shoulder with the right hand and say, "As the Light Touches the Dark", then, with a sweeping motion raise your arms above you and then lower them so your hands are parallel to the ground and say:

> *Lucifer, Father of Witches!*
> *Horned One, Devil, Dark and Fair.*
> *Hekate, Mother of Witches!*
> *Triple goddess of magic might.*
> *Great Vessels of the Day and Night,*
> *Of sun and Moon,*
> *of Heavenly and Infernal Fire,*
> *I dedicate this rite to you!*
> *Come, Guide me on the Cunning Road,*
> *I shall follow the light betwixt your horns*
> *And the torches that you bear*
> *As I welcome you to this circle!*
> *In the Devil's name, So it is!*

Now the Compass Round has been laid, you can begin to Tread the Mill. For this you can choose to walk in a dextral or sinistral circle, depending on if your rite has more to do with building up (dextral) or banishing (sinistral) energy. There are many chants that can be used while you are walking the circle, drums can be played, songs can be sung, fun can be had. I suggest you begin to make up your own circle chants, but you can use those found in books to very great effect. Remember, though, that the guiding power in your work as a witch will be the spirits of the land on which you are practicing and working, so a chant or song more personalized to that spirit will go over better than one meant for spirits across the Atlantic. I will include a possibility here, one that I have used with more Southwestern roots, but feel free to modify as usual.

Spider of the Northward Road,
Spin the web to snare the Toad,
Black as Night that Fades to Day
Guide me as I Tread the Way.
Stag that Grazes in the East,
Run Before the Fearsome Beast,
White Your Tail, Gold Your Head,
With Me Walk the Milling Tread.
Southward Slithering Scarlet Snake,
Life You Give and Life You Take,
Gird the Circle by Venom and Scale,
Writhing as the Witches Wail.
Bear Who in the West Does Walk,
Red of Paw that Silent Stalks,
Dig the Root to Wake the Flame
That Blazes in the Horned One's Name.
Black Horn, White Horn,
Red Faced Beast,
Flame on the Head and Under the Feet.
Grey Spirits, Black Spirits,
White and the Red,
Walk with me now
as the Circle is Tread.

Continue to Tread the Mill and repeat the chant as often as you feel necessary. The important thing is to raise the energies you need and create the liminal space. It might take just a few circuits, or it might take dozens. You will know when the Tread is complete because the air will feel thick and electric and the shadows grow more intense.

THE DEVIL TAKE YOU!

In the lore of witches, at least as viewed by the witch hunters, the basic ideas are that the witch would go down to the crossroads and ask that the Devil appear to them. If he did, they would offer themself to him and he would suckle a bit of their blood, mark their body, or in some other way make a show of the deal being made. On the second meeting, often after the witch had travelled to the sabbat on their distaff or the back of their familiar spirit, they would have carnal copulations with the Devil and thus become his lover.

In truth, the witches' pact is not with Satan, the Adversary, and not really with the Devil. It is with the witch's own self. The rites we perform as initiations, either solitarily or in a coven, are made through the Devil as a spirit, but truly with ourselves as a promise to nurture our highest good, our power, and our relationships with the spirits, to act with as much integrity and honesty as we know how, and to nurture the disciplines of the witch so that we may develop spiritual strength as we travel the crooked path. A witch bows to no one.

To be initiated one does not have to go through a ceremony with a coven. Initiation is a pact between the witch and the Devil, a tutelary androgyne of both celestial and terrestrial origin, and all that is required is a strong desire to wander the crooked path and a dedication to developing the arts, not a covenant with a group of other witches. You may choose to join a coven, but it is not necessary to your development as a witch. Covens can be helpful, but they are also fraught with their own political and social tensions and not all covens are headed by people with good intentions. There are many stories of witches being sexually assaulted in their coven, often by the person filling the role of "high priest" or its equivalent. A covenant should be made between people who love and trust one another, not merely to gain power and knowledge, or to feel more authentic in the craft. Your power and authenticity stem from within.

I think it is better to call it a dedication rite, rather than an initiation, and it needn't be overly formal. The witch does not have to call the full compass to perform the rite of dedication and it can be performed more than once. I like to do it once per year at the Vernal Equinox, though you can choose whichever time suits you best. Go to any place that resonates with you, where you can feel the power that rises from the earth and feel the presence of the spirits.

Take with you the besom, the knife, the nowl, the cord, the stoup, the trencher, the thurible along with a lighter and some coals, the incense of your choice, some good wine and a tasty treat, and anything that you may want to dedicate while you make your pact. Clear the space with the besom and your cleansing exhortation, walking the circle nine complete times (nine is the number of mastery). In the place that you have chosen, kneel upon the ground and place the tools before you. Pour a little wine in the cup and put your treat on the trencher, just so they are prepared before they are needed. Take the coals and light them, then sprinkle some sacred incense into the thurible. As the smoke rises say:

As the Herbs of Arte Burn,
And the smoke does turn,
Let the Earth Serpent wake,
To hear the pact I now make.

Take a deep breath and begin to feel the energy rising in the circle. You don't have to gather a ton of energy, just enough to make the rite work. Now you can make an offering of rum or wine by pouring a small amount on the ground, and an offering of your body, such as spit or blood by nicking your thumb with the knife, a pin, or a lancet (you by no means have to) before calling to the spirits and the Man in Black.

Now is the hour I choose my path,
Freely and without compunction,
For all time; past, present, and future.
I accept unto myself the Witches' Art,
Its secrets, and its responsibilities,

by the breath and water of my body,
It is so.
Spirits of the land and in this place!
Hear me!
Spirits of the ancestors,
both familial and greater! Hear me!
Spirits of the Sun and Moon,
Spirits of the Day and Night,
Spirit of the Crooked Road,
Spirit of the Witches' Might!
Hear me!
By spider web and antlered head,
By serpent skin and cavern bed,
Spirits, spirits!
Hear me!
I call out to thee,
Horned One, Black Tom, Janicot!
Be here and accept me as I accept you.

Take the cord at either end and place your left hand beneath your left foot and your right hand on the crown of your hand and say:

I now and forever pledge all betwixt
these two hands
to the Witches' Art and the crooked path.
I pledge to tend the Twilit Grove,
To be daring in my actions,
To use my will with wisdom,
To keep the witches' silence,
And to go about the witches' work.
I shall daily keep the craft.
Between the hands,
between the horns,
Within the sacred fire,
I do make pact and pledge myself

to myself
In covenant with the spirits
And in the Devil's name. It is so.

Take the cord and wrap it around your waist. Take the cup in your right hand and say as you raise the glass, "To the Land, to the Sky, to the Waters of the Earth, and to the Cunning Fire, in the Old One's Name! Drink a draught, the spirit is caught," then partake of the wine and pour a little out for the spirits. Take a bit of your treat and hold it up while saying, "The fruits of the forest and the field are ours, in the Horned One's name! Take a nip after the sip," then put some aside for the spirits and eat the rest.

This is a symbolic feast, what Gemma Gary calls troyl and Robert Cochrane called housel. It is meant to bring you into communion and relationship with the spirits and the Horned One. Before you go, take the nail and plunge it into the ground or into a suitable container (you can even choose to hammer a nail into a piece of wood every time you make the pact and keep it on your altar) and say:

By this action so the pact is fixed,
for all time, past, present, and future,
in all aspects and dimensions of reality,
in the Devil's name and
by the authority of my Self.
It is so.

Then you may gather your tools. Before you leave be sure to say thank you and good-bye to the spirits and leave them your offerings. I usually say, "Merry meet and merry part until the crooked path unites us." Then the pact is made and voilà! You're a witch!

You may also choose never to make such a pact, which is equally valid. Witchcraft is about claiming personal sovereignty and power, so whatever you feel speaks to that best for you, do it. I value the witches' pact because it makes me feel that I have made a powerful, open declaration of my commitment to my path and my truth, but it isn't for everyone. Always do as you will, not as you are told in a book.

VENERATION

I include this as one of the seed arts of witchcraft because respect for the value and power of things, people, and places, and a willingness and desire to treat each and every moment and everything in it as a spiritual sibling and as a spiritual equal are essential to what we do. Cultivating reverence, not deference, in one's daily life takes work, practice, dedication, and mindfulness. This includes not only animate members of our reality, like cows, chickens, worms, beetles, bees, and people, but books, dishes, blankets, rocks, incense, mirrors, cucumbers, nettles, phones, beds, shoes, cars, and anything else you can think of. Everything has a spirit and everything partakes in its share of the divine.

Our coven's brand of witchcraft is animistic, which is the belief that all things have spirit and life (even plates, dust, and hair all the way up to tsunamis, tornados, and the multiverse) with which we can commune and make relationship. We believe that spirits can be contacted even after physical death and that all spirits are equally important, powerful, and unique. In animistic systems there is often the belief in reincarnation and transmigration of souls and practices that allow disembodied or other dimensionally bodied spirits to inhabit objects such as charms, spirit houses, and certain tools. We also believe that we can be called upon by the spirits as we call on them. There is no distinction between the sacred and profane.

When thinking of animism be sure to remember that it is by no means a religion of any kind, but rather a worldview, a perspective that may be part of a given religion (such as Shinto) and is perhaps the oldest perspective, the fertile soil from which our greatest theologies have grown, including Christianity. There is no push toward worship of any deity, however, only a cautious respect of spirits who require appeasement through offerings or who need to be kept at bay through protective spell work and ritual, though animism does not preclude theism. It is, in fact, often found with a pantheon, a slew of spirits, and an ancestor cult. Not all witches are animists, however, which is perfectly fine.

Veneration is not only about giving reverence, but also learning how to accept it. Many people feel that they are unworthy or undeserving of the attention and love of others, let alone their reverence, but this is because we have been sold a story that tells us that the "right thing to do" is usually a self-denigrating one. We must give up our earthly attachments, our pleasure, and our pride to be "good". This is folly. Witchcraft is, at least in part, a practice of self-remembering and empowerment, which on its own will lift others up without having to give all of yourself away.

By reverence I do not mean the Christian type that asks you to give everything to your elders, authorities, and ultimately to the Abrahamic God. Already in that system is a hierarchy of "power over", where one must defer to someone who is "more" than oneself. In witchcraft reverence is not synonymous with deference, there is no virtue in ceding dignity and power to those who have not earned it by showing through their actions that they wish to share power, that they also hold you in reverence. Just because someone is older, has authority, or calls itself a "God", does not make a person, spirit, or thing intrinsically right and worthy of more respect than any other spirit in the multi-verse. This type of reverence is demanded and given out of fear, not love.

Please do not take from these words that I in any way denigrate fear and laud love. Spirituality in our society has said a lot of negative things about fear, basically making it love's opposite, though this is untrue. Fear has just as much power as love, it's just harder to see its good side because it doesn't give us the "warm and fuzzies". Not only is fear part of the feeling of awe that gives rise to reverence, it is an alarm system, telling us what might be dangerous to us, what to watch out for. It also alerts us to where our courage can be found. Without fear there can be no courage, for when we face our fear it becomes the mother of bravery. When we choose to disregard our fear and leave it unprocessed, however, it becomes the "mind killer", the "little death" in the words of Frank Herbert, and suddenly mole hills become mountains and the forward momentum we feel suddenly stagnates.

For the witch, fear is not a frightening subject or sensation and deference is not the same as goodness. For a witch it is more virtuous to think for oneself, admitting when one is wrong but also knowing when one is right and having the audacity to stand up for Truth. To revere a thing means to be in awe of its beauty, of its power, of its strength while also acknowledging its imperfection and its frailty; it means to see the wholeness of things. When one begins to recognize wholeness, really allowing all and everything to be as it is without judgement and without confusion, then true reverence can begin to grow out of that thing we call love. Which leads us to the question; what is love?

Philosophers, poets, musicians, and artists of all stripes have tried for millennia upon millennia to suss out the answer to that question and I have no more definitive an answer than they have had. What I have come to understand of love is that it is a state of consciousness and a deeply held feeling, but it remains dynamic and cannot truly be pinned down with thoughts or words. Like witchcraft, love is experienced. What I can say is what love is not. Love is not a commodity and cannot be traded or bartered with, cannot be used as a weapon, and it cannot be a source for obsessive, aggressive, or possessive behaviors and thoughts. Those thoughts and feelings arise from conflicting and unclear desire, from a deep place of misunderstanding, but not love.

So, veneration is simply holding something in reverence, which means "to stand in awe of" "and "to honor." It is

71

the art of loving things, of giving respect and consideration, of being mindful, and of accepting veneration from others and not settling for less. This comes hard for many of us, so this seed may take a bit of work to grow. A daily meditation practice will be of use to the witch, as it helps to develop gratitude, serenity, and stillness, all essential to growing one's sense of sacredness.

This brings us to the important distinction between religion and witchcraft. Witchcraft is a practice, something a person does, not a religion. Even a Christian can practice witchcraft (it does happen, the case in point being my own grandmother…and most witches for the last two millennia, actually). Alternatively, you can be part of a nature-based religion and not practice witchcraft (this also happens). Really, what matters is that you identify as a witch, but also walk the walk in whatever fashion the walk manifests for you, be it in a church, in your living room, or in the forest wildly dancing in the nude.

To recognize the intrinsic value of things apart from their use to you is a skill in and of itself, one that needs to be practiced. A simple exercise to work your gratitude muscles is to choose any item in your home at random and meditate on it. Remember everything has a spirit, so ask the item's spirit to make itself known to you before you ask it questions. If you're having trouble making connection, tap the object three times saying, "Awake! Awake! Awake!", then add a "Hail and welcome" or a simple "Howdy!" for good measure.

After you've spent a bit of time with the item ask questions like the following: Does it hold a special place in your life? How does it enrich your life and in which ways? Can you name the last time you handled the item before this moment? What emotion(s) does it inspire in you? What kind of relationship do you have with the object and would you like to deepen it, or should the relationship end? Focus and answer these questions honestly and with as much detail as you can muster, then write about your meditation in your Liber Lamiae. Gratitude is basically thankfulness, but with the added feelings of affection, appreciation, and reciprocation, and it can be difficult to articulate; it is a complex emotion made from many others. These questions are meant to help you identify and expound on why you may or may not be grateful for the item you have chosen. If you find that connection is difficult, or you just don't get a good sense of the item, perhaps it is time to move it along.

You will notice that connecting to the spirit of things becomes easier when you have brought your mind to stillness and you are approaching it from a place of calm. If your mind is racing and you have a million things going on around you and the television is on and there's music going and you're feeling rushed because you need to make dinner before your entire family arrives and you aren't used to stilling your mind, perhaps choose a better time to start your gratitude exercises. Stillness and serenity do not just happen; they require intentionality. Energy follows intention, so make the conscious choice to sit or lie in stillness, simply watching your thoughts without judgement and without angst, until they become slower and slower, calmer and calmer. Again, it takes practice to do this with any proficiency, so be easy with yourself as you begin to build your practice.

As for what to do during veneration, it really depends on what the spirits want. I have a personal spirit, a familiar, who asks for a special altar made just for him, with a goat skull, a Sulphur crystal, and his own pitcher of honeyed rum. It is basically a spirit house, a place for my familiar to touch base, recharge, and rest when he wants to. I light candles for him, talk to him, and he comes to me for help when he needs it (which isn't often). I also have an altar built for Hekate, the goddess of witchcraft, made from a hand carved wooden cabinet from Greece and a hand carved wooden statue of the goddess made by an artist in Ukraine. It is decorated with candles and keys, snake skin and power items that I use in the work I do for her. I also light candles for Hekate, and give her offerings of coffee and sweets, sometimes grave-yard dirt, money, and incense.

Another of our venerative altars is one dedicated to Santa Muerte, the Holy Death, who is a folk saint of Mexican and New Mexican origin. Appearing as a female grim reaper, she is the dark side of La Virgen de Guadalupe, one of the forms the Virgin Mary takes. She wears differently colored robes depending on what she is doing, like red for love magic, gold or yellow for money magic, and black for protection. She may also simply wear white because, magically, white can stand in for any other color. On my altar is a skeleton wearing the color of robe most appropriate for the work I'm doing (I usually just keep her in a white robe, though I have several color options), pillar, taper, and cathedral candles, rocks and crystals, money, cigarettes, various powders I use for thaumaturgical purposes, divination items, etc. Anything I want to have blessed, petitions written on paper, enchanted candles, photos of clients, and whatever Santissima asks for goes on the altar. I also bless donations to charities on her altar, especially those going to LGBTIQA+ or feminist causes, as she is the patron saint of the outcast, the black sheep, the non-status quo, and those who are unjustly diminished by our society.

I also have an altar built for the Witch Mother and the Witch Father, which together are the Devil of the witches. It is also an altar for various other spirits and my ancestors, a place where I lay offerings and have spirit bottles. As you may have guessed, my whole house is covered in altars, in-cluding those my husband sets up. Don't worry if you don't have space like that; a single altar will usually suffice, or a single altar space with items that can be switched out de-pending on which spirit needs to be worked with, petitioned, or offered to.

Perhaps having a permanent altar is problematic for you. That is alright. Set one up when you need it, carry around an altar poke (a little pouch with tiny altar things), draw one out on paper, or simply ask Nature to be your altar and leave offerings at the base of trees (if those offerings are natural and bio-degradable and non-hazardous to wildlife). Just because you don't have tools doesn't mean you cannot venerate the spirits and your ancestors, nor does it mean you can't be a witch. Your wand can be carved from rare wood and encrusted with gems, or it can be a toothpick you got from the fast food joint you ate at, or a stick off the ground, or maybe you don't have one at all. The magic is in you, in the spirits, and in your Will, so no tools are really required.

If you can't afford to offer a bunch of different things to a bunch of different spirits, don't worry about it. Work with a comfortable amount of them and make it clear that you may not always be able to provide what they request, but that you will negotiate. Spirits often love to haggle[1], so make your terms clear, ask for the spirit's terms, and be a bit flexible to make the relationship as smooth as possible. I find that the more rigid a spirit is the less I want to work with them, but learning to compromise with spirits like that can have benefits. Feel it out, think it over, and proceed with cunning.

The above is just a small glimpse at what veneration can look like. Some spirits will ask that you give part of your earnings to charity, which in itself is a form of veneration to the beings who benefit from the donation and the people who work for the charity. Sometimes veneration is randomly giving away some service or product, or helping your mother move, or leaving roses at the altar of a local chapel, or planting trees. Veneration is giving, but don't forget to venerate yourself and give yourself a spa day, or even just an

---

1 Some spirits do NOT like to haggle and expect you to respect their requests. Make your own boundaries firm and clear and, if you cannot work with that spirit at the time you first make contact, tell them that you are open to talking about making relationship after a year has passed. If they accept, then revisit your terms when the time comes. If they do not accept, there are plenty of other spirits that may be a better fit for you. Don't get discouraged.

hour alone, a hike, a night out, a fancy dinner, or a movie, or anything you can offer yourself that will make you feel enlivened, empowered, and magical. Remember that you are a spirit and need to be taken care of just as much as your ancestors and familiars do.

Another facet of veneration is taking responsibility and giving it up when necessary. We as witches must learn to accept the consequences and rewards of our own actions, pick up the burden of our own lives, and allow others to do the same. Sometimes its just as easy to accept the responsibility for another person as it is to shunt the blame onto them, but we must stop confusing our responsibilities with those of others. When we are not holding ourselves and others accountable, we are damaging our own power and theirs, either losing the opportunity to work on our imbalances or stealing the opportunity from other people. To paraphrase the words of Jesus the Christ, "Render unto me that which is mine, and render unto you that which is yours."

On the same note, we must learn to ask for help when we need it and to not feel guilty for it. We must also learn to give and accept help when we honestly can. Taking responsibility and being accountable does not mean that you have to do it all on your own, only that you recognize what needs to be done and make it happen in whichever way you can (within reason and while maintaining your dignity, whatever that means to you).

I think that the seed of veneration is essential to grow before any of the others, so let this be your first work. Learn to revere things whole-heartedly and the other seeds will grow more easily and more powerfully than you can imagine. Think of this tree in the Twilit Forest as a kind of companion plant, the one you grow because it takes care of other plants in the garden and helps the whole eco-system flourish. The seed of Veneration is largely about living with an open heart, for when the heart is open your possibilities are limitless.

76

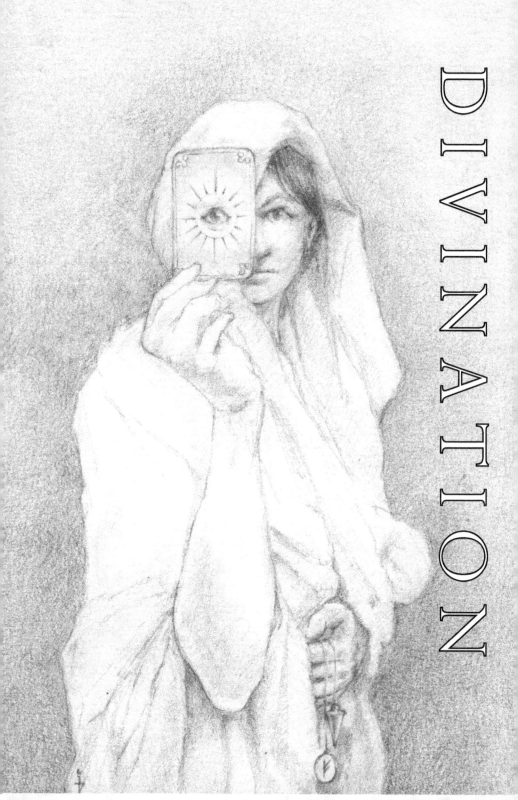

DIVINATION

Divination is one of the fundmental arts of the witch. Without it, we can get lost and bogged down in our own passions and opinions, so it is imperative to cultivate some sort of divinatory practice with which you may get consistent results. The most used divination tools are tarot cards, runes, and pendulums, but you can use anything. There are so many classes and books devoted to the use of these tools and so many ways they can be useful to your practice. If you can consistently read pertinent information in someone's used chewing gum (you can call it cummiomancy), I say do it!

The important thing to remember is that you are not necessarily reading the future, but divining information. You can divine the location of something lost, whether a person is sick or afflicted by spirits and the correct ritual to perform to help them, to find ley lines (also called dragon or serpent lines), or to discover what is closest to the truth or toward your highest good and the good of all concerned. The future sometimes comes into it, but, because time is non-linear, all future events are mutable, immutable, or have happened already. Divination can allow you to know whether your goal is attainable, and if so, what you can do, right in the moment, to achieve the end you desire.

My divination practice usually consists of tarot, rune, and pendulum dowsing, though the various methods have their own pros and cons and should be chosen accordingly. The nature of divination is subjective, so using a secondary or tertiary form of divination to double and triple check your work is a good idea and helps to maintain as objective a viewpoint as possible.

DOWSING

The methods for dowsing are various, but the most often used tool is the pendulum, a weight at the end of a string or chain. Keeping one in your poke or wearing a necklace that can be used as a pendulum keeps one of your most useful tools close to hand. Dowsing is extremely useful for discerning yes/no information, percentages, and for clearing or building energy. Programming the pendulum is a simple procedure of repeating instructions to the item you are going to use to help keep clarity in your dowsing. There is a comprehensive, free PDF document for the use of pendulums and their programming called A Letter to Robin: A Mini-Course in Pendulum Dowsing by Walt Woods, but the following are simple directions for the programs I use in my craft.

While you are dowsing remember to let the hand holding the pendulum relax completely, from your neck to your shoulder, down your arm, all the way to your fingertips. I tend to wrap the chain or rope around my fingers, so I have about three inches between my hand and the pendulum itself. The program I use for my pendulum is a back and forth motion for "yes" and a side to side motion for "no", with diagonal swings indicating that my question wasn't quite right or perhaps irrelevant. To program these into the pendulum, consciously start the swing and repeat what the motion means three times, so programming a "yes" swing would require swinging the pendulum back and forth (toward and away from your body), while saying, "Yes. Yes. Yes". I find it helpful to hold the pendulum over my other hand while I ask questions and during programming; you can feel the energy moving through your body beneath the pendulum, which helps to keep you more honest.

To program the pendulum for building or dismantling energy, swing the pendulum over your other hand in a dextral (clockwise) or sinistral (anti-clockwise) circle, respectively. As you spin the pendulum dextrally say something along the lines of, "As the pendulum swings toward the right, in the path of the sun, may all good and beneficial things be added unto (the item you are blessing), all things that are toward my highest good and the highest good of all concerned, for all time, past, present, and future, in all aspects and dimensions of reality. Az ze[1]". For the reverse, begin the swing sinistrally and say "As the pendulum swings toward the left, against the sun, may all negative, non-beneficial energies and entities, and anything which is not toward my highest good and the highest good of all concerned be removed from (the item you are clearing) for all time, past, present, and future in all aspects and dimensions of reality. Az ze."

The best questions to ask your pendulum are yes/no format, such as "Would citrine be the best stone to use for this operation?", or questions about percentages of things like beneficence or maleficence.

Hold your pendulum in one hand and hold the other out in front of you with your fingers splayed and palm toward the ground. Furthest toward the right side of your hand is "0%", the finger on that side is "10%", the space between the furthest right finger and the finger to the left of it is "20%", all the way over to the furthest left side of the hand which is "100%". Trust the swing, as it will go toward the most appropriate finger or space to give you the most correct information. If you have clarifying questions like, "Is the number between 70% and 75%," then switch to the yes/no method of asking and ask for each number between 70 and 75.

You can also use the pendulum to discern what "level" a spirit is and whether the spirit is benevolent, malevolent, or neutral. If a spirit is overly benevolent, it is just as dangerous as one which wants to harm you, so knowing how powerful that being is can helpto keep you safer for longer. Hold your hand in front of you as if you were going

---

1   "And so it is".

to ask about percentages, but think of the middle finger of your hand as "0". The space between the middle finger and the finger to the left is "level 5 negative", while the space between the middle finger and finger to the right is "level 5 positive". The finger to the left is "level 10 negative" and so on up to level 25, these being the most powerful (see diagram 1). Once you've figured out the strength of the spirit, continue with questions about its nature, using the yes/no format (Is it intending harm toward me? My loved ones? Is it a spirit which needs to be exorcised immediately? Can I exorcise it? Is it non-human? Disincarnate? Fragmentary?).

The important thing with dowsing is that you remain calm minded and honest. If you feel that you are having trouble with impartiality, take a moment to check in with yourself and ask what is going on inside you that keeps you from being neutral. When it comes to divination, especially a form that can be so subjective, neutrality is key to accuracy and ultimate success. Ask the question and wait for the pendulum to swing. It may take a while to really start feeling the energies moving the weight, but over time it will get to a point where you no longer need the tool itself to get a good reading. I will often put my hands in the position for pendulum dowsing and simply follow the energy with my hand alone.

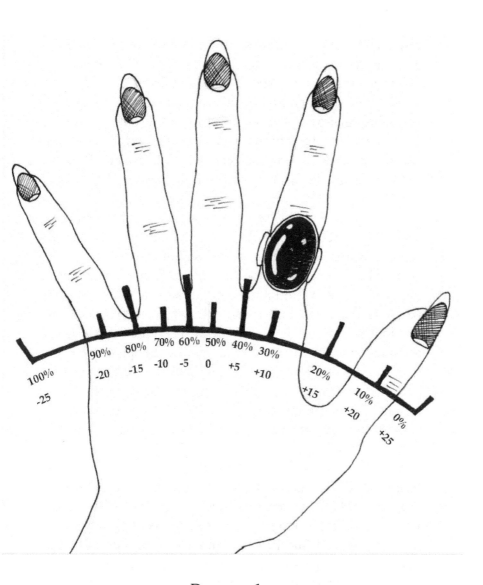

DIAGRAM 1
*Using the hand to find percentages
and power levels*

SCRYING

The word scry is short for descry, which means "to discern". What the witch does in the practice of scrying is to discern images in water, crystal, glass, and other reflective surfaces, or things that are in some way hypnotic, like fire, smoke, and cream poured freshly into coffee in order to discover information or to (possibly) foretell events. In media it is often a scrying tool that is used by the fortune teller or psychic, such as the enormous crystal balls used by Professor Marvel and the Wicked Witch of the West in The Wizard of Oz.

The crystal ball is not only a recognizable tool, but also a very useful one. It functions in a similar way to the scrying mirror and the reasons to use both are basically the same. They are excellent tools for thaumaturgy (spell work) because they help to train the concentration and focus of the witch, help clear the mind, and help project the psyche outward into another object. They are also excellent aids to necromancy (working with the dead), giving the spirits a reflective, liminal surface to manifest in, making it easier for the practitioner to see them. It was with the use of mirrors and crystal balls that John Dee and Edward Kelly discovered the angelic language of Enochian and developed their angelical system of magic[2].

Set up your mirror or crystal in a semi-dark room, a place that is quiet and where you are unlikely to be disturbed. Light a candle or two and place them behind or to the side of your tool and relax, letting your thoughts flow through, without judgement. I find that the harder I try to stop thinking that much more persistent my thoughts become, so allowing and surrendering to them makes it easier to focus and to have visions. As your thoughts are playing through, gaze into the crystal or mirror with loose eyes, without effort; straining and grasping will get you nowhere.

---

2   Jason Louv, John Dee and the Empire of Angels: Enochian Magick and the Occult Roots of the Modern World (Rochester, VT: Inner Traditions, 2018).

You may experience a sort of mistiness in the glass called "clouding", which is perfectly normal, though it doesn't always occur and sometimes seems to happen only within the eyes of the witch. It looks as if everything around the crystal or mirror is surrounded by mist or static. Sometimes the visions don't truly play in the crystal, but in the mind as if projected from the crystal, which is no less "real" than seeing images within the crystal itself. I find that the latter experience is the more common one. You may also experience the tool you are using becoming brighter while everything around it dims or recedes into darkness when you are scrying.

If you have a hard time seeing anything in a clear glass, try a darker one. Obsidian scrying mirrors are available to buy and small ones are not very expensive, or you can get a piece of black stained glass from the local craft supply store. A black mirror can be easily made by stretching black velvet over the backboard of a picture frame and a crystal ball can be made darker by placing it on or in front of a piece of black velvet or dark paper. If the room is dark enough a clear or silvered tool will likely not be terribly distracting, though I prefer to work with darkened glass in most cases.

An interesting experience I have had with the crystal ball nearly every time I've used one is that it tends to "shimmer" with a blueish light that extends about half an inch to three inches away from the surface of the sphere and will reach into the glass and swirl gently. It can be manipulated by adding energy to the sphere with the hands and by slight movements of the fingers, making the swirling of the light more or less intense. There can also be an orange halo just off the glass that will undulate through the blueness, or there can be no such light show and the visions will still come. Scrying is really about states of mind, focus, and the willingness of the witch to surrender to visions as they come without judgement and without grasping.

Other forms of scrying rely on the reading of symbols in a physical object, such as tea leaves in tasseomancy. You can also read symbols and signs in wax poured into water, wine stains on a cloth, an egg broken into warm water, or anything else that may make or leave a readable image. The important thing to remember about any such practice is that the symbols you are seeing and the interpretations you give them are unique to you and if another reader were to pick up the same tea leaves or egg cup, they would read something almost completely different. The item you are reading is reflecting your own inner vision and is not straight forward by any means.

Tasseomancy is one of the best known of these arts today. To read the leaves the witch will place loose leaf tea, not too finely broken up, into a cup on a saucer (preferably a beautiful set, for ambience) and then pour hot water over them. Don't let it sit for too long, as you want the querent to enjoy the tea and a bit of chat before the reading. When the tea is almost gone, but not to the last drop, swirl the contents and turn the cup over with gentle force, just to make patterns with the tea leaves on the side of the cup, then begin the reading. In her article on tasseomancy, Sarah Anne Lawless indicates that the handle of the cup is closest to the time of the reading and that the reading can be sliced up by month leading away from the handle to the left and back around to the right (dextral). Anything near the rim of the cup is surface knowledge and is currently known or about to be discovered, while the deeper into the cup you gaze the deeper hidden and less likely to be known the information will become.

There are tasseomancy tea sets that come with handy saucers marked by the zodiac, making time easier to tell; just line the handle up to the month of the reading and go from there. These can lead to stultification during the reading, however, and can be exorbitantly expensive, so learning how to do a down-home reading with a simple cup is going to be more useful than learning with a fancy tasseomancy set.

Egg reading, or oomancy, is actually quite a lot of fun and helps to do two things in one go; divining for information and balancing the energy of the client. I learned to do this from books and watching one of my mentors perform the whole operation, which consists of rubbing the client with an egg, starting at the feet and rubbing away from the heart. Work your way up the leg, front and back (always rubbing the egg toward the feet), starting the hands as you get to the hips and working up through the arms, abdomen, and thorax, rubbing up and away from the heart as you get into the head and neck.

When you are over the heart itself you can rub the egg in a spiraling motion toward the right, starting in the center of the heart and moving out toward the sides of the body, remembering to do this on the front and back. While performing the egg clearing, think of all of the unbalancing or unnecessary energy that does not serve your client or lead them toward their highest good being transferred into the egg, like a little treasure box. You can also start from the head and brush the egg down the body, now always down toward the feet, and stop in areas where it feels like there is stagnant energy or blockages that could be harming your client or keeping them from progressing.

Now the egg is full of your client's energy and can be used for oomancy. Take water that is on the hotter side of warm, but not boiling or scalding, squeeze a bit of lemon into it, and have the client crack the egg into the cup. The white will begin to turn from clear to milky and form patterns and symbols that can be read just like tea leaves. The yolk will tell you about core issues, the things closest to the yolk are direct influences on the client and are very important while the bits furthest from the yolk are less pressing, but may be part of deeper patterns of behavior that keep your client from their goals. When reading the yolk, if a white spot appears it may be a sign of mal de ojo, the evil eye, and a further cleansing or hex breaking may be necessary. A spot may also be an indicator of a marriage or pregnancy. If the yolk breaks it is a sign that the client is leaking energy or is being preyed upon and needs to be attended to soon, where an unbroken yolk may mean that the client's energy is fine, or that they are holding onto too much of it; the interpretation will depend on the rest of the reading. Blood in the yolk can mean disease or heart break and double yolks may indicate a fractured spirit that needs to be called back to unity through retrieval work, but may also indicate multiple births, or a possessing/corded entity.

When it comes to scrying, do what works and trust your gut. Your intuition is the best guide to interpretation that you could possibly have, so working to develop that faculty by practicing various methods of scrying is a first-rate idea. See what works for you and experiment with how symbols work in your craft, gain a bit of accuracy and proficiency in each type you learn, then stretch your symbolic legs by reading for others. The more practice you have with scrying the easier your time will be when it comes to working with clients.

CURIOMANCY

Casting or throwing the bones, what I call curio-mancy, is an extremely fun and personal form of divination, which technically belongs under the header of scrying, but with which I will deal separately. This is one of my preferred forms of divination as it utilizes the old trinkets we hold onto without really knowing why, along with some items of great sentimental value. Each curiomancy set is unique to the witch who uses it and the meaning(s) attributed to each piece are completely the auspice of the reader.

The pieces are each small items, usually no longer than the pinky finger, and represent people, places, and events that may be of importance to the querent. Remember that each item is alive, has a spirit, so treat them well and ask them to guide you honestly so you know you can trust the reading more fully and the reading will be easier to perform. The items in the bag can either help or hinder you depending on their mood, so make sure to use items you have a long standing relationship with, that each piece is consecrated, and that each piece knows its basic meaning.

Some of the pieces in my own collection and what they represent are a plastic body builder (a male presenting person) and a small, plastic cameo of a feminine face (a female presenting person), a large shell (a male presenting elder) and a small one (a female presenting elder), a knotted cord (to show connection between events and chronic issues), an ammonite fossil (a long standing pattern of behavior that relates to nearby items), a glass heart (relationships), with about 80 other items with various meanings. These I keep in a leather bag which I upturn over a white cloth with a large circle drawn on it.

Whatever items land nearest the center of the circle are the most pressing to investigate, while those furthest to the edges of the circle are less pressing, but possibly important depending on their placement and proximity to other items. The things near the side of the circle closest to the reader tell about things that enliven, impassion, and agitate the querent; those to the left of the circle deal with emotions and relationships; those furthest from the reader are indicative of ancestral connections to events and issues and the things the client least wants to deal with; the right side of the circle deals with their mental states and thought patterns. Of course, any of those categories can be dealt with anywhere in the circle depending on which items land where, but use the quarter system as a guideline. Anything that falls outside of the circle can be placed back in the bag, unless an item within the circle is touching it, or the item is mostly in the circle.

To read the curios takes practice and is much more like analyzing a painting than doing a spread for a reading. Just like with the crystal, relax your body. Have your list of meanings and your liber lamiae close by, as you will want to take notes about the reading and how the curios interrelate reading to reading. As you work your way through one part of the reading and move to the next grouping of items, you will begin to realize how complexly events, issues, and traumas are woven together and just how easy it is to get befuddled by the twists and turns these relationships make. Remain as objective and honest as possible while maintaining awareness of your intuition, the guidance of spirits around you, and the voices of your items.

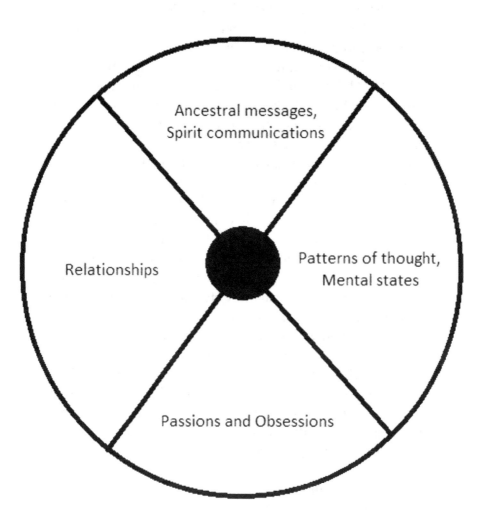

DIAGRAM 2
The circle for the casting of curios.

GLYPHOMANCY & ARITHMANCY

The use of glyphs and numbers to divine information is likely as old as written language, though there are certain systems that have gained some fame. Ogham, or the tree alphabet of Old Ireland, is used as a divinatory tool, as are the Greek alphabet, the Hebrew alphabet, and Japanese kanji. To my knowledge, though, the most famous system of glyphomancy is runemal, the magical system surrounding a set of twenty-four symbols called the Elder Futhark, used by Germanic and Nordic peoples as letters and as magical devices between the 2nd and 8th centuries. From the 8th century forward the runes transformed into the Younger Futhark and the Anglo-Saxon Futorc, leaving the knowledge of how to use and read the Elder Futhark forgotten until it was deciphered in 1865 by Sophus Bugge, a Norwegian linguist. The history and use of runes are incredibly rich areas of study, one we cannot spend too much time on.

Personally, I rarely use the runes for divination, preferring to work with them as sigils and magical engines in their own right. If, however, you want to use them for divination, a brief list of the runes and a few keywords for each will be provided here. They are divided into their traditional aetts, groups of eight runes in three categories assigned to a deity, the first rune of each group being the first letter of that god's name.

To cast the runes, simply have a set in a bag (this works best) and turn the bag over before you, reading the runes where they land. You may also choose a certain number from the bag (for numerologically important reasons of your devising), then throw those down and read them as they land. They can be read upright and reversed and may have different meanings if they are top-toward-right or top-toward-left; they are as flexible as the All-Father, Odhinn, himself.

Another possible way to cast is to roll a six-sided die and an eight-sided die, using them to roll for the coordinates of a single rune within the aett system. Freya's aett corresponds to 1 and 4 on the 6-sided die, Hel to 2 and 5, and Tyr to 3 and 6, while the eight-sided die will correspond to the particular rune within that stave, so a roll of 5:7 would leave algiz as the answer to your question, where 3:2 would lead you to berkana.

Freya's 8		Hel's 8		Tyr's 8	
Fehu ᚠ (F)	Money, Success, Bestowals	Hagalaz ᚺ (H)	Destruction, Wrath, Transformation	Tiwaz ᛏ (T)	Warrior, Authority, Courage
Uruz ᚢ (U)	Physical Strength, Power	Nauthiz ᚾ (N)	Fate, Need, Desire, Death	Berkana ᛒ (B)	Birth, Fertility, Survival, Growth
Thurisaz ᚦ (TH)	Discipline, Shaprness, Protection	Isa ᛁ (I)	Challenge, Ice, Frozen, Stilted	Ehwaz ᛖ (E)	Communication, Slow Travel, Burden, Work
Ansuz ᚨ (A)	Power, Odin's Rune, High Magic	Jera ᛃ (J, Y)	Hope, Peace, Companionship	Mannaz ᛗ (M)	Self, Humanity, Social Order, the Physical Home
Raido ᚱ (R)	Travel, Quickness, Rage, Hurry	Eihwaz ᛇ (AE)	Defense, Trust, Protection from Surprise Attack	Laguz ᛚ (L)	Water, Flow, Life, Speech, Fluidity
Kenaz ᚲ (C, K)	Inspiration, Knowledge, Cunning Fire	Perth ᛈ (P)	Chance, Hidden Things, Deceit	Inguz ᛝ (NG)	Seeds, Caring, Children, Close Family
Gebo ᚷ (G)	Gifts, Relationships, Covenants	Algiz ᛉ (Z)	Protective Circle, Cheild, Ward, Cutting	Othila ᛟ (O)	Homeland, Inheritance, Spiritual Family
Wunjo ᚹ (W)	Happiness, Joy, Pleasure, Addiction	Sowilo ᛊ (S)	Victory, Magic Power, Spells, Life Force	Dagaz ᛞ (D)	Breakthrough, Daylight, Awareness, Revelation

DIAGRAM 3
The Elder Futhark Runes and a few key words

HEBREW GEMATRIA

In Kabbalah the Hebrew alphabet is a work of art, the abstract given expression, the divine given form on earth. According to the Kabbalah the letters are the bones of the universe, the very fires of Heaven from which all is created. Each letter holds within it a spiritual essence and every word is a vessel that contains a complete harmony of those spirits, a spiritual resonance. Each letter not only stands for a phoneme, but a number, meaning every word has a numerical value and some words hold a value in common. Those words resonate at the same spiritual level and in some sense are facets of the same spirit.

There are many methods of gematria, though the one I prefer is Mispar ha-Panim (the normative value system, or face number) that attributes a basic number to each of the twenty-two letters. Take as an example the Hebrew word for "truth", emet (אמת), where א is 1, מ is 40, and ת is 400, which, when summed, equal 441. Other words that share this value in common will share in the essential spirit of emet. You can take this a step further and add the numbers of the sum (4+4+1) to get 9, the number that represents the Torah and the Law of Judaisim.

To work with another example, we will take the word for "witch", mekhashefah (מכשפה), which sums to 445. Another word with the same value is mik'shah (מקשה), which can mean "field of melons/cucumbers", but also "twisting". The PIE word -weik, which means "pliant, to bend, to turn, to change", is where the word "witch" and many words with connotations of bewitchment and spell casting derive from in English. The section "Gematria" of 777 and Other Qabalistic Writings by Aleister Crowley describes various uses and ways of performing gematria, while the section "Sepher Sephiroth" is a useful reference for the lay use of these Kabbalistic/Qabalistic numerological systems. It is not the most extensive reference guide but can be of great use to the beginner.

NUMEROLOGY

Along similar lines to Gematria is numerology, which simply observes and manipulates numbers and numerical patterns and derives meaning therefrom. The witch can add numbers, seek out patterns of numbers, repeating numbers, etc. and apply meaning from there. Much like Hebrew, the Latin characters can be given numerical values in the "9 chamber" system (See Diagram 4).

With this system one can make any word into a number and discover another layer of meaning in the words the witch chooses to use. The word "stang", for example, would be $1+2+1+5+7=16$, which reduces to $1+6=7$, so hidden meaning surrounding the stang can be found in the number 7. You can also do this with your own name, with character names, and so much more, though I really do not put much stock into "life path numbers" and the like; it is a little too arbitrary and "fluffy" for credulity. The numbers only go from zero to nine, but all have symbolic meanings that the witch will discover repeated in many occult works, such as the tarot and in the making of tools, potions, and spells. Number symbolism is very important to what we do. Some of the basic symbolic meanings of numbers are given in brief in diagram 5, with which you may experiment and explore the world of numerological correspondence.

NINE CHAMBERS

1 A J S	2 B K T	3 C L U
4 D M V	5 E N W	6 F O X
7 G P Y	8 H Q Z	9 I R

DIAGRAM 4
The 9 Chamber System

NUMBER SYMBOLISM

0	The void, the abyss, the negative space that gives meaning, the vagina/womb, the return
1	The monad, unity, wholeness, the phallus, stillness, primal chaos, power, essence
2	Birth, separation, choice, the feminine body, the temple, schism
3	Work, complexity, the masculine body, the divine, the goddess, and the godhead
4	Balance, the elements, the square, the earth, the compass, celebration, youth
5	Marriage, challenge, the child, the created, sex, marriage of opposites, life
6	Freedom, the senses, adulthood, the philosophers' stone, attainment, victory, generosity
7	Mystery, magic, sorcery, the hidden, vision, manifestation, menstruation, the lunar cycle
8	Strength, speed, growing power, the wheel of the year, the solar cycle
9	Mastery, the end before the beginning, gratitude, rest, respect, growth, responsibility, old age

Diagram 5

Key words pertaining to the numerology of the first nine digits.

CARTOMANCY

PLAYING CARDS

Older than the tarot by at least a century (though probably much older), the four-suit deck of playing cards developed in the Far East, most likely China. Though Johannes Gutenberg is given credit for the invention of the movable type printing press in1439, a truly revolutionary technology that allowed the mass production of books and printed media, Asia had been in command of similar technologies for centuries, since about 1040 CE. The ability to reproduce images on paper made it easy for Asian printers to create decks of cards that spread rapidly and cheaply, though playing cards did not make it to Europe until the late 14th century from an Arabic source.

Though tarot evolved from suited playing cards, they are not read in the same way whatsoever. With a modern playing card pack, at least a French/English style pack with red and black cards separated into hearts, diamonds, clubs, and spades, the basic spread I would use begins by laying down one card in the middle of your reading space to represent the querent (a signifier card). I never choose the signifier consciously, though some authors say that the King of Hearts represents male-presenting clients and the Queen of Hearts represents female-presenting clients. I find this is too exclusionary, so I prefer to let the "cards fall where they may", as it were.

Next, lay a card to the left of the signifier, one to the right, one above, and one below, then fill in the spaces above and below the cards on the right and left of the signifier, leaving you with a block of nine cards. These are the things more important to the querent, what is in the immediate sphere of influence. The card to the left is the immediate past, the one to the right is the immediate future, the one above is the most pressing external influence, the one below the most pressing internal influence. You can include another ring of cards that represent an outer ring of influence that must be read as a kind of tapestry, without the benefit of positional markers.

A regular pack of playing cards can also be used for yes/no questions, or for simple three card draws. A single card spread is enough to get a yes or no answer; a red card means yes and a black one means no. For more in-depth questions, like those that are time-sensitive, or require a vision of simple influences, designate a meaning for each of three cards (morning/afternoon/evening, past/present/future/, etc.) and then lay your spread.

The most famous system that descends from the four-suit playing card pack is the Lenormand, a thirty-six card deck which mixes playing cards with symbols commonly found in tasseomancy and coffee ground readings (such as the lord, the lady, the clover, the mice, etc.). Originally a game called Das Spiel der Hoffnung (the Game of Hope) developed in 1799 by Johann Kaspar Hechtel in Nuremburg, it posthumously became conflated with Marie Anne Lenormand, a French cartomancer, who gained quite a bit of notoriety during the reign of Napoleon, even becoming a close confidant of Empress Josephine and giving readings to Tsar Alexander I. Though her deck and other occult items were burned after her death by her devoutly Catholic nephew and we have no real idea what her cards looked like for certain, several decks of playing cards meant for fortune-telling were given her name, though Hechtel's Game of Hope remains the most widely used style for the Lenormand deck.

The difference between the Lenormand cards and reading a simple playing card deck is that Lenormand cards are like words in a sentence and are never really used in single card spreads. They are syntactical, meaning that the first card is usually considered as the subject of the sentence, while the following cards are modifiers of it. You can, of course, choose to ask simple questions, like, "what will my afternoon be like?", then lay down two to five cards in a string. The big spread in the Lenormand system is the Grande

Tableau, which uses all thirty-six cards laid out in either six rows of six or four rows of eight and one of four.

Again, in the Lenormand the signifier card is traditionally the Lord or Lady depending on the gender identity of the client. This is, however, too exclusionary, so shuffle the deck and have the client choose a signifier card at random from the deck, then shuffle that card back in before laying the cards out. Wherever the signifier card is in the spread is the focus of the reading.

In the row that card is in, any to the left signify the past, where those to the right signify the future. In the column the card is in, those above are influential thoughts, while those below are important impulses of the querent. In the Grande Tableau, the farther from the signifier to left or right the further backward or forward in time the card represents, while the farther above the card is the less present to mind that thought will be and the farther below, the deeper buried the impulse may be. Cards diagonal from the signifier on the right signify conscious (toward the top) and unconscious (toward the bottom) possible paths for the querent, where diagonals to the left represent strong external (toward the top) and internal (toward the bottom) influences.

To discover information about certain topics (love, health, wealth, etc.), look for the card that represents that thing within the spread and read it as a nine-card block, just like in the above description of the playing card spread. The further the topic card is from the signifier, the less important it is for the querent at the present time. The middle four cards of the spread can be read as a sentence describing the core issue the client is working with and can become the center of the reading rather than the signifier (all four act as the signifier rather than the one your client chose). The Lenormand system lends itself to lots of nuanced interpretations, flexibility, and a deeply personal tone that makes it one of the most fun and fulfilling types of cartomancy I know of.

8	2	6
4	1	5
9	3	7

1= signifier, 2= influential thoughts, 3= important impulses, 4= past, 5= future, 6= conscious influence, 7= unconscious influence, 8= external influence, 9= internal influence.

DIAGRAM 6
Card placements for a 9 card tableau.

TAROT

Likely the best-known form of divination in the world, tarot is an Italian descendant of playing cards. The earliest ancestor of the deck we know today originally developed in Milan sometime between 1420 and 1440 as a game called Carte da Trionphi, a trump taking game similar to bridge. The earliest extant examples of these cards were all commissioned by one of the most powerful families in Italy and the rulers of Milan, the Visconti-Sforzas, with the earliest mention of "triumph cards" being in a commission letter from 1440. The original decks were hand painted, gilt works of art that evolved between Milan and Ferrara. Later, in Northern Italy, a woodblock version of the deck evolved that today is called the Tarot de Marseilles. During the war of 1499-1504 the Visconti-Sforzas were overthrown by Louis XII of France and Pope Alexander VI and, in the pockets of returning soldiers and the bindings of books, the tarot found its way to France.

Between 1500-1509 descriptions of tarot trump images and wood blocks for their production begin to appear in France and Germany and we begin to see the game developing as part of popular consciousness. Just when the use of the cards turned toward fortune telling none living can say, but it likely developed in multiple parlors, salons, and bar rooms as a sort of drawing of lots, as really just another game. We know that by the mid-1700s there were individual divinatory meanings for at least some of the cards, though they likely all had fortune telling purpose by this time. There were also growing sanctions on tarot by the Church because they were believed to be evil and a distraction from piety (more as a type of gambling than magic).

It is also in the 1700s that we see the first famous cartomancers and the introduction of tarot into the occult circles of France. In 1770 Jean-Baptiste Alliette, better known by his magical name Etteilla and considered the first professional tarot reader, wrote the first known pamphlet on the use of tarot cards for divination. In 1781 the scholar Antoine Court de Gebelin published the eighth volume of Le Monde Primitif, a historical encyclopedia of world history (from his armchair perspective, of course), and describes the "Egyptian origins" of tarot. This is the first time that we see the cards conflated with a mystery tradition and where much of the Egyptian lore surrounding the tarot comes from. After the publication of de Gebelin's book, Etteilla wrote a second pamphlet in which he elaborates on the Hermetic symbolism in and possible Egyptian roots of tarot called How to Entertain Oneself with a Pack of Cards Called Taro. The writings of both Etteilla and de Gebelin are the main reason that tarot has been cemented into our culture as an occult system.

In 1804, a disciple of Etteilla, Melchior Montmignon D'Odoucet, published a three-volume work titled The Science of Signs of Medicine for the Mind, Known Under the Name of Card Drawing, which is one of the best collections of Etteilla's teachings and where many of the meanings for the minor arcana stem from. Later, in Paris, one of the most famous magicians ever to have lived, Eliphas Levi, published a book called Dogma and Ritual of Transcendental Magic, which is one of the first books to correlate the tarot with the Hebrew alphabet and thus to the Kabbalah. His work influenced later authors, such as Kenneth MacKenzie, S. L. Mac Gregor Mathers, Robert Chambers, Paul Christian, Oswald Wirth, and, perhaps most famously, the magician Papus who codified and expanded on Levi's work.

That brings us up to the early 1900s, when, in 1909, the most famous tarot deck ever to have been printed was published in London, the Waite-Smith (often called the Rider-Waite) deck, which has formed the foundations for a huge portion of Western thought on tarot. Though A. E. Waite conceived of the deck, it is the illustrations by Pamela Coleman Smith that have allowed the deck to endure. Smith was already an eminent illustrator who had written several books and was prolific in her art before entering the Golden Dawn in 1901, where she first met Waite. Her unique and powerful style truly gave a new life to the tarot, especially because hers was one of the first decks to fully illustrate the minor arcana and to tell a narrative with them, making them both easier to read and more palatable to the general public. The majority of beginners' manuals and decks today follow the example of the Waite-Smith deck, which itself is based on the teaching of the Golden Dawn.

In 1951, with the replacement of the British Witchcraft Act of 1735 with the Fraudulent Mediums Act of 1951, tarot decks were able to be published with impunity and were distributed widely, particularly the Waite-Smith deck and the Oswald Wirth tarot. In 1960 Eden Grey published her book The Tarot Revealed, which helped to popularize the cards and paved the way for their addition to the New Age movement, which was about to ride into the world on the coat tails of mesmerism, spiritualism, and theosophy.

It was not until the 1970s, with the work of Stuart R. Kaplan, that tarot really took on its current popularity. He wrote a book titled Tarot Cards for Fun and Fortune-Telling that introduced the cards in a fun and popularizing way, making the cards seem like less of an esoteric system of symbolic meaning and more of a parlor fortune-telling game. He also published four encyclopedic volumes about the history of tarot and started the company U. S. Games Systems, currently the largest publisher of tarot decks in the world. Eden Grey published her second book in 1970, The Complete Guide to the Tarot, which is the first place that the "Fool's Journey" is described. Then, in 1971, Paul Huson published his book The Devil's Picturebook, one of the first works to properly couch the cards in the world of witchcraft and paganism, making it one of the most staple accounts of tarot in the witches' repertoire.

Of course, a brief history of tarot would not be complete without mentioning the pioneering work of Aleister Crowley, who broke from the Golden Dawn and published many of their secrets, including a tarot deck that was altered to be more in line with Crowly's own Thelemic magic, one he called The Book of Thoth. The paintings created for the deck by Lady Frieda Harris were visionary artworks that gave life to the philosophies and magical teachings of Crowley. Though the cards and his system for using them were published during his lifetime in a leatherbound book, the deck itself was not published until well after his death. It was printed by the O.T.O. as a poor photo reproduction in 1969.

This is the other major system that has influenced tarot today, with many decks being made in the vein of The Thoth Tarot. The system draws very heavily on astrological associations, the beings Crowley encountered in his work (such as Babalon and Leviathan), alchemical theories, and the revelatory teachings of Crowley's Liber Legis, or Book of the Law. It is basically an artistic codification of the entirety of Crowley's teachings and is a true marvel of occult invention.

All of this to say that tarot is a marvelous tool with an extraordinary history, fueled by the genius work of occultists, magicians, historians, and witches over a period of nearly 600 years. Every reader of the cards and thinker that adds their work to the "Magnum Opus of the Grand Work of Tarot" is an essential part of the system, an integral part of the magic that the tarot evokes and wields. By using any deck, you are tapping into this collective power.

The best deck to use is the one that resonates most fully with you, the one you like the best and feel the most comfortable with. The idea that you must be given a deck is preposterous. The deck does not have to be kept in a secret box, nor out of the hands of others, but can be handled by clients, left on your altar or the coffee table, and treated as a friend (I've come to recognize that each deck has a personality all its own and that they can indeed become your best friend. Some are even willing to gossip with you). You can read at any time and you need not light a sacred candle and rub crystals all over them to get them to work for you; you just need to make a relationship with the deck and practice reading. You can also use more than one deck. Some decks like to tell dark stories, some like love stories, some prefer rambling tales connected with many spreads, and one deck may be better for one client over another, so leave your options open.

I am not a proponent of exclusively using spreads with placement meanings, as I prefer to intuit meaning in a generalized layout of three to ten cards, sometimes using clarification cards to get deeper information about aspects of the reading. My method is to clear the cards before handing them to my client (I tap the deck three times and blow on it). I then ask them to hold the deck while thinking about their life, what they want to ask about, and simply sitting with the emotions that well up. This helps to inform the cards as to what is going on with the client before I shuffle. I then lay out an initial line of four cards, which I read more like lines of poetry than components of an equation. Then, once I have the feel for the initial line (which is often about the situation at hand), I lay out a line of three, then a line of two, and a final "apex" card that leaves me with a triangle shaped layout I can then interpret like a painting. If any clarifications are necessary, I ask for guidance and pull cards at random from the deck until the point is made clear.

I also use the seven-card spread mentioned by Paul Fenton Smith in The Tarot Revealed, which is shaped sort of like a chevron with a card in the middle. The left-hand side positions are the past-present-future cards, those on the right-hand side are the influences-expectations-outcomes positions, with the middle card representing the key/answer to the situation. Another spread I commonly use is to lay out three cards in a row, just to get an idea of what is going on with a question, or up to nine cards for a more in-depth view. There are, however, multitudinous spreads the witch can choose from that are a mere internet search away.

Creating one's own spreads is of benefit to the reader, as well. Decide which positions you want in your spread (past-present-future, growth, health, whichever headers you choose), write them down individually on sticky notes, and play around with the shape of your layout, trying different combinations that may feel more or less right.

The same playfulness can be given to the divinitory meanings. The cards have been attributed traditional interpretations, but they are meant to adapt to contemporary issues and to be flexible in their use. Whatever you intuit in the cards is what they mean to show you and following that will make your readings more unique and genuine, though having a healthy understanding of the tradition will help curb some of your subjective judgements. It is not my intention here to rehash what has been well-documented and retell a story told a thousand times, so I will not include the meanings for the Lenormand or the tarot in this book, though there are many out there that will give a good understanding of the tradition. What you see in the cards is far more important, though.

If you need or would like to, reach out for clarity in a reading by asking the Tarot itself for guidance. The tradition, the system, the entirety of Tarot is a type of egregore. It has a life and power all its own, so you can reach out to it whenever you would like to. Your deck also has a spirit and life of its own, especially after you work with it over a long period. It becomes a tulpa, or thoughtform with enough etheretic energy of its own that it is fundamentally alive. Ask it for help and it will help you.

* * *

Whichever method of divination calls to you, practice it until you feel capable of using it intuitively and autehntically, without the use of books, and until you can get consistent, accurate results. Daily use of your tools will benefit you, as will carrying them with you and sleeping with them under your pillow or near your bedside. Start with doing readings for yourself, building relationships with the spirits that want to help you in your work, and then begin doing readings for others. The more divinations you do, the better you will become at using your favorite modalities and the more your confidence will grow.

Once you gain in proficiency, I encourage you to get creative. Come up with your own spreads, create a new system for the runes that works for you, find a way to use four pendulums at once, read the shadows cast by the leaves of a tree as they fall across a tablecloth marked with patterns of your own making. The world is an amazingly complex, beautiful place and you are the only one who sees it the way you do; please, when you're ready, share your vision with the world and make it that much bigger and brighter!

HEDGECRAFT

One of the most intoxicating and dangerous of the seed arts of witchcraft is the hallmark ability to "send forth the spirit", to travel beyond the everyday type of consciousness, to fold your spirit into another shape, and travel into worlds unknown in the act of "hedge riding" or "hedge walking". The spirit sent forth is the fetch, or etheric body/ double of the witch, a wonderfully adaptive energetic part of our being that can do so many useful things. This is one of the more "shamanic" practices of the witch, using drums, singing, psychedelics, meditation, and visualization to view and effect various realms and to speak to spirits. It requires a shift in consciousness, which can be trained by the witch to happen more easily over time without the use of drums and drugs. Entering a dream-like trance can be made easier with the use of various tools of the subconscious world, especially "anchors", which are marks left in the mental body that can help to shift consciousness on command and may have correlates in the physical world (like crossing the fingers, touching the temples, and other various hand gestures).

When you have gained proficiency in this part of your craft the multiverse will open to you, worlds upon worlds of color and sensation where spirits of all sorts will speak to you and give you answers to questions, where you can travel great distances at a thought. It is as easy as breathing, once you get the hang of it, and with the appropriate training it is also possible to do it relatively safely, though there is always a bit of danger in the practice.

Because the hedge witch lives between the worlds, I consider hedge riding to be a form of Toad magic. Toad teaches us to live both in the water and out of it, to jump high across the hedge, and land safely on the other side. Toad is a great guide to us. The hedge is the border between the everyday world of the city or village and the world of the forest, the wild places where the old gods dwell. It is thick and full of thorns, nearly impassable, unless you know the secret places where the foliage thins, and those who live on either side can dip and dive between the leaves to gather the delectable berries that ripen across the hedge. The hedge rider, the haegtessa, the Toad-born wise woman who wanders through the brambles in search of treasures from the spirits beyond the boundary is our teacher; Toad is our guide.

The reasons to learn to ride the hedge are many, though the main one is knowledge. Across the hedge is an infinity of possible worlds with spirits to populate them, including the dead and the ancestors we venerate, the gods, the elements, and all the powers we work with. By sending forth the spirit the witch may work much more directly with the spirits and powers, thereby increasing the amount of personal power they have to share with the community and helping to strengthen the relationships with the spirits so integral to our work.

Across the hedge we find familiars, learn to fold the fetch, and in other ways work with our own spirit as well as others. Unlike ceremonial magicians, we do not always wrench the spirits from their normal habitation and force them under our control with magic; we coax and woo the spirits, leave them offerings, learn their likes and dislikes, listen to their stories, and become their friends. Some of them are far wilder than others and need to be treated like any other wild thing, with respect and caution. Some ought to be avoided altogether.

Healing can also be accomplished while hedge-riding, by sending the spirit to the aid of another person. The witch can even travel into the etheric world of another (the lower astral) and encounter the spirits that are most helpful to the client, manipulate the client's energy to better affect health, and lift curses and such from the person. The witch can remotely view other locales to check up on situations and to cleanse energies over long distances. The opposite is also true; the spirit can be sent to cause maleficium, to lay jinxes and curses, thus damaging another person. When you can ride the hedge, you and your power are much freer.

Hedge-riding is not about gaining power, however. It is about growing in knowledge and understanding, becoming wise, which naturally leads to greater power, though it hopefully also leads to knowing how best to use it. It is also meant to grow relationships, which amplify the witch's power. We ought not seek power over another being, but power with others. When you share power there is always a growth and flow of power, a balance, while to seek power over others leads inevitably to imbalances, illness, and strife. Seeing the hedge as a community is key to our work. Various members of that community may ask to work more closely with you, or vice versa, and may become your familiar(s), the spirit partner(s) of the witch.

HEDGERIDING SAFETY

Safety is of paramount importance in this part of the work. Warding the space, laying traps, and having the appropriate tools are essential to being able to travel safely and to return to safety if things get hairy. These are simple actions and visualizations that can greatly reduce the likelihood of problems occurring while the witch is traveling or that can quickly get the witch out of trouble and to a safely warded area.

Practitioners will have multiple items throughout the house that have a protective quality, things like altars, artwork, bits and bobs hanging from windows. A witch's house is often well protected without needing to take very many extra precautions. There is, however, a plethora of ways the witch can protect themself from the vagaries of the world beyond the hedge. Firstly, the witch is wise to ward the working space. A ward is a protective barrier built by magic that surrounds a place and keeps it safe and sacred. The word "ward" is derived from the Old English weard, meaning "a guarding, protection; watchman, sentry, keeper". Wards can be as simple as a visualized magic circle of protection or as complicated as a golem or other magical protector. Another option to protect the space is to mix water with salt, bless and enchant it, and asperge with it in a circle around your working space.

To enchant the water and salt is simple. Take a bowl, preferably glass with no markings on it, and fill it with water. Take another bowl of earthenware and put into it a small amount of non-iodized salt (use what you have at home, though, whichever bowls and salt you have around). Using both hands make a triangle between your thumbs and forefingers over the bowl of water and say, "Awaken, Spirit of Water. Let all impurities be shed from you and may all good be added unto you". Do the same with the salt but replace "Spirit of Water" with "Spirit of Earth" and make a rectangle with your thumbs and forefingers rather than a triangle. Add the salt to the water and hold your hands over the bowl saying, "By magic might I call you forth, spirit of water and spirit of earth. Mingle your spirits, create new life, that guards me and holds me and protects me from strife". Make the sign of the pentacle over it with the fore and middle finger of your right hand (the Sign of Benediction), then circle it seven times, visualizing golden light coming from your fingers like honey and filling the bowl with brightness.

Now you can use it to create a protective barrier around your space, to consecrate items, and for any other form of beneficium. If you want you can make a large amount of enchanted water for future use you can add 40% grain alcohol to it (128 oz. of water would need 52 oz. of alcohol), which will help to preserve the water and protect it from molding. The salt also helps, but the alcohol preserves more strongly. You can alternatively bless a bottle of vodka, which is 60% water and 40% alcohol already and is just as readily made holy and sacred by your withcy powers, then go about your day. The choice is yours.

The circle of protection doesn't have to be made of salt and water. The witch can choose to make a physical circle with tape, salt, chalk, corn meal, or whichever herbs they choose to use, or they may choose not to use one at all. I often do not and feel a lot of freedom in choosing not to. Some witches have a piece of long nylon cord they use to lay out a physical circle with every working (usually with a nine foot diameter), though, personally, I think the mental version works just as well. You may also choose to lay traps throughout your house and put up amulets, charms, and enchantments to help protect against spiritual intruders and malignant energies seeking to disrupt your work. Traps can be simple, things like God's Eye charms, broomsticks over the doorways, witch balls, mirror traps, spirit snares (sort of like bird cages made of sticks), or the witch may choose to use runes or sigils drawn directly on the walls and the floor or on paper taped to various surfaces in the working space. Another way to protect yourself is to suffumigate yourself and your space while riding, which has the added benefit of creating a space that feels liminal.

Wearing amulets and talismans during the hedge ride is also a good option. I usually have several on at all times; rings and necklaces, a hat, a few tattoos. An amulet is a magical item that repels energies and protects the wearer, often against things like the evil eye or other common energetic maladies, though the jewelry of witches can get much more specific, helping to repel particular entities, spirits, or energetic patterns. A talisman, on the other hand, draws energy toward itself and can be used to attract energies the witch wants in the space, protective spirits and powers that may benefit their flight and keep the witch safe. Both are types of charm, enchanted items instilled with the power of a spell to effect the world in various ways. The most familiar is the lucky charm, though there are charms for love, better dreams, or anything else the witch can think of. They also come in a number of forms, sometimes being simple written or spoken formulae or pokes stuffed with herbs, parchment, and ephemera, cords tied with knots and hung with stones, or any of an innumerable array of things. Wearing them or hanging them around the working space can be highly effective in guiding the spirit and protecting the body.

I think it is a good idea to have a poke filled with things that may come in handy while hedge riding, such as small charms and brick-a-brac that have power for those who know how to use them. Things as simple as a root from an herb that offers courage, two iron nails tied together in a cross, a small vial of egg shell powder (cascarilla), a knotted piece of twine, gem stones that help with clarity, etheric travel, increase, and grounding, anointing oils, snail shells, bottle caps, etc. You may also include spell scrolls in your hedge poke, things that may be needed to summon up a little bit of help. The witch may also get to a point where these things are no longer needed in the physical world, their magic and mind are strong enough to keep them safe and sound without the use of magical props, but I think it is best to proceed with caution, especially when just starting on your journey toward proficiency in hedgecraft.

I have mentioned the use of guardians, things like golems, that might be of use while hedge riding. Traditionally the golem is a creature out of Jewish lore, a being made of virgin clay and blood and given life by the secret names of God. The best known golems are Adam and Lilith of Genesis fame and the Golem of Prague created by Rabbi Judah Lowe ben Bezalel to protect his people from anti-Semites in the late 17th century. You don't have to fashion one from clay if your crafting skills are lack luster, but you may be able to find a suitable porcelain doll for the task. These can be enlivened and given a fetch, an etheric body, that can perform various tasks and protect you and your home, so long as you treat the golem with respect. A simpler option is to ask the spirits of the physical working space to protect you and to keep forces that may interfere with your work at bay.

You can also ask spirits, particularly ancestors, to take up residence in your home by giving them spirit houses or soul crystals to inhabit. Soul crystals are quartzes and other common gems that have been enchanted and buried or kept in a bottle as a new body-on-earth for the spirit of an ancestor or elemental to inhabit. Burying the crystal is just a way to protect it and in no way impedes the movements or power of the entity inhabiting it, unless the point of your spell is to bind the spirit, which you may choose to do for a number of reasons.

You may also choose to prepare tools for more direct use in the world over the garden wall, what I call hedge weapons. The knife and the wand are suitable for this purpose and can be included in miniature in your poke, held in your hands, or laid near your person while you are "hedgesploring". You may feel better using things like rattles, brooms, staves, mirrors; the witch can use whatever they can think of to use as an offensive measure should the need arise. Usually these will go unused and the witch will rely more on cunning and wit than on brute force, but sometimes aggressive and dangerous spirits respond best to a blast from your wand or a slash of the sword than to gentle negotiations.

There may come times when you are ensnared, trapped, or ensorcelled while over the hedge and will need a tool to extricate yourself, or you may find yourself well in over your head and need to fend off attacking forces while you figure out how to get back to safety. Conversely, one of the spirits which you have contracted may get into trouble while doing a job for you and come asking for help, at which time you will need to be prepared to fight by their side. Even with these precautions in place the best laid plan may fail.

These precautions help prepare the witch to perform

the work. You may choose to do none of them or all of them and then some. It is entirely up to you. Remember, however, that the world beyond the hedge is dangerous and unpredictable, so it behooves us to be prepared not only with our tools, but with our skills. The better able you are to turn that world to your will at a moment's notice, the better able you will be to perform the objective of your flight and avoid issues while doing it. One of the most useful skills you will develop is to formulate and hold in your mind a clear desire and objective, which will help to guide you through the Wood. The clearer in your mind your desire is, the faster and more efficiently you will be able to find it (or it will find you, which is often the case).

The reasons for hedge riding are just as various as the ways to do it, though there are some categories we can loosely put in place to help guide the journey. One of the primary reasons is to commune with spirits, especially ancestors and tutelary spirits that can help us to develop our craft and help us to understand our work better. They can also be asked questions about how best to use an herb (though the plant itself is often the best to ask these questions to, either directly or while across the hedge), how to make a spell work better, symbols to amplify our power, o deepen our understanding of certain otperations, and where to find lost items (spirits of place, genii loci and house spirits, are also great at helping with these issues, especially misplaced keys).

PATRONS AND DEITIES

Among these advisory spirits the witch may come across a patron, a powerful spirit or deity who wishes to have a working relationship with them or a spirit tied to their familial line, though family for the witch has a broader definition than in common parlance. In my own experience this is a spirit I have come to understand as ancestral and call Aunt Maggie. She lives in a cottage in the woods and I always find her sitting by the hearth spinning wool into yarn or simply gazing into the fire, sitting crooked and talking straight. She has become as dear to me as any other member of my family and I cherish and respect her wisdom and power. I also work with various spirits who give me what I have come to call the "download", as it often comes with a gentle touch or a bout of glossolalia that is later processed and understood over time. Deities also form a strong bond with witches, and sometimes show up in our visions across the hedge, giving us guidance and instruction, or telling us what needs doing. Whatever deity you make relationship with, make the relationship strong and communal.

Deity is both real and unreal. Some believe that any deity is merely a mask, an archetype that represents a deeper part of the human psyche, where others believe that deities exist wholly and completely of themselves, that Hekate, Lilith, Lucifer, etc., exist in the universe just as completely as we do. The truth, so far as I have been able to understand it, is that both of these beliefs represent reality, that the Horned One is an archetypal image of the Divine Masculine within ourselves, but also the real and present Devil of the Craft, from cloven hooves to hornéd head.

Peter Paddon said in his A Grimoire for Modern Cunningfolk:

> "There is quite a difference in opinion among various Pagans as to the nature of deity. For some, they are living, breathing entities in their own right, while others see them as archetypes, or representations of deep-seated facets of our own psyche. The whole argument of whether they come from within or without is debated fiercely and eternally on various internet forums, but ultimately the only opinion that matters is your own, formulated from your own experience. For myself, I always answer "both", not only because there are differences in

the nature of different deities, but because I believe
— based on my own subjective experience and in-
teraction with the Gods and Goddesses I work with
— that they truly do partake of both."[1]

Something I try to keep in mind in my own practice and
something I impart to my students is the Law of Paradox,
that all things exist and do not exist concurrently throughout all time and space in all dimensions, worlds, and realities; Everything is separate, everything is one. The better the
witch is able to keep this in mind, the stronger their magic
will be.

In the vein of deities are tutelary and guardian animal
spirits, which represent the egregore of your family. The tutelary animal is more of an overarching, spiritual personality
you can communicate with during hedge walking, kind of
like the fetch of your ancestral lineage that you may interact
with as an ancestor in and of itself. They may also be the
essential spirit of all eagles, bears, possums, ants, or any animal you can name, the spiritual template or oversoul for that
species. These are powerful spirits and can clarify aspects of
yourself and your place in the craft, but, as per usual, proceed with caution because they can sometimes ask for more
than you are willing to give. Make the details of your desired
interaction clear before going forward.

FAMILIAR SPIRITS

You may also want to find a familiar spirit that will
help you in your craft work and gathering information, a spirit with whom you have a friendship and can send on magical
errands. These can take the shape of animals but are usually
powerful spirits who take a form compatible with your own
nature. Sometimes they simply arrive at your side or have

---

1   Peter Paddon, A Grimoire for Modern Cunning Folk (Green Valley Lake,
CA: Pendraig Publishing, 2010), Kindle Edition.

been with you for many years before you notice them, or you may search and never find one.

Because of the symbiotic nature of this relationship you and your familiar must both get something out of the relationship and a contract will be made to ensure that neither party is left resentful. What is asked of you can be as simple as companionship or to make daily offerings, but sometimes you may be asked to do a certain kind of work (such as healing, teaching, etc.) that different spirits will want to help you perform. I have spirits that prefer divination work, others that prefer healing, and some that prefer retribution work. The task will depend on the relationship between you and the spirit and, if the contract isn't upheld, the spirit may leave entirely, not show up when summoned, or start to play tricks on you to get your attention, so be aware and do as you promise your familiars you will do. The relationship between a witch and a familiar is one of the best-known aspects of the craft, though that relationship is certainly not guaranteed. It is something to be sought after respectfully and deeply cherished.

We know that familiars often take an animal form and have names like Pyewacket or Greymalkin, come to the witch as the spirit itself, or can even take on human form, like the familiar of Bessie Dunlop, a spirit who she called Thomas Reid. She said Tom Reid came to her in about 1572 and that he was at one time a human soldier, a barony officer, who had been killed at the Battle of Pinkie. He looked like a dapper old man who carried a white wand. He said he lived with the "fairies of Elfhame" and would advise her on how to heal people, where lost things could be found, and even foretold the death of her child and her husband's recovery from a severe illness.

After she was arrested for witchcraft, Bessie told her questioners that Tom Reid had been ordered to help her by the Queen of Elfhame, who had disguised herself as an old woman, knocked on Bessie's door, and asked for a cup of water, which Bessie happily gave. Though Bessie Dunlop was a boon to her community, she garnered unwanted attention which eventually lead to her being sentenced to death by strangulation and burning, never seeing help from either her clients or Thomas Reid. The spirits do as they do and must always be considered wild, even if they are your helpful friend, and, in some cases, there is nothing they can do to help you if you should get into trouble, so you must always be cunning.

The witch, at some point, may also meet the fetch mate, a being which Lee Morgan compares to incubi and succubi due to their more-often-than-not sexual relationship with the witch. These are daimonic, not demonic (a Christianized idea of malevolent spirits in the service of Satan), a type of familiar spirit which exist as arbiters between humanity, gods, and the realm of spirit. They are often tutelary and sometimes take a sexual interest in the witch. When I think of the fetch mate I think of the Grigori, or Watchers, the angels which were set to watch man in the Book of Enoch but developed relationships with humans and begat a new angel-human hybrid, the Nephilim. Some consider witches to be the descendants of the Nephilim, but I think a less elitist way of looking at it is to think of the relationship between a tutelary spirit and a witch as essential to learning the deepest ways of working with your personal power (perhaps with a sexual component, perhaps not).

SHAPESHIFTING

Across the hedge, the witch learns to shapeshift, to fold the fetch into an animal form that can leave the physical body and journey through the world of spirit and, sometimes, effect the physical world directly. This is one of the most tantalizing bits of hedgecraft, though it is also one of the most feared and dangerous aspects. The fetch, or etheric double, of the witch is normally very similar to their own body. It is possible to "fold" it into other shapes, though, creating a magical body that can travel through the Wood and help the witch perform tasks and travel the spirit world in a different way, to perceive it through the eyes of the animal-form. In order to make it work well, the witch must dive deeply into their core, facing their light and shadow and all in between, so that they have total mastery of their form.

It is also wise to seek council from the Totemic spirit of that animal family. If you find that you transform into a hawk, find Hawk beyond the hedge and ask for its help, or ask Wolf, Bear, Salmon, Egret, Cockroach, Pigeon, Shrimp; whichever animal it may be. Some of them can be volatile, wild, so proceed with caution; damage to the fetch can have lasting consequences in the physical body and the everyday world.

Perhaps you will also learn how to fold the fetch over your physical body, melding them together, and, by so doing, become a true therianthrope. This is vastly more dangerous than the shapeshifting of the fetch alone, but can be incredibly helpful because you can effect the physical world, perhaps even being seen by those who normally cannot see the unseen. Because you are more "real" in the physical world, you can suffer real and lasting damage to your physical body. There are lots of stories about witches who are caught off guard while in the shape of an animal, such as a cat, and get their paws cut off, the paws quickly becoming severed human hands and leaving the witch bleeding to death. Pursue this practice with caution.

REMOTE VIEWING

With practice and proficiency, the witch can learn to remotely view other locales and see what is happening in the real world in real time and, eventually, interact with it. In my experience this is one of the hardest aspects of hedgeriding, where other witches find it to be a natural extension of their abilities. My best friend in high school could close her eyes and just... whoosh! While she was in a trance state we would ask her questions about what she saw.

She never remembered what happened and today refuses to believe that anything did, which is common among natural seers; an inability to remember the journey and what they saw. In fact, regular vivid and lucid dreaming are often the hallmarks of the naturally adept haegtessa, and it takes just a bit of tweaking to remotely view things, though it may still be difficult. Persevere and the worlds will open to you.

HEALING AND "DEEP DIVING"

By developing the ability to ride the hedge, the witch has the opportunity to view and influence the energetic bodies of another person for the purpose of healing. In my own practice I do what I call "deep diving", which is to send forth my spirit, my magical body, into the etheric world of another person and there remove blockages, realign energies in accordance to what the body tells me is necessary, and to help my client move through emotional issues, illnesses, and long held guilt, shame, and fear. I try to be as non-invasive as possible, but this can be a profoundly felt experience. While this is happening, it is best to remember that the witch is seeing symbols and signs with meaning only to the witch that will guide the session, not necessarily what the client is seeing or personal experiences of the client, though that may occur at times. While performing these services the session is always client centered and the witch holds neutral space for the client, remaining as judgement free and adaptive as possible.

CROSSING THE HEDGE

There are many and varied ways to get across the hedge, some based purely in visualization, some requiring the use of tools such as drumming or the unguentum lamiarum (witches' unguent), a hallucinogenic ointment that will be described in the wortcunning chapter. You do not have to take hallucinogenics, of course, and can choose to use simple visualizations that alter consciousness.

Before beginning to ride, make sure that you've taken the appropriate precautions as mentioned above and that you've chosen a place and time that you are unlikely to be interrupted, your phone is on silent, you have used the bathroom, etc. If you have a flying ointment apply it before you start and be as comfortable as possible. You'll find that as you begin this process every little pain will feel like the most important thing happening, but this is the conscious mind trying to maintain total control; keep relaxing through it all. I suggest you lie down for the flight as it helps to fully relax the body.

Before we take our initial steps toward true flight we need to set up some inner parameters and safeguards, a warded space called the LOCUS within the lower astral world of the witch where the fetch can return to safety. Once you are relaxed, bring to mind a place. Any place will do whether you have been there or not, but it is wise to make it a place that makes you feel safe. It may take a few sessions to bring this lace into vivid detail and you may need to wander a bit before you find the best locus for you.

When I started the practice of hedge riding it took me several weeks to feel sure-footed in my locus and I had to learn to bring the world into focus through my Will, first falling through a misty void that coalesced into a blurry scene that eventually became a tangible place of power for me. This power takes time to develop; be gentle with yourself. When your locus finally coalesces, begin to focus on minor details of what you can see, textures of things, color and vibrancy, depth, distance. Once you get the hang of seeing what is there, begin to stretch your other senses and discern scent and sound, what the air tastes like, what the air remembers. Start with one and work your way up to more. Try not to overwhelm yourself.

Once the surroundings become clearer, look down and at your hands. Notice if they are yours, if they are even human. Whatever you see, allow it. These are the hands the fetch has manifested and they are a clue to your inner nature, a point of further rumination when you come back from your flight. They may change throughout the journey, too, which we continuously allow. Eventually the magical form will become more static, but, for now, it is learning about itself. From your hands look at your wrists, your arms, until you've scanned your whole body. Take note of what the fetch looks like; this is the beginning of your magical body, a sort of costume for the fetch, and is of the greatest importance across the hedge. It is not only a safeguard for your fetch but is what others will see if they run into you while riding.

You may find that your magical body has a human body but the head of a rooster and the feet of a goat, or maybe it has the head of a fish, a human face in its stomach, and the wings of an eagle. Do not fear it, these are symbolic representations of powerful parts of your spirit seeking manifestation in the astral world. In paintings and depictions of the witches Sabbath there are often images of men and women, some riding distaffs and brooms, some dancing, and sometimes surrounded by things that look like monsters. To my mind, these are not monsters, demons, or evil spirits, but other witches in their magical bodies who have come to join in the festivities with their toad-born siblings. What non-initiated dreamers take for twisted and ugly features the witch understands as the shifting nature of the spirit realm and emblems of power.

Now, in one of your hands you will find an object, small and recognizable, something you will leave in your locus as the ANCHOR. This is a tool that will help you to return to this exact spot at a moment's notice whenever you want or need to. Before you put it down examine it, making sure you know its texture, color, smell. The anchor that comes to you can sometimes be surprising. Mine is an angel statue I bought for my sister one Christmas and never gave to her that now represents Aradia on our altar. It could be something of great importance to you, or maybe the napkin holder that sat on your grandmother's dining room table, a favorite childhood toy, or something as simple as a surveying flag.

Now that you've established a clear and present magical body for your fetch and you've placed the anchor, look to your right. There will be an object of some sort, a landmark. Take note of what that is, how close it is, and whether it has markings on it. Do your best to remember these details. If there is nothing close to you cast your mind further to the right until you run across something that stands out to you. Once you get used to this you can travel a very great distance faster than thinking. Once you have explored to the right, return to your original spot by thinking of your anchor, then look to the left and see what is there. Again, if there is nothing, cast your mind further to the left and, once you have found a suitable landmark and discovered enough details about it to bring it to your memory, return to your starting point and turn around.

This is possibly one of the hardest things to do in the spirit world, a uniquely odd sensation that the mind tends to resist. If you can do it once, you can do it easily ever afterward. Behind you will be a doorway of some sort, a cave, a hollow tree, a phone booth, something that you can enter. This is the path to the Underworld and, once you see it, it beckons and pulls you close. Before you choose to go through this door, which you will soon, you must set up the rest of your warded space, so make the clear and conscious choice to turn from it.

When you do, you will find a structure before you, a large building. This is what I call the Interior Castle, the doorway to the etheric world of yourself and others. If it is a great distance away, "flex" your powers and build a bridge to the doorway. Before the door will be a creature, possibly your childhood self, a mentor, or something wholly non-human. Who or whatever it may be I call the Guardian at the Threshold, who is meant to protect your spirit from intrusion. As you approach, this being will try to challenge or trick you and this you must meet with cunning and skill; you cannot force your way through. Entry depends on gaining the trust of the Guardian. If you run into trouble on the bridge, return to your anchor and try again later. At this point you have accomplished the important tasks; seeing the fetch body, laying the anchor, and seeing the great edifices of your lower astral locus. Keep in mind that this is my experience and one that is similar to the experiences of other witches I've talked with, but may not be how you experience your hedge ride. Always trust yourself and your abilities; don't second guess your experience because it does not correlate with another person's story.

Eventually you will also want to explore the above and the below within the locus, travel up and down, as these can be pathways to other parts of the spirit realm and may be very different than what our physical body experiences as earth and sky. Eventually you'll be able to travel not only in static directions, but diagonally, in swirls, in bursts and bubbles between dimensional boundaries, in truly limitless ways. The key to this whole process is learning to simply surrender while maintaining your cunning and being able to meet challenges you have not even dreamt of. The world over the hedge can be beautiful and tantalizing, highly educational, but also exceedingly dangerous, so you must always be on your guard and trust in the spirits you've learned to work with. That said, now that you have an idea of what the fetch body looks like (for now) and you've set up a place that is warded and safe, you are ready to begin the process of learning to cross the hedge.

Begin relaxing the toes, then work your way down the feet to the heels, up the calves and shins, relax the knees, the thighs and hamstrings, the glutes, pelvic floor, abdominals, low back, chest, and mid back, upper back, shoulders, upper arms, forearms, wrists, hands, fingers to their tips, the neck, the jaw and tongue, the soft palette, the chin, cheeks, eyes, forehead, ears, scalp to the ends of the hair. Relax everything. As you begin to feel tensions leave the body, let your mind begin to drift. Whatever comes through in your thoughts, allow it without resistance. Surrender is the first part of the training and begins to prepare your fetch and your spirit for lightning-fast action. Once your thoughts begin to thin and you can see the spaces between them try to catch a clear glimpse of what is on the other side, within those spaces; bring your thoughts to stillness there. Parts two and three of your training are patience and unwavering focus.

Walk closer to the image; if it begins to jitter about or it begins to blur, return to stillness and bring it back to focus. Walk closer and closer until you are absorbed by the other side of the hedge and the image you were seeing becomes the world you are inhabiting. Just as with the locus begin to sense this world in its every detail, as much as you can, and draw yourself further and further into it. Once you are fully there, ask that you be taken to a place that will bring you into contact with the spirit that is most important to your highest good and the highest good of all concerned. You will either be instantly transported there, be drawn there in a swirl of colors and sounds, a door will open near you, or a spirit (often one that wants to be a familiar) will come up to you and ask you to follow. You may be unable to hear or understand voices at first but try to get the general sense impression from the spirits and the environment so that you understand what is being asked of you or offered to you. Remember, not every spirit has your best interests in mind, so keep your senses open, your cunning sharp, and demand their honesty.

Wherever you end up, so long as you discern that it is safe, spend some time there talking to the spirits of the place, interacting with them, exploring the location, and trying to

127

find things that stick out to you (those are important details). This practice is largely experimental and experiential, so it will take time to grow your proficiency; do not despair if you're not a master your first time, or if you can't get or stay across the hedge the first time or the first hundred times. Keep working at it.

Throughout the years you will build friendships with multiple spirits who will want to stay close to you, you will find that your magical body changes, that you learn how to do strange and wonderful things, and that your craft becomes more and more fluid. There are always times when it isn't as fluid as it seems it should be, which are times of growth for you. These are times to celebrate, not fear, because it means you have been growing and now must figure out how to wriggle from the confines of your magical molt, like a snake from its skin.

HEDGERIDING WITH THE DEAD

No discussion about hedgecraft is complete without going over the interaction of the witch with the dead. In tales of the Sabbath it is said the witches not only cavort with demons and the devil, but the spirits of the dead and damned. As you may have picked up, I do not believe in damnation or the Christian Devil, but it is true that witches gather together with other magical beings, the dead, the Horned One, and the Great Lady, High Queen of the Witches, both of whom were discussed in the chapter "Sympathy for the Devil". Again, there is nothing to fear from these creatures (usually) so long as the witch stays aware during their flight. The dead can be great friends and allies, and the art of making relationship with them is one of the ultimate traditions of Craftwork.

In most of the lore about witches and their ability to "fly by night" the idea of their propensity to comingle with those who have shuffled off the mortal coil plays an integral part. Witches themselves are somewhat a part of the world of the dead already and not completely a part of the mortal realm, rather inhabiting a space between the two, what I call the Twilight. Travel to the Underworld is possible during hedgerides, of course, but so is travelling what are called "death ways", something akin to the idea of ley lines, energetic pathways running through and over the earth that are travelled by spirits and feed the land like arteries of spiritual force. A witch out of their body can use these ways to travel very quickly from place to place.

***

Hedgeriding, though essential, is a dangerous practice. Spirits don't always have the best manners and some can take afront easily, leading to arguments, battles, and stand-offs between you, your familiars, and the spirit in question (especially along the Death Ways). I've had my fair share of run-ins with spirits I had little knowledge of how to deal with, but by maintaining flexibility and being adaptive, I've always made it out with my rear end intact, though my tail feathers may end up a bit singed every now and again. Follow the suggestions for safety found in this chapter, take it slow, and do not jump before you really feel ready and you will end up a hedgeriding master in no time!

NECROMANCY

Of all the witches' arts it is necromancy that has garnered the most ire, even from within our own communities. Many witches desire acceptance in the world at large and the darker aspects of our art are the sacrifice for it, especially those that are considered "creepy" or "icky". Necromancy is, after all, the original "Dark Art". The word itself comes from the Greek nekros (dead body, corpse) and manteia (divination by means of), but it eventually became known as "nygromancy" in the 14th century, the Black Arts, under which title all of magic was eventually buried. In my opinion that makes the practice of witchcraft necromancy from the start.

Though necromancy, in the strictest sense, is merely divination by means of the dead, raising their spirits to garner information and answers or to discover secrets, it has become synonymous with the Abrahamic concept of "witchcraft" and has been almost wholly conflated with demon worship. For some, the very admission of having practiced necromancy makes them the vilest villain, who has probably fornicated with the odd corpse or demonic force and brought ruin not only to their own soul, but those belonging to everyone who associated with them. For witches like me, though, the aim is not to damn souls and woo corpses from their graves to make a zombie army of Christian devouring monsters, but only to raise spirits, both human and non-human, for the aim of communication.

ANCESTORS

The ancestors and the dead are handy keepers of secrets and tend to know the location of hidden things, so their comradery comes in useful for the scrupulous witch. They also can help guide readings and treatment sessions with clients, even telling a witch about a novel combination of herbs that might help and the proper way to prepare the remedy. I have had multiple moments like this, when a grandmother enters a reading and tells me the best way to offer difficult information or comes to comfort my client, or when a recently departed loved one comes through the cards to say "goodbye". I've also been in situations when I am performing energy work on a client and a departed spirit comes and offers to help, shows me where blockages are hidden, or even tells me secrets that the client may be hiding that are leading to energetic issues. Necromancy may seem like the stuff of myth, but it is rather useful once you get the hang of it.

The idea of "ancestor" is a tricky subject, one that deserves a brief explanation. When we think of ancestors we tend to think linearly, going back from our parents to our grand-parents and so on. The linearity of time, however, is merely our perception of a much more complicated concept that, in fact, is non-linear. All of time exists at once and, with proper training, can be perceived, at least in part, as more of a cloud of moments that the witch can observe and learn from or bring into manifestation. In The Haunting of Hill House, the Netflix original show, the character of Nell describes time in a most perfect way, saying, "Our moments fall around us like rain, or snow, or confetti." Our ancestors are all of those to whom we are connected by blood, spirit, circumstance, or magic throughout all time, past, present, and future, throughout the multiverse, and all of them can be helpful and relationships can be cultivated with them because they exist HERE and NOW.

Ancestors are different from non-human spirits, but

also different from disincarnate entities and ghosts. Some of them are powerful spirits in their own right, some are gentle guides, some are astral imprints, but most fall into two basic categories: The Greater Dead and the Familial Dead. The Greater Dead are a host of spirits who changed the world during their lifetime, whose names are still known, remembered, and venerated by many people. They are the spirits of people like Martin Luther King Jr., Mark Twain, Etta James, and also the ancestors of our art like Gerald Gardner, Doreen Valiente, Sybil Leek, and Robert Cochrane. Sometimes they can be reached, sometimes they cannot; they do as they please. There are also some spirits who seem to have gone beyond a place where they can be contacted, or even felt, a phenomenon I call Silence. What that means for them I do not know.

It is mostly with the Familial Dead that I have experienced Silence. These are the spirits of family members and friends, people who are close to us during their life or who have been close to or important to our extended family. What I have experienced is a period of about a week during which the spirits are easy to contact, then increasingly greater difficulty until they vanish into whatever leg of the journey is next. Some go almost instantly into Silence. This tends to happen less for the Greater Dead because there is still so much energy being offered to them through the living as we continue to tell their stories, read their books, and emulate them. I've made some big claims, but I cannot say I know what happens after death, only what I can feel and garner from hedgeriding and from the deceased.

Something to be aware of is that there are thought-forms that take on a life of their own and play the role of spirits, especially of the Greater Dead. These are less the spirit of a particular dead person and more what the living think the dead person would have been like. These are technically egregores, a thoughtform given autonomy and life by the energetic and magical power of a group of people (i.e. fans and adherents). These can also be of great service to the witch because they carry with them much of the disseminated knowledge of the deceased and seem to attract various remaining fragments of that person's etheric body, thus gaining a fairly well-rounded and deep persona, though they cannot technically be the actual spirit of the deceased. This doesn't mean that you ought not make relationship with them, just be aware that they are not the deceased and may have motives of their own. Proceed with caution.

Traditionally, the hearth is where the family would gather to tell stories and was the centerpiece of the home. The art of necromancy, in the way that we practice it, is all about making relationship with the ancestors, the spirits, and the dead and inviting them into our personal space (with strict guidelines in place, of course) to tell their story. Many people now do not have a true hearth, but you can make a hearth altar that will work just as well. It is one of the easiest ways of making a point of connection and communication (not worship) between you and the ancestors. Place a large, flat stone (about as wide as your lap) down on a table, in front of a heater, or even near your stove if there is room, though anywhere will work. Put your ancestor altar, the bone, and the thurible there as well. If you can, make this your working space and use it as a point of power in your workings, especially hedgecraft and necromancy. On the ancestor altar can also be a scrying mirror, or a wishing mirror, a thurible and incense, candles, and a collection of spirit jars, which are temporary houses for the spirits you work with.

Spirit jars are easy to make. Inexpensive, beautiful bottles work better than old salsa jars and are easily found at thrift stores. Fill it partly with crushed egg shells and partly with graveyard dirt[1], add some herbs that help spirits to

---

1 A note on graveyard dirt: Some authors have written that mullein leaf is a suitable substitute for graveyard dirt, but I disagree. To obtain it go to a graveyard and, if available, take soil from a freshly dug grave and leave an offering of honeyed rum and a nickel (or any silver coinage, so long as it is worth at least

manifest or that make them more comfortable (things like mugwort, wormwood, mullein, and fennel), and a few things spirits like, such as tinsel, colorful string, and small mirrors. I am unsure why spirits have the same tastes as cats and parakeets, but I know they like shiny objects and bright colors. If you want to make a spirit bottle devoted to a particular ancestor, maybe a grandparent who passed away, an uncle who was versed in the occult, or the cousin who was always the person you could confide in, then place into the jar a personal effect of the deceased, such as ashes, belongings, or a photo (or a combination of these things). It is important that you do not fill the jar completely, but leave plenty of room for the spirit to live in. Whenever you call on the spirit you can invite them to take residence in the spirit jar and, when you are finished with your work, the spirit may choose to stay or leave according to its desire.

The veneration of our ancestors is a major part of necromancy, calling our ancestors to our altars to give them offerings and attention so they may help answer questions and offer us aid in our magic and divinations. Usually this does not necessitate the use of rigorous rituals, but more of a shift of consciousness, like that used during hedgeriding. Peter Paddon, in A Grimoire for Modern Cunningfolk, talks about "tapping the bone"[2], which is simply tapping the knowledge of our ancestors to help along the reconstruction of folk magic into a new and powerful craft for the modern

---

five cents). If a fresh grave is unavailable, take dirt from a grave of your choosing, but always make sure to pay for it. All kinds of interesting and terrifying things can occur if you take the belongings of the dead without leaving appropriate payment. The first time I took graveyard dirt I did not leave an offering and woke up in the middle of the night with a middle-aged couple standing over my bed, holding hands, and staring down at me accusingly. Things in my living room were vibrating and items on my altar began to fall over. I apologized and went back to the graveyard the next day to make my offerings and payments (with interest).

2   Peter Paddon, A Grimoire for Modern Cunning Folk (Green Valley Lake, CA: Pendraig Publishing, 2010), Kindle Edition.

practitioner.

In the book Besom, Stang, and Sword by Christopher Orapello and Tara Love Maguire is a method for reaching out to the ancestors by taking the bone, referenced in "The Witches Toolbox" chapter, in your lap while you sit cross legged, thus making your body into a skull and crossbones (the symbol of the ancestors, the connection of the Above and the Below, and the Initiation at the Crossroads), and rocking back and forth until the consciousness shifts. Once you have achieved the switch and feel like the air has "thickened" around you, ask your question aloud before turning inward and meditating on the question and receiving answers in the form of impressions, voices, or any other sensations which arise[3]. It isn't necessary to set up a circle or compass round for this operation but, if you do, remember to open sacred space by thanking the spirits and ancestors and leaving an offering for them.

Granted, many of the rituals you will read about involve the exhumation of corpses, the sacrifice of black animals, and various other acts you may find unappealing. There are plenty of rituals that do not include those things and, as always, please feel free to create your own rituals, so long as you take the appropriate precautions and perform them in the truest spirit of the operation, giving it the full respect a spell of this kind deserves. The act of summoning a spirit can be dangerous and, if not done properly, invasive and angering to the spirit itself, so it behooves the witch to perform their magic wisely. It is best to make relationship with those spirits and ancestors that want to have a relationship with you, rather than forcing spirits to do your bidding. The ancestors are powerful allies when they are treated well and can be negligent or malicious when they are treated poorly.

Important to note is that through our actions in the

---

3   Christopher Orapello and Tara-Love Maguire, Besom, Stang, and Sword: A Guide to Traditional Witchcraft, the Six-Fold Path, & the Hidden Landscape (Newburyport, MA: Red Wheel Weisner Conari, 2018), 188-193.

world, through our work, through healing our own spirit, our own body, and our own mind, we can heal the ancestors that have gone before us and the relationships that they left broken. Our ancestors can be powerful allies, but they did not lead perfect lives, just as we do not. By actively working to help the communities our ancestors injured, by working to heal the environment and maintain as sustainable a life as we can, by consistently remembering and observing ourselves and how our interactions with the world create ripples that effect it for better or worse, we can begin to heal the wounds we were born into. We do not have to live in the wound, acting from a place of uncontrolled fear and hatred, of overwhelming pain and sorrow, of bigotry and willful ignorance; we can heal the wound and become stronger, more understanding, and wiser. Necromancy ought not to be considered a practice of subjugation, but of healing.

CONJURECRAFT

One may need to compel a spirit to manifestation in the physical world, though rarely. If the spirit you want to work with refuses to come to you and no other spirit has the information you need (which is almost impossible), then it may be necessary to force the spirit to talk to you, though such strong arming should only be used when all other avenues have failed[4]. The operations necessary to compel a dead spirit from the astral to this one can be very dangerous because the witch is at risk of possession, entity attachment, and angering the spirits in a way that may lead to a variety of ill occurrences, including death, because the spirit has been displaced by magic might instead of being allowed to make its own decisions.

Offerings are an easy way to coax a spirit into doing what you want or working with you. People tend to be more

---

4   Paul Huson, Mastering Witchcraft: A Practical Guide for Witches, Warlocks, and Covens (Bloomington: iUniverse, 2006).

pliant after they receive something thoughtful and spirits are quite the same, especially if you build up trust over time. On the ancestor altar leave a small offering plate and a cup and place offerings on the altar regularly. I also leave offerings for the spirits and powers I work with and anything else the spirits ask for or I think they might enjoy. When I refresh the offerings I either dispose of the old ones, thanking them for helping the spirits, or leave them as offerings for the tree I have designated as an ancestor guardian in my front yard.

The ancestor tree is another point of contact at which you can leave loosely tied, natural fiber prayer ribbons (clouties), spirit houses, and other offerings. Any tree will do, just begin leaving offerings at its base and speaking to it. When I leave offerings at the base of our ancestor tree I ask that it provide a sheltered place for the ancestors and spirits to rest, for the fairies to live, and I ask that it act as a guardian over our home and our family. We loosely tie natural fiber yarn on the branches to pray for rain and snow, or, to give the spirits something diverting, we hang spirit bottles, bird feeders, lights, and all sorts of fun and magical things, always thanking the tree for its kindness and its support.

Making relationship with spirits is important, but there are times that you will need to trap a spirit because it has become dangerous or bothersome, for which you can use a spirit jar. Spirits are drawn to them and they may just wander into it. If you paint it with trap symbols (pentacles and sprit seals as found in the Lemegeton), it may work to hold onto spirits until you can cleanse or release them. Boxes filled with herbs, string, and bent nails are useful, as are glass fishing floats and netting, holiday ornaments filled with colorful yarn and mustard seeds[5], or jars filled with beans, salt, and white vinegar and a mirror glued to the inside of the lid. There are so many kinds available and many more

---

5   Spirits feel compelled to count seeds, beads, and grains, so filling your trap with mustard, peppercorn, fenugreek, salt, and things of that nature will keep them busy.

waiting for you to invent them.

You may also make a number of god's eyes and hang them throughout your house, particularly over windows and doors. They are merely two sticks glued or tacked together (rowan, tamarisk, or tree of heaven work nicely) and wrapped in red or multi-colored yarn spiraling out from the center. You have likely made them before, as the popsicle stick version is often a craft project in kindergarten classes. Mirrors can act as spirit traps, too, but facing mirrors toward one another or breaking the mirror will release the spirits, so you have to be careful with these.

You will know the traps are full when mischief starts up in your home; things falling off shelves, pictures falling off the walls, inexplicable clumsiness, cold spots in your house, or the traps may fall, shatter, or become cloudy. At that point, transmute the energy trapped inside by throwing the flammable ones into a fire or burying the ones that cannot be burned for a full lunar cycle. You can also wash them in running water (the faucet works) and ask that the spirits held within be taken to a place in better accord to the highest good of all concerned. Placing your traps in direct sunlight is also an act of transmogrification. A stunningly beautiful type of spirit trap is the spirit tree, which is a tall post with many rods coming out of it (almost like a coat rack) and covered with cobalt blue bottles. Tradition holds that spirits get caught in blue glass, so having a spirit tree outside of your home protects you and yours by night and at dawn the spirits that have been caught are – poof! - transfigured. If your house is prone to spirit intrusion or you live along a Death Way[6] or near a cemetery, this might be a good idea for a new garden decoration.

---

6 Death Ways are the paths the spirits of the dead use to travel from place to place or from the place they died to the nearest vortex, or spiritual gateway, that will lead them to the Underworld. They are often found between cemeteries, especially very old ones, and they often follow the rivers of etheric energy called ley lines.

141

Binding spirits is another option, especially if you have cleared the same entity more than once and it keeps coming back, or it is particularly malevolent and needs to be bound for safety reasons. Consider, however, the ethical ramifications of spiritually chaining an entity to an item, and, before you proceed, think about all of the stories of angry Djinn and ghosts that have been trapped for far too long and go bonkers after they escape (which they inevitably will). Make sure that whichever object you are going to use as a binding agent is suitable for this purpose. Anything will work, but some things work better, especially things that are sympathetic to the cause. You will have to do some research and divination to figure out exactly what might work best, but a general binder is just a vessel filled with bone dust, dirt, spirit consoling herbs, and powdered beef jerky. You can also make a figure out of clay, plaster, or ceramic to make a poppet, which often work better than jars for general bindings.

Take your binding agent to a place where the spiritual energy is high, or where you know the spirit you are trapping can be found. Set the stang up in the middle of the area you intend to work in and place the cauldron before it along with the binding agent and the bell. You will also need your thurible, a binding incense, holy water, the fresh root of a binding herb, sanctified vinegar, and some red thread. Measure the thread by holding the end to your heart and then extend your arm fully to the side. This is one length, from heart to fingertips, and you will need seven lengths for this spell.

Use your thurible and suffumigate the area, walking in a circle with your smoke and spreading it with a feather or fan while saying, "Spirit, you may not rise as this smoke rises. You are bound within this space and cannot leave." Then take a bowl of holy water and with a root of dandelion or calendula asperge it in a circle around the space, saying "Spirit, you may not follow as this water flows into the earth.

142

You are bound in this space and cannot leave." Make a third circuit and use your fingers to sprinkle a mixture of salt, ash, and red wine vinegar around the space saying, "By the power of the Three in One, you are bound in this space and you cannot leave. Az ze."

Go to the center of your space and kneel before the stang. Pick up the bell, sound it once, and call out, "Spirits who protect me, be here now!" Sound it a second time and say, "Ancestors who guide me, be here now!" Sound it a third time, saying "Spirit I have come to bind, harken to my words!" If the binding agent is a vessel, leave it open; if it is a poppet, simply place it in front of you. Swing the bell over your head in a continuous circle and ring it loudly as you say your spell:

I come to this place made sacred by the Holy Rings of Three
And summon, conjure, and abjure you,
o malevolent spirit!
By the power of the Three in One and the Emerald Flame,
By the authority of the Ancient Ones and all the power of
The Crooked Rose, I bind you to this vessel/poppet!
I bind you! I bind you! I bind you!
You are bound, for all time: Past, Present, Future!
You are bound, in all facets of reality throughout the mul-
tiverse!
You are bound, by the authority of the Ancient of Ancients!

Clamp the lid tightly on your vessel or pick up your poppet and begin to wind the thread around it while chanting, "You are bound, o spirit." Continue chanting and wrapping until your thread is out. Then place your binding agent in the cauldron and say,

As the womb of the Mother births us to freedom,
so can it birth us to captivity.
By the power of the Father of Witches

and the power of the Mother of Witches,
by the Holy Light of Lucifer and the
Sacramental Blood of Dionysus,
by the Power of the Septenary Goddess,
the Double Three,
and the Three in One,
by the beating Heart of Witchcraft,
I birth you from the Midnight Womb of the Earth,
bound and harmless in all ways and for all time.
Az ze!

Now the spirit ought to be bound to the agent, making it less immediately dangerous (if the binding holds), but also grumpy. Take your binding agent out of the cauldron and wrap it in soft, white cloth, then in red cloth, then in black cloth, which act as layers of protection so other magics cannot meddle with your binding. Put it in a box and place the whole thing where no one will ever touch it again; lock it up, bury it in a place of power, or place it in the middle of a body of running water, then forget about it.

A personal story about binding spirits: When I was sixteen and far too naïve to be dealing with powers like these, I decided to help a friend by creating a sort of "golem" out of clay and summoning a spirit (just some scrappy little fellow with a penchant for mischief) to inhabit it, something we could set upon her stepmother, who wasn't really that bad, but at the time seemed like something straight out of Cinderella. The house they lived in was full of spirits, cold spots, and time loops; I don't know why, some places just are. We chose a suitable corner in the upstairs bedroom and summoned the spirit and chained it to the clay figure, which was rather difficult (that should have been my first red flag). Once the spirit was secured, we took it to a magically charged place outside, a corner of the barn where we had seen multiple spirits, especially children. We shallowly buried it and set it on its way to cause trouble for her "wicked" stepmother.

The situation escalated quickly. That day her step-mother started feeling ill, worn down and clumsy. The next day all four of her tires were slashed while she was at work and her illness worsened. On the third day she was mugged. We decided the spell had gotten out of hand and needed to end, so we returned to the spot where we had buried the doll and began to dig. We shoveled out a hole about a foot deep and two feet wide, searched through the displaced soil, but could not find the figure. I scooped all the dirt back into the hole and, as its creator, commanded the figure to appear. I stuck my hand into the loose soil and there it was, barely covered in dirt. We took the figure to a stump they used to chop wood and I released the spirit, thanked it for its service, and chopped the head of the figure clean off with a hatchet. Their step-mother began to feel better and her run of clumsiness and terrible luck cleared up[7].

I include this here because the conjuration and command of spirits has traditionally been included under the category of "nygromancy", or the Dark Arts. Necromancy is not so cut-and-dry as "talking to the dead", anyhow. In my experience, necromantic rituals and rites are not necessary for contacting the deceased because time over the hedge is non-linear, so hedge-riding suffices and works much better for getting the information I need. There are times when the rites are called for, but when summoning a spirit to the circle it may have difficulty taking form because what is summoned is not the full spirit but a fragment of the personality that the witch or magician must bind to this realm by providing a temporary etheric form for the fragment to speak through.

---

7 A story like this may seem wild, but this is magic, this is witchcraft; this is dangerous. These are the red claws and blood-stained teeth, the nettle whip and choking grip of the witch and we ended the spell before it could reach a much bloodier end. This is a cautionary tale; do not perform these rites without being willing to take responsibility for the ways the magic can snowball out of your control.

POSESSION & EXORCISM

The fragmentation of the spirit becomes worse over time as more and more of the fractured personality degrades, so freshly deceased people are easier to contact than long dead ones. The messages are often not clear and sometimes the spirit cannot be compelled to give the information in an easily understood form, so the witch must find other means of discovery. These fragments can also be "hungry", lusting after a more permanent connection to the etheric body provided for them, so they may try to enliven a connection to it by draining the life-force energy of the witch. We must always proceed with utmost caution.

These etheric fragments are parts of the personality which may hang about for a period of days or years and can become attached to objects, animals, places, and people. Without a physical body acting as a tether to keep together the thoughts and emotions of what I call the Lunar Body (of which we will talk later) the whole thing begins to disintegrate and return to the World Soul or River of Spirit from which the ether that inspirits all living things on Earth is derived[8]. The strongest parts of the personality, however, those emotions that are overwhelming in us, obsessive thought patterns and long-held habits, can find a way to continue a type of life by lodging themselves in the nearest etheric field they can.

This is the phenomenon of disincarnate entity possession (an idea similar to the Jewish dybbuk). Whole spirits do not need to possess or embed themselves in the Lunar Body of a living being in this way, though non-human entities and the Greater Dead can speak through the mouths of mediums using similar methods. Once a fragment embeds itself in a host it will begin to affect the host's behavior, health, and thoughts and may be able to nearly overtake the

---

8   This Life-Force Energy runs through the land as the ley lines, fairy lines, death ways, serpent veins, dragon lines, and so many other names. These rivers of energy are part of the World Soul that we share with our planet.

host completely. To remove the fragments requires clearing, banishment, and exorcism.

If an entity attaches itself to a person, the possessed may begin to experience sensations, thoughts, and cravings that feel like they are coming from some other mind (because they are), or like there is too little space in their body to fit their spirit, or like one of their eyes does not belong to them, or a slew of other related symptoms. It can be highly disconcerting. On the other hand, a person may never notice these fragments. A good friend of mine was a paramedic for years and I have removed several spirit fragments from her that never caused noticeably adverse symptoms. I can feel spirit fragments like this in the cemetery sometimes, though the graveyard is often silent and still. The presence of a witch or other person who can feel and speak to the dead will wake the spirits and the longer you stay in the graveyard the more spirits will gather; your attention garners theirs. You can also find yourself attacked by various non-human spirits and disincarnate entities at the cemetery, so wear protection and be cautious when you go[9].

Fragments are not ghosts. In my experience a ghost is more of a recording of a certain person at a certain time in the ether, like a tired old re-run; they do not notice the

---

9   Precautions and Protections for the Cemetery: 1) Sprinkle salt in your shoes before you go, 2) wear a sprig of rosemary or juniper in your sock, 3) remember spirits are drawn to bright colors, so wear as much black or white as you can, 4) wear a hat to protect the spiritually vulnerable spots on your head, 5) wear a cardigan or jacket that covers your waist past your butt, or wear a wide belt, to cover more of your puntos vulnerablés, as my teacher calls them, 6) wear a protective amulet, like a ring engraved with the Seal of Solomon, or a piece of selenite to ward off spirits, 7) make sure to touch the gate or walk way before entering as a sign of respect to the dead, 8) take silver coins and a bit of rum to pay spirits with, especially if you're grabbing graveyard dirt, 9) and take your blasting rod or devil's whip to thrash your feet after when you leave, just in case. Do not in any way desecrate the cemetery by leaving burning candles, incense sticks, or other trash about because you will leave with an angry spirit. Just follow this general rule of thumb when doing any work, even outside of the cemetery: Don't be a dick and you'll probably be okay.

living. Sometimes a ghost is actually an anachronism, a window through time where the fabric of reality sort of folds through itself and denizens on all sides are haunted by each other. These "hauntings" will only end when the pattern of energy has been altered by the destruction of the haunted place, through magic means, or simply with the balm of time. Something like a poltergeist or other interactive spirit is likely a non-human entity, psychic energy, or other power. Fragments are merely pieces of an etheric body, of a personality, that carry a strong emotion or desire. That isn't to say that you can't interact with a fragment, as they can sometimes take form if there is enough etheric energy concentrated near them (which is why these experiences can get worse the more fearful you are, as strong emotion creates a surge in energies.

Ghosts are also different from disincarnate entities, which are fragments that take on a sort of spiritual life of their own and can cause harm to the living, like Samara from "The Ring". Sometimes they are the spirits of those who die violently and seek revenge or try to continue living by taking control of another sentient being, usually a close relative or friend, but anyone will do. You may also feel these old and powerful spirits in family houses, religious places, centers of community activity, prisons, or in places where something momentous happened, such as battlefields. Some non-human and disincarnate spirits will also try to stand in as a summoned spirit, especially if the actual deceased has gone into Silence, so you have to be cautious and ask plenty of questions, demand honesty, and above all treat each of the spirits with whom you work with great respect and cunning.

Disincarnate entities and fragments of the dead usually don't have the same qualities as other spirits, such as ancestors and non-human spirits like brownies and fairies. They may retain much of the same shape they had during their life, but time may make them appear less and less human. They may only retain part of the knowledge they had while living, as well, remembering only certain things like pain, sorrow, love, and rage. They have a hunger, a drive that keeps them tethered to the world, making them single-minded and dangerous. When summoning these spirits, using the Triangle of Art[10] is a good idea, then calling on powerful spirits you have a relationship with (Hekate, Lucifer, Lilith, the Greater Dead, or strong ancestors) so that the "shade" cannot easily aggress against you.

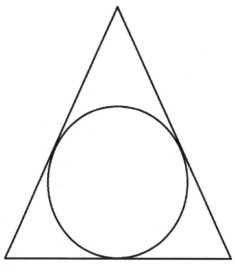

DIAGRAM 7
The Triangle of Art

Exorcism, the removal of spirits and astral fragments of the dead, is an art unto itself and needs to be understood before you start working with necromancy. In the above story about my friend's stepmother, I was very, very lucky not to have suffered some extremely ill effects from the spell I

---

10   The Triangle of Art is a specially designed symbol, a circle within a triangle, which is meant to contain and constrain summoned entities. It can be made of salt or cornmeal, ink and paper, possibly metal or crystal, or it can be summoned through visualization and will power. The circle is a spiritual portal that allows the spirit to enter, but the triangle holds it by the power of the Trinity.

had done and the way I exorcised the spirit. The spirit wanted to leave, I think, but sometimes they do not want to go and need to be coerced or forced to leave. The methods of exorcism are numerous and most are fairly simple, though there are some that are fairly ritualized and lengthy, such as the Catholic method. The tools you will need are few, only a pendulum and a command of hedgecraft, though, for more stubborn or malicious spirits, you may also need several other items. I like to have a pendulum handy at all times, so I always wear a necklace with a heavy pendant or a poke with a pendulum in it.

Many of the books written about exorcism are from a very Christian perspective with a focus on punishment rather than transformation. The techniques work, but we want to shift the focus from threats and sadism to movement and evolution. As witches, we understand that these spirits, ghosts, and entities have intrinsic value and need to be treated with the same respect and care as anyone else. Let us also be clear that we are surrounded by them, all sorts of spirits, all the time. They are like a menagerie of fantastical insects and animals of all shapes and colors, some like twinkling starfish, some like snails, some like rainbow-colored smoke, or angels, or origami; they can look or feel like anything and not all of them were once human.

To perform an exorcism, start by using your pendulum to figure out what you are dealing with. Ask what level of power they possess and whether they are of a beneficial or malicious nature (refer to diagram 1 in the Divination chapter), then begin to whittle down what you or your client needs to do to exorcise the entity. You may need to use one or more alternate forms of divination to get to the bottom of the issue, though the pendulum is one of the exorcist's handiest tools and can be used not only as a diagnostic tool, but a weapon. Once you begin the exorcism you must complete it, or things may just get worse.

Other energies to remember to clear include all cords

that the entity may use to feed off of the host, residual energies they may leave behind, and objects associated with the entity. Objects are anchors the entity may have left inside of the etheric body to help find the host body more quickly or thoughtforms that will continue to control the host. It is also important to close any non-beneficial portals and vortices the entity may have opened in the client and fill in the spaces left by the exorcism with whichever energies are toward your client's greatest good and the greatest good of all concerned. Once you have successfully exorcised an entity it will not return, but another may fill its place if it gets the chance, so be thorough.

THE FOUR BODIES

In order to better understand why the above is true it is important to understand how the soul is basically constructed. Various religious and mystical systems list multiple "subtle bodies" that are part of our existence. The Upanishads mention five bodies, the Rosicrucians believe there are seven bodies, and some newer systems list dozens, layers upon layers of increasingly subtle forms. In the system I use there are four bodies, though they should all be considered aspects of the same Soul Body or Vessel. The least subtle and heaviest is the Planetary or Edenic Body (also called the Gross Body), the physical form created by the combined energies of the planetary spheres and the stars, the physical elements of the Earth itself, and various energies from the environment (food our birth-giver ate, music they listened to, people they spent time with, and innumerable other factors) that acted upon it in the womb, all governed by the blueprint of genetics.

Next is the Lunar or Free Body, also called the Body of Breath, the fetch, and the etheric double that permeates and enlivens the physical form and processes the subtle energies the Edenic Body requires through energetic centers and

151

pathways. This is the part of the spirit which can leave the proximity of the Edenic Body and travel the Astral Plane[11]. This body consists of three layers, the Fetch or Animal Body, the Emotional Body, and the Mental Body. Because of this layering we can learn to feel emotions and remember what happens in the Astral Plane, though it may begin to fade quickly at first (like when you wake from a dream and can't remember what it was about). Practice will help the witch build up the Lunar Body and the Astral World will become more and more real to its senses. In the above when I have mentioned the etheric body this is the part of the soul I am referring to. The Lunar Body is also the house of the personality that dies with the physical body and, as it degrades, becomes the source of the fragments we discussed earlier in this chapter.

Then come the lighter parts of the soul that rarify after death instead of sinking back toward the Earth. These are the Plutonian Body and what we shall here call the Corpus Lamiae. The Plutonian or Spiritual Body, also called the Evolutionary Template, is the part of the soul that may be considered immortal, though it is really a collection of various spiritual vibrations that coagulate into one body that can pursue a particular goal, the life's evolutionary "purpose"[12].

---

11   The Astral Plane is the Astral Body, at least in part. The Astral plane can be broken into two levels, the Lower Astral and the Upper Astral. The Upper Astral is the area where we can meet outside of the Edenic Body, where the Witches' Sabbat takes place. It is a world in and of itself and is shared by everything with a Lunar Body. The Upper Astral connects to our Lunar Body, though, and in effect becomes another "body", which is in fact the Lower Astral Plane, something unique to each of us. My Lower Astral is different from yours and yours from everyone else's. However, this is the realm that we can travel through to help a person through energy work or "deep diving", sending forth our Lunar Body into their Lower Astral to effect change and increase health.

12   I think it is best not to think that your life has one, fated purpose. When we say "evolutionary purpose", it describes the multitude of choices which you are most likely to make according to the habits you have garnered over lifetimes, so it is changeable and highly flexible. Do not waste your time looking four your one purpose, your one path, your one love, your one anything. Life is to complex and beautiful for such limitations.

The reason this is called the Plutonian Body is that it manifests through the Gateway of Pluto, only reincarnating when Pluto the planet enters a suitable position and can draw the Evolutionary Template into an appropriate body. Pluto moves slowly around our sun, averaging about twenty-one years in each sign of the zodiac, and is considered a generational planet that describes what each generation is here to work on to progress toward our collective evolution. In each person's natal chart, however, Pluto can give us clues as to what that individual's evolutionary "purpose" is.

The Plutonian Body is a conglomerate of energies that benefit from working together and they may have been incarnated multiple times, which is partly where past life memories come from. Part of your Evolutionary Template may have been Cleopatra's or Joan of Arc's, perhaps even a great deal of it, but yours will also be made of parts from other previously incarnated vibrations of average people (and sometimes animals) as well as energies that have never incarnated before. You have never lived before and are unique throughout all time and all realities across eternity.

Upon death the Lunar and Edenic bodies disintegrate and return to the Earth while the vibrations that create the Plutonian body, hopefully having been rarified during their Earthly sojourn, will slowly separate and "rise" past the Upper Astral and the Gates of the Ancient of Ancients[13]. They will later re-conglomerate in a new pattern and into a new incarnation when the Plutonian aspect is right.

The final body, the Corpus Lamiae (witch's body), is special because not everyone possesses one. Some are born with it, natural witches who have always had some control of their power, where others create one through developing the Six Seed of Arts and doing the work of a witch, learning from teachers and spirits, and collecting sprowl, which allows us to do our magic. In fact, this body acts like a vessel

---

13   Gate of Death

for the energy and grows in relation to your practice, your personal evolution, and your Will. Once the Evolutionary Template has been involved with the Corpus Lamiae it leaves an eternal and indelible mark[14] on those vibrations, causing them to come together again and again, leading that person toward the Craft and toward the awakening of their personal power and awareness, the Cunning Fire. There is a saying, "Once a witch, always a witch"; it holds true.

I call this body the Corpus Lamiae here because of the scope of this book, though other people have called it other things. The idea of a constructed body or soul is not original to me in any way. Many people have thought that magical and meditational practices, seeking toward constant awareness of self, movement practices (like yoga and sacred dance), the creation of art (especially music), and much else can begin to build this fourth body. There is also an idea that the fourth body can act as a vessel for the others, excluding the physical body, thus maintaining much of the builder's essential self after death and allowing for a form of immortality. I'm not sure this is true, but perhaps can explain the

---

14   Genesis 4:15: "But the LORD said to him, 'Not so; anyone who kills Cain will suffer vengeance seven times over.' Then the LORD put a mark on Cain so that no one who found him would kill him. 16 So Cain went out from the LORD's presence and lived in the land of Nod, east of Eden." This is the Mark of Qayin that can be recognized in another person almost instantly once you start developing your powers as a witch. The word for "mark", 'ot, can also mean "self, existence" and is basically the same idea as "I am the Alpha and Omega, the First and the Last, the Beginning and the End", the name that Jesus Christ uses for himself in Revelation 22:13 and the name Adonai uses in Isaiah 44:6. The word is spelled with an aleph (the first letter of the Hebrew alphabet), a vav (which means "and"), and a tav (the last letter of the Hebrew alphabet). The name Qayin means "possession, acquire". The word Nod means "to wander", but if you use Gematria to work with the name Nod you get the number 60, which is the value of the Hebrew letter samekh, which means "support" or "protect" (and relates Nod to the word matate, or "Broom"). 60 is also the value of the word genizah, which means "treasury, treasure chest, storehouse". The Corpus Lamiae is the store house in which we build/acquire our God Self that radiates that telltale power of witchliness, the Mark of Qayin. Another way of looking at it is that the Mark of Qayin helps us identify our own and leads us to one another, like a built-in magical GPS.

154

mythology of the revenant and the vampire and their ability to shapeshift, fly, and travel the astral plane[15].

SELF-CENTRISM

I think there is an important point to make here. There are major veins of thought in the world today that say dissolution of the ego is the most fundamental aspect of true "spiritual awakening", that selflessness and self-effacement are the only way to know your truth. Thinking that you as "Sarah" or "Duane" is un-important or bad in some way, that you have value only as part of a larger, spiritual whole, and that your ego is the thing that separates you from that, is preposterous and poisonous. The idea that your desires and your urges lead to suffering is only partially true, because they also lead to pleasure, survival, love, rage, longing, joy, peace; all the deep and gut-wrenching energy of our intensely rich emotional lives. They are nothing to hide from and there is nothing wrong with your animal tendencies, your emotional pulse, nothing to feel guilt and shame over. You are partly divine, yes, but also part beautiful beast. You are the Baphomet, Divine Androgyne, the Magician, the Witch. There is not a path to magic; you are the magic. Here, do not think of the ego as the puffed-up partridge of self-importance that the popular mind paints it as, but as your personal genius, your own spirit, and the center of your beautiful individuality.

We, my darlings, are incalculably valuable as we are and our flaws do not make us imperfect; it is through the cracked places that our sovereign nature shines most brightly. It is in those jagged, painful places that part of our power hides. They are like treasure boxes, caverns filled with gold

---

15   If you are interested in all sorts of blood-thirsty monsters and spirits, check out Nigel Jackson, The Compleat Vampyre: The Vampyre Shaman, Werewolves, Witchery & the Dark Mythology of the Undead (Somerset: Capall Bann Publishing, 2001).

and jewels. They should not be covered up or viewed as an ugliness, nor as something that makes us inferior, incomplete, or unevolved. Our wounds are something to be explored and understood because they are where our strongest emotions are hidden. Emotions are of paramount importance in craftwork, especially the ones that make us wild with joy or rage, the ones that make us want to run screaming, and it is only through accepting responsibility and ownership of them that we can tap their potential. Self-empowerment through self-responsibility is one of the mightiest gifts of witchcraft, in my opinion, and returns power to its true owner: us. We must learn to dance with the Devil; we do not cower in the light.

The idea that the ego is an illusion only to be dissolved also allows the pseudo-spiritual person to run from taking responsibility for their actions because it was the "ego" that did it, not the "real" self; the heaviness and pain of living isn't real, only an illusion, so it doesn't matter. So many half-lit thoughts and half-digested philosophies have given us a crisis of meaning and a crisis of truth. We hide behind "spirituality", which has become an emotional vapidity that threatens to lead us over a cliff, our yoga mats and crystals crashing with us against the sharp rocks of reality. We wrap ourselves in spirituality, like a cocoon of ignorance, and forget; we go bloodless on the banks of Lethe. A witch, however, is bathed in blood and refuses to pretend living in the land of the living dead.

These words must come with a caveat. The light is essential to the dark and they must exist in harmony and the two must be allowed to create a whole spectrum of experiences. I am not advocating for pure emotional abandon and a removal of the lighter side of spirit altogether, but the acceptance of pain as a part of life. The trend I have seen in many magical and New Age communities is an abandonment of the dark side of spirit, a complete exsanguination of it. The blood of spirit is replaced with the embalming fluid of "love and light", which only gives the corpse of the spirit an illusory, lively flush. We cannot turn from either light or dark, but must live in the twilight between them, following the crooked path that wends through the Twilit Grove, exploring the meadows, the side-trails, the lovely darkness between the ancient trees. Witchcraft follows not the straight and narrow path, nor the middle path, and certainly not one with any goal, but one that wildly wanders where it pleases and revels in its own Selfhood.

A distinction must be made between egotism and what I think of as self-centrism. I am someone that sees value in the ego and nurtures and supports it, does the work to educate it, and desires to stay wholly and completely myself. There is a secret part of ourselves that is only for us, that cannot truly be shared, that needs to be held in sacred trust and hallowed solitude; the heart of our genius. Being self-centered is not thinking that the universe revolves around the self. Rather, it is the quality of being centered within self as the source of power and Will, the crucible of magic and manifestation, and the understanding that the personal genius is of equal value to all others. You are a god unto yourself, so develop your power and your understanding, sharpen your cunning, your tongue, and your craft, and walk through the multiverse draped in your own radiant glory.

HEDGERIDING FOR NECROMANCY

Keep the above in mind when you decide to try travelling to the Underworld, the Land of the Dead, to seek out spirits. I have been there myself, it just is not what I expected and isn't always the same. Sometimes the Land of the Dead is a vast, misty world submerged in water, ankle deep at the entrance and steadily deeper as you go, but I've also seen it as a dark forest with a red door in the center, and as a deep ravine between impossibly high cliffs dotted with caves. The Land of the Dead is what it needs to be and cannot be mapped or truly trusted. What I found useful is to leave a magical double of a mirror I have in my working space in the world of the dead that I can use like a walkie talkie. You will need to make a relationship with the spirits who rule that world, the psychopomps and the guardians of the dead, before doing so.

Consider that without a grasp of hedgecraft it would be easy to get lost and enter places that you don't intend to. Other than the locus and places like it, almost nowhere you go over the hedge is safe, especially places like the Underworld. Always keep your wits about you and your defenses up. Remember that the traditional role of the cunning person, shaman, or witch is to protect people from the spirits and the unseen, and for very good reasons. To ride the hedge is to hurl yourself into the lions' den; proceed accordingly.

Another place that is sometimes (if not always) connected to the Land of the Dead is an inky blackness, devoid of form, where the Unity of Chaos resides and where the Devouring Serpent, Apophis or Leviathan, waits. This creature is meant not to destroy but to dissolve into constituent parts the various bodies of all beings, perhaps as a natural process after death, perhaps as a guardian of Creation, I can't say. It is possible to make it through this place in one piece, though it is dangerous. You must maintain a very good sense of self and ego; otherwise dissolution is hard to resist.

Before you decide to explore the realms of the Dead and of Chaos, work on strengthening the ego, because these are places that try to dissolve you, coax you to stay, convince you that you belong there. Sometimes when you come back from a journey to the Land of the Dead you will experience obsessive thoughts about your own death, or the death of loved ones, like voices whispering about the thousand-thousand ways you and they may suddenly perish. The Abyss may leave you feeling despondent and lost, formless and disconnected. If this happens, spend some time soaking in the sun, spend time with friends or in a place with lots of people, or take yourself and a friend out for lunch. Sometimes it can take days or weeks to feel right again, but you will. We must explore the dark and lonely places, but we need the balance of the light to stay whole and sane.

There is also an underground world that I sometimes go to, though it is not what I think of as the "Underworld", but the Faery Realm. The dead certainly sometimes can be found there, especially those that were good hedge riders, dream walkers, or were close to the fae during their life, but you will mostly find non-human spirits here. This is a labyrinthine world of winding tunnels, vast caverns, and wonderous creatures. The citizens may ask for strange favors, ask that you solve a puzzle before they help you, or try to trick part of you into staying with them, which makes this a dangerous place. To get there once you are across the hedge, sink beneath the black soil, crawl under ancient tree roots or into their hollows, look for sacred rings of mushrooms, stones, or beneath the hollow hills; seek the places Underneath.

The practice of Necromancy and the development of this Seed Art are dangerous, so do not go about it willy-nilly. Read through this and the Hedgecraft chapters again before galivanting off to the cemetery with a handbasket full of candles and jars, or you may end up in the basket yourself. Before you do any conjuration, exorcism, or exploration of the Underworld make relationship with your ancestors; they will protect you during your operations. Set up an appropriate altar and begin leaving them offerings, build a rapport with them, and practice your divination skills with them. The more practice you have under your belt, the safer you will be.

WORT CUNNING

One of the guiding virtues of the witch is a deep and abiding love of nature, a faith in the power of the earth and the spirits in the land, which helps the witch to cultivate an ability to utilize the power inherent in plants to create magic. The word wortcunning literally means "the wisdom of working with plants", a combination of magic and medicinal herbalism, or the art of how to make relationship with the spirits of plants in such a way that they can teach you to help or hinder another person. Historically, the wortcunning person would have been the village healer, councilor, or protector against malicious magic. Cunning folk are often trained by someone else who has this cunning, but also gain a large amount of their wisdom directly from the spirits of plants and place, the genii viridis and the genii loci.

Each and everything has a genius (an indwelling spirit and intelligence). Each develops personality and proclivities, and each is influenced by time, place, and choice. Each individual plant, down to each blade of grass, has its own genius, and each of those is invigorated and under the protection of the genius loci, the spirit of the meadow, glade, or mountain that you find the plant in. These spirits are often fairies and other non-human entities, sometimes groupings of entities (there is a place near my home that is protected by a troop of brownies), though they may just as easily be the spirit of an ancestor who guards the land and protects the spirits there (like the Norwegian nisse and Swedish tomte).

According to Daniel Schulke in his Viridarium Umbris, "Bound up in the Genius of the plant are its preferences in life, its emotive soul, and other distinctive and peculiar traits like unto the unique personalities of angel, man,

163

or beast.["1] Each has its own preference for how it wants to make relationship to the witch, how and when it is to be gathered, and how it is to be used thereafter. Remember that you are not working with "just a plant", but a powerful spirit who will do well or worse by you depending on how you treat it. It is the work of the cunning person to make relationship with each genius and its attendant spirits in order to understand the power of the plant and use it to its fullest potential, pairing and grouping plants where necessary and bringing forth the greatest power of these wild spirits for the betterment or detriment of the community.

The Greek pharmakon means not only an herbal remedy or poison, but also a spell, and the practice of pharmakeia was the use of plants and charms, amulets, and sometimes human sacrifice to either remedy or create illness. Some interpretations of the Bible equate it with witchcraft and, in animistic fashion, the word pharmakis can be used to describe either the practitioner of pharmakeia or the pharmakon itself. This set of words very excellently demonstrates the ambiguous nature of the herbal arts in witchcraft.

Within the Seed of Wortcunning lies a coiled serpent with one fang of ivory and one of ebony, one that heals and one that poisons, but the venom that comes from either is the same. All plants can be poisonous and all plants can be healing; the dose makes the poison. Of course, there are some plants that are extremely powerful and can be harmful in very small doses, sometimes merely through touch, so we must learn to treat them with respect and how to make relationship with them safely.

THE POISON PATH

A term coined by Dale Pendell in his Pharmako- trilogy, the Poison Path is in the midst of a renaissance thanks to

---

1   Daniel Schulke, Viridarium Umbris: The Pleasure Garden of Shadow (Hercules, CA: Xoanon Limited, 2005), 3.

the psychonautical studies of the 1960's. There are currently multiple online groups devoted to it and many practitioners are turning to poisonous plants for their efficacy as pain killers and for their psychoactive properties. The Poison Path is not something that is only the purview of the witch, for many peoples over time have used psychoactive and poisonous plants as medicines and as teachers, as the sacred gods of the viridis mundi[2].

Before travelling this road it is essential that the witch be properly prepared with training, particularly under the tutelage of an experienced pharmakis. There are many books on the subject, but nothing can replace experience. It is also a good idea to sit for a long while with one of these allies, as they are very powerful and learning to work with them can be challenging, so it is best to not overburden oneself trying to learn about a whole encyclopedia of plants.

The largest family of plants on the Poison Path is the Solanaceae, or nightshades. These plants have petals that mimic that five-pointed star that is so much a part of our Craft. Many grow berries of various shapes and sizes, and many are lethally poisonous or will drive a person mad in the right amount, though some we eat as regular parts of our diet (such as tomatoes, eggplant, and potatos).

There are, of course, the psychoactive allies that have gained in popularity since the days of Terrence McKenna, Timothy Leary, and Albert Hoffman and we have learned more about them in the intervening decades. From the jungles of South America to the snow-shod paths of Scandinavia, these allies have likely been in use for as long as humans have existed, if not longer. They are the magical teachers that shift and alter our consciousness, dissolving and coagulating our perception, and causing radiating fractals of Astral Light as they educate our souls.

---

2   The Green World.

UNGUENTA LAMIARUM

Also called flying ointment, the unguent is a soft salve usually made with animal fats and poisonous herbs with a transdermal, hallucinogenic effect. Once the fat was rendered and clarified, the herbs would be warmed in it for a period of hours to days, which turn the fat green (another name for the ointment is green salve). Then, once it was prepared, it would be rubbed on the body to aid in having visions. Some of the old recipes call for use of some fairly toxic plants, like hemlock and aconite, which can cause severe complications in the user such as heart failure and respiratory paralysis. My suggestion is to learn to make one from an experienced herbalist or buy one from that person. With the recent increased popularity of witchcraft and herbalism there are a few available on the market.

Some of the herbs used, like henbane and datura, give a feeling of lightness and tingly floating in the air, a sensation like floating on water coated in the most dazzling glitter, helping the witch in sending forth the spirit, stretching the Lunar Body away from the Edenic Body, allowing it to fly off across the hedge to gather information, meet others in the spirit world, or confer with the Devil of the witches

There are many accounts of the use of the unguent, some Early Modern accounts even saying the fat used to make it came from newborns or the fat of hangmen. Personally, I've never used the fat of a baby to make anything, preferring to use things like ghee or duck fat that are easily purchased at the local Co-Op. Other stories about it are that witches slathered the handles of their besoms with it and used them as dildos (there is NO evidence for this), or rode them around a great bonfire in order to take flight to the sabbat and the arms of the Devil. Why, if they were already together around a physical fire, they would need to use the unguent to get together across the hedge, I don't know. Also, a giant bonfire would attract some attention from those the witches would have been wise to stay hidden from, so I am doubtful that it actually happened that way.

Many travelers of the Poison Path, attempting to know more about their authentic power and to deepen their relationship with their magic, their spirits, and their ability to help their people, have made ointments and unguents with psychoactive properties. There are global accounts of medicine people and cunning folk who use unguents made from hallucinogenic plants and other preparations made from entheogens and psychedelics that are used during trance work and sacred rites, including cunning folk and witches.

BIOREGIONALISM

It is easy to exoticize the plants of the Poison Path and fall back on the European staples of magic, but the witch must always keep in mind the health of the land and its inherent wisdom. My teachers have always said, "What you need will grow near you," and there is a powerful grace in this. It is our responsibility to become acquainted with the land around us and make relationship with it, allowing it to teach us how to tap into its power in a healthful, respectful, and potent way.

To start, learn the history of the place you are living in. Who are the Native people who lived there before colonization occurred? How can your work honor them without appropriating their culture? Is there a long history of violence, or has it been relatively peaceful? Can you find the history of the house or apartment you are living in, or the major landmarks closest to your home? If you are interested, are there other practitioners of magic living close to you and what kind of work do they do? Is there a Pagan Pride or other day of celebration for witches and community in your area? Also learn what you can about the land itself. Things like average temperature, wind patterns, rain fall, and other abiotic characteristics of your region will determine its overall energy and nature and will in some ways govern the kind of organisms that make a home there. How do they act on the soil, the animals, the plants? Do you live in an area that was formed by volcanic actions, flooding, or glacial movement? Those things determine to a large degree the kind of beings that will live in your region.

The Native inhabitants of the Albuquerque region, where I live, are largely descendants of the Tiwa and Keres Pueblos (of which there are nineteen within an hour of the city), but also the Dine speaking peoples, the Apache, and the Comanche. Native peoples have lived in this region for at least 12,000 years, subsisting on this often difficult terrain. The land here is desert and conifer forest, and though it has become increasingly dry over the millennia, the risk of years-long drought has always been an issue. It is worse now that our major river, the Rio Grande, has been incarcerated by a series of dams that strangle her and leave the riverbed almost completely dry in the Winter and Summer. It is a year-round possibility to walk out into the middle of what once was a mighty body of water that flooded the entire Rio Grande Rift Basin, which stretches from central Colorado to Chihuahua, Mexico.

Here in Albuquerque, we live in a half-graben called the Albuquerque Basin, one of the largest basins in the Rift, which was formed through the activity of shifting tectonic plates and the venting of the three Albuquerque Volcanoes to the West. To the East we have the most prominent part of the environment here, the Sandia Mountains, which were formed about 10 million years ago when our little block of land descended and are one of the most biodiverse areas in the Southwest.

Because of the sudden elevation changes that occur between the Sandias and Albuquerque[3] there are four life zones that blend together from top to bottom, leading from

---

3   The highest elevation in Albuquerque is about 6,700 feet and the highest point of the Sandia Mountains is 10,678 feet, which only takes approximately 47 minutes to drive between.

cactus and juniper dominated limestone soil areas to juniper-pinon scrubland, up through conifer-oak forest (which is quickly shifting toward locust and elm forest), and up to a much colder zone dominated by gamble oak, aspen, and cold-tolerant conifer species. A rich array of plants and animals also call the Sandias home, some of which are endemic only to our little mountain range. Also toward the East are the Manzanos and Manzanitos, which are largely juniper-pinon scrubland, but are additionally home to the maple dominated Fourth of July Canyon, named for the amazing coloration of its foliage in Autumn.

In whichever region you call home, there is an expert who can teach you about the land and the plants that grow on it. I teach an herbal medicine and wortcunning apprenticeship from May to September, and I am only one of several herbal mentors here in Albuquerque. Wherever you are, I'm sure the situation is similar, especially with the increasing popularity of holistic modalities, herbalism, and esoteric studies. Look into foraging classes that can teach you how best to take care of and subsist on the land and how to look for animal sign, as these skills will be useful during herb hunts.

Learning to use invasive plant species instead of rarer, possibly endangered plants in your magic and medicine is more sustainable and responsible than simply using what the old grimoires tell us to. Classes that focus on invasive and local plant medicines are becoming easier to find, though they are still rare and often a bit lean on content, but if you can find one, I suggest you take it. The more skills you acquire of this sort and the more familiar you become with the land you live on, the more powerful your relationships with local spirits will grow.

Also, if possible, look for a teacher who has a good relationship with the spirits of the land, who doesn't shy away from talking about magic and the feelings they get from the plants. Look for someone who talks to the herbs, the animals, the wind, and the rain. They are hard to find but well worth the search!

TOOLS OF WORTCUNNING

The wortcunner may use whichever tools are handiest, though there are some guidelines that will make working with and gathering the plants a little easier. First is the wortcunner's blade, made of sharpened bronze, which suffices for most gathering purposes. If possible, get a curved blade, the more crescent shaped the better, though a straight blade will work just as well. Try to avoid steel and iron blades, as they may offend the spirits of the plants. The lore is clear in the fact that fairies and other etheric beings are averse to iron, so using any metal with the qualities of that metal may prove harmful to your remedies and charms, though an appropriate bronze knife can be acquired for only a small investment. Other options include gold, silver, and copper, though these metals are rather soft and, at least for the two former options, costly.

The blade can also be made of glass or stone, so long as the edge is sharp enough to slice through stems, twigs, and small roots. Obsidian is a good choice, as are flint and agate (really anything that can be knapped). The handle of the knife can also be of bronze or stone, though it can be of some natural material, such as antler, bone, leather, or wood. Signs, symbols, and sigils can be carved into it to help with keeping it cleansed of malicious energies and sanctified for the work of the wortcunner.

The wortcunner will also want to carry a cross-body bale meant for the collection of herbs. This can be made of leather, which I prefer, or can be a weatherproof camping bag made with synthetics. So long as it can carry and conceal your gatherings it will do. The bale ought to be able to safely hold your wortcunning blade, a ball of twine or yarn to make bindles with, and a jar of blessed offering water that you can use to thank the plants you collect.

A wooden staff will also come in handy for the wort-cunner, especially if it comes from your local area. This can be the working staff, or it can be one that is used only while gathering. Either way, it is used to open the way for the wort-cunner, to announce your presence to the genius loci of the area you wish to work in. Knock the ground three times with the staff and then address the spirits of place:

Hail to the spirit who
guards this place!
Hail to the spirits who
inhabit this place!
Hail to the powers that
abide in this place!
By the authority of the
Seven-Faced Goddess
And in the Devils name,
Allow me safe passage
through your domain!
I come peacefully to gather for the Art
And promise you no harm.
You are myself and my family
and we are one.
Az ze.

Also carry with you a journal that will serve as your Liber Herbalis, or book of herbs. Record the herbs you find and where, the state they are in (nursery stage, blossoming, fruiting), the time of year, the time of day, and whatever experiences you have with them. If you care to, also draw the plant in your book, which may help you to understand its spirit a bit better.

You will need jars, honey, vinegar, bee's wax, and all of the other tools and ingredients any herbalist would use, but also nails, bones, snakeskin, and many other ephemera

171

for use in your charms. While you are out gathering, look for feathers, bones, thorns, owl pellets, pieces of quartz, and anything else that may pique your interest or be of use to the charm you have planned. If you make your needs known to the spirits, they can help you complete your gathering more quickly and help you find hidden treasures along the way.

MAKING RELATIONSHIP

Speaking with the genii viridis takes practice, time, and the ability to listen deeply. It is absolutely essential that we ask the permission of the spirits before we gather anything and, if we have not learned to commune with them, we may not hear what the wishes of the plant actually are. If you always get answers in the affirmative, you are probably not listening deeply enough and must spend more time learning to quiet your mind to hear the voices of the plant spirits.

A good place to start is with simple meditation exercises, such as concentrating on one's breath and consciously moving energy through the four bodies. Then, if you have little experience with this kind of thing, begin taking care of some house plants, listening for what they need, where they want to be in your home, and how they want to work with you. If you have the space, try your hand at gardening, too. A luscious garden is a powerful draw for spirits that may be able to aid you and your Craft and indoor gardens absoultely count. Once you have a good grasp on taking care of a domestic plant, then try your hand at making communion with wild plants.

Go to some hiking trail or wild place (always be safe, though. Don't wander into a wilderness without being prepared and without telling anyone) and wander until you come across a plant that "stands up" for you. My teacher says, "When a plant is interested in you, it will stand up," making itself known and noticeable. Whatever that is, go to it, introduce yourself, and sit down with it. Examine not only

172

its physical body, but its Lunar Body as well, learn about its spirit and feel it with every cell in your body.

Try to clear your mind as much as possible, just letting thoughts drift through as they may, and see if there is anything that seems out of place, like something is trying to grab your attention. That may be the plant making relationship to you. Pay special attention to song lyrics that pop up in your mind, random poetry, or quotes, and also to bodily sensations (tingles in the belly, throat, and spine, heat waves, chills, and anything else that may come up). These are all symbolic signs that act as the voice of the plant. One day you may hear the voice, but at first you may only feel it.

FOOD AS MEDICINE

It is also important to make relationship with our food in a healthy, empowered way. The wortcunner understands the importance of all plants and their powers in our lives, whether we think of them as magical or as part of our diet. The plants we choose to eat can be nourishing to our bodies as well as treat common maladies, such as inflammation, and help to keep our immune systems strong. They are valuable in keeping our minds and bodies in tip-top shape so we can remain focused on our craft. If our relationship with the food we eat is a healthy one, our bodies will become healthier and our spirit will thrive.

This begs the question; what do we mean by "health"? A healthy relationship to food can look different for different people. I think we tend to get too caught up in what other people are doing and what "authorities" say on what is healthful for our bodies. I say eat what honestly makes you happy and honestly makes you feel good. If that means no meat and no gluten, then so be it. If it means no coffee, so be it. If it means veganism, so be it. If it means three double cheeseburgers, a donut, and a beer, so be it. Your diet is yours and your relationsihp with the food you eat should bring you joy, not shame. If a food really and truly makes you feel stronger, more aware, gives you more energy, and makes your body and mind thrive, then eat that food no matter what society tells you about it, though I urge you to eat whatever it is in moderation and maintain variation in your diet.

What I think is the best diet is immaterial, but I will give you my opinion, anyway. We evolved to eat meat, which is incontrovertiable. The archaeological evidence is there to prove that our ancestors knew how to work with fire and cook food and that they ate meat and animal byproducts. It is one of the primary reasons our brains were able to develop into the miracle they are today, the simple availability of cooked protein and animal fat that the bodies of our ancestors were able to absorb. Not to mention that there is a large amount of evidence that our earliest Homo sapiens ancestors were eating loads of seafood, which absolutely counts as meat. If you don't believe me, read the book Catching Fire: How Cooking Made Us Human by Richard Wrangham.

So, a little bit of meat and animal byproducts, not a lot, is essential to our diet and for the proper functioning of our brain and nervous system. A much larger portion of our diets ought to be made up of vegetables, fruits, nuts, dairy, and fermented foods. The "All-American" diet, veganism, raw food diets, and any other such limiting thing is, in my opinion, not the most beneficial for our bodies. Our ancestors were opportunisitc eaters and would not poo-poo a hot dog in preference of lettuce.

If you have a problem with eating meat or animal byproducts, but would like to start, I suggest saying a charm over your food every time you eat, offering venerations to the animals that died for your meal. Buying meat from small, local farmers that you are familiar with is a wonderful way to make sure you are eating meat from animals that have been treated well and slaughtered as humanely as possible. The amount of meat you need to eat in a day is not very much, so, though local meat is more expensive, you can eat less of it. Add in lots of local produce, which is usually pretty cheap and can often be purchased with social assitance money.

In Japan there is a certain type of spirit called Ubusunakami (the protector of the land, basically the genius loci of the place you were born and the place you live) that exists in the land and the beings who inhabit it, that makes up a part of your essential being. It suffuses the four bodies and is fed by the energy of the land. Eating the local meat and produce of our bioregion is not only the most healthy for our bodies but for the land we live on, our local economies, the plants and animals, the water, the air, and everything else around us. Farmer's markets are the loci of health for any community.

Again, when we are absolutely honest with ourselves, to live is to feed on the life of another being, even if that being is a vegetable. Everything has a spirit and to eat is to kill; we must kill to survive. Let's fess up to the fact and do so conscientiously and with intentionality rather than shame and guilt, which are more likely to make you sick than eating a bit of meat every day.

DOCTRINE OF SIGNATURES

Beginning in the work of Paracelsus and finding further cohesion in the work of Jacob Bohme and William Coles, amongst others, the Doctrine of Signatures states that the medicinal use of a plant may be discerned in its physical form. A walnut looks like a brain because it is good for the brain, and St. John's Wort is perforated because it helps with skin wounds. This is an anthropocentric viewpoint and only works to a point, as the physical character of a plant can tell us some things about its medicinal uses, but not all about them. It goes without saying that a plant can be poisonous without looking poisonous, so relying on the Doctrine of Signatures without critical thought is a good way to end up as porest floor fertilizer.

The physical body of a plant also tells us about its planetary resonances, which elemental energies manifest through it, and which spells it may be the most useful for, but not all attributes are seen in its morphology. One must always take the time to understand the plant and do the research necessary to properly identify the herb and learn how to use it safely. Remember that "the dose makes the poison," so be certain of dosages before using plants internally.

There are, of course, magical and spiritual attributes that can be recognized by looking at a plant and preparations that do not need to be consumed. Thorny plants are often protective, particularly if it is a thorny hardwood such as black locust, and plants with purple flowers are often useful for opening the pathways to the spirit world (though some, like aconite, do so by killing us, so be cautious and make no assumptions). The Doctrine of Signatures is a useful springboard, but should not be used in a definitive manner or as a replacement for proper training and scholarship.

PLANETARY RESONANCE

Timing is an important factor in wortcunning because each plant has an affinity for certain planetary energies and elemental powers, which in turn are strongest at certain times of day or night and on particular days of the week.

Each hour of the day at which the planting or gathering is performed is ruled by a different planetary energy. These planetary hours are not sixty-minute intervals, but vary in length, and are attributed only to the seven classical planets, leaving out the outer planets Uranus, Neptune, and Pluto. There are twenty-four hours in a planetary day, though the cycle is from sunrise to sunrise, rather than midnight to midnight as it is with a calendrical day. Thus, different locations will have different planetary days and the planetary hours for different areas will vary.

Planetary hours are also divided day from night, with day hours being calculated from sunrise to sunset, and night hours being calculated from sunset to sunrise. The length of these periods will be longer or shorter depending on the time of year, with day hours being longer during the summer and night hours being longer during Winter. They're only evenly dispersed on the Vernal and Autumnal Equinox.

The planet that rules the first hour of the planetary day will be the ruling planet for that day of the week[4], so the first hour for Sunday would be the Sun, the first for Tuesday would be Mars, the first for Friday would be Venus, and so forth. The sequence of planetary rulers for each hour is always the same: Saturn, Jupiter, Mars, the Sun, Venus, Mercury, and the Moon. Calculations for these hours are not very difficult, but there are calculators online that make them more accessible. Of course, this information is only useful if you know the planetary ruler of the plant you are working with, which requires a bit of memorization, though there are guidelines one can use that will make the assessment of astrological attributions more intuitive.

Plants are also strongly influenced by the moon and will flourish or be at highest potency when planted or gathered during a particular phase. Most plants will be at their best when planted under a full or new moon, though I prefer to leave the new moon for planting baneful herbs as the dark aspect of the moon is associated with command and cleavage of powers. The full moon and second quarter moon shed the most light, thus leading to better and healthier plant growth. The water in the soil during these phases is swelling and will harbor the seeds better than at other times of the month. The third quarter and new moon are better times for harvesting and maintenance of the garden.

Also take into account the zodiacal sign that the moon is in before deciding to plant or gather, as the power

---

4 Monday=moon, Tuesday=Mercury, Wednesday=Jupiter, Thursday=Mars, Friday=Venus, Saturday=Saturn, and Sunday=Sun.

of each plant will amplify under the auspice of certain stars. Take the Artemesias, for instance, which are aligned to the moon and, for the most part, the zodiacal sign of Cancer. If the witch plants such herbs as mugwort and wormwood on a full moon shining in the sign of Cancer, the seeds will bear stronger plants than if they were to be planted during the day or when the moon is in another sign, such as Capricorn.

The Moon

Lunar herbs have a nighttime affinity and often grow best at night or in the shade. They sometimes have a silvery sheen or a shininess to the leaves that is reminiscent of the shining moon. They may also be found close to water, though this is not a certitude.

In medical astrology the Moon is associated with the chest, chest tissue, the left eye, the venous system, much of the endocrine and limbic systems, the reproductive system, the urninary system, and the lymphatic system. Lunar herbs are aids to movement, particularly of the various fluids in the body, though they tend to gently coax those fluids through the body and moderate their flow. They are nurturing and may also help the person taking the herbs to become more nurturing and clearer headed.

The plants under the rulership of the Moon are often anthelmintic (something that gets rid of parasitic worms), like the Artemesias, or are associated with the growth or clarity of psychic powers, especially prophetic dreaming and hedgeriding.

Many Lunar herbs help to clear the Etheric Body, which will help with clients having nightmares or repetitive dreams. They can help the client "get the message" and then move forward.

Mercury

Mercurial herbs are often hollow-stemmed with feathery leaves and racemes or umbels of flowers at the end of a stalk. They also tend to have an overall balance from top to bottom, hardly ever looking overly bushy or lopsided.

They are herbs meant to soothe or cool the skin, such as lavender, or tend to have a proclivity for the lungs and respiratory issues, like osha and yarrow. Mercurial herbs also have actions that help the overall nervous system, the internal sysytem of communication of the body, like oats, periwinkle, and skullcap. These herbs will help with focus, memory, and acuity.

Use Mercurial herbs in spells meant to help with communication and to make contracts more binding. THey are are useful in business and legal matters. The god Mercury is a psychopomp, so the herbs sacred to the god will help you to get in touch with the spirit world, even helping to make hedgeriding to the Underworld and the Underneath easier.

Venus

Venusian herbs are often soft to the touch and may have flowers with "meaty" petals, like roses and magnolia, and they are usually highly aromatic. Many of the herbs we consider culinary (thyme, basil, rosemary, and many others) are Venusian.

They have an affinity for the heart and circulatory system, but also often act as aphrodisiacs and help to increase sensations of pleasure. Venus rules over the throat, the kidneys, and the skin and hair. Herbs which aid with these areas of the body will probably resonate with the planet. Venusian energy also leads many of the plants under its rule to be good for ovary-having bodies, such as red clover and violet.

Herbs under this planet's rulership are, of course, used for things like love spells and relationship events, like weddings. Resonance with Venus, who rules over relationships, leads Venusian herbs to be versatile and able to be mixed well with others, bringing them to harmony.

The Sun

Solar herbs are filled with the energy and power of Dionysos/Apollo and are powerful aids in the growth of one's skills, particularly divination, poetry, and the visual arts. They can also be powerful aids to manifestation spells and petitions for prosperity.

They are usually yellow in color and love the sun, following its path through the day. Sun flowers and calendula have flowers which will move to always have their face to the sun. These plants are best harvested during the height of the day, at sunrise, or during a solar hour.

Solar herbs will have an affinity for healing burns and redness in the skin, like St. John's Wort, an herb which also helps to increase feelings of self worth and decrease feelings associated with depression. The Sun rules over herbs with effects that help to increase happiness and similar emotions, which makes them ideal as additions to remedies meant to help a person get over long illness, chronic pain, and general sensations of depletion.

Mars

Martian herbs are hot and sharp, like the god of war himself. They tend to have prickles or thorns and sometimes pointy leaves with veins that are long and parallel. The flowers of these plants may even resemble weapons, like the spear-like flower of the ginger plant.

Herbs of Mars promote digestive motility, like turmeric, and create heat and rubifacience in the skin and mouth, like chili peppers. Martian plants can be stimulating and are found in beverages and treats that provide energy, like coffee. They have effect on the sympathetic nervous system, the arteries, the brain, pelvic cirulation and functinoanlity, and have similarities in their actions with herbs of the Sun when it comes to the heart. Where the Solar herbs are more gentle and encourage the blood, Martian herbs will make the heart beat more quickly and move the blood more forcefully. They will also help with cardiovascular conditions and will aid in reducing or regulating blood sugar.

Magically, use Martian herbs to quicken a spell, for strong protection, or for attack spells. They can be used to armor your workings and to exorcise spirits from a place. Martian herbs are also part of spellwork meant to get rid of unwanted neighbors and enemies.

Jupiter

Jupiterian plants tend to be spreading and have big, rough leaves. The Boraginaceae family of plants is ruled by Jupiter, as are most of the Rumex genus of plants. Herbs that fling their seeds are under the auspice of Jupiter, as well, like castor bean and filaree (Erodium cicutarium).

Herbs which resonate with this planet will have an affinity for the liver and the digestion, but also for rough, dry skin conditions. This group of plants has a tendency to raise the spirit and make one feel slightly inebriated, as is the case with kava.

These plants are used in spells for increase, luck, prosperity, and happiness. They are also used to strengthen and exacerbate spells, to make them grow. Be careful, though, as this use can make a spell get out of hand if one isn't careful.

Saturn

Saturnine herbs are mostly of the baneful variety like aconite, hemlock, and belladonna. Saturn is the god of time and a lord of death, so his rulership of poisons makes sense. They may also have flowers that come from joints in the stalk, flowers that come directly off the stalk. They may look "leggy", long and thin with sparse flowers coming from a base of large leaves close to the ground. The leaves may look ragged, as if they had been torn apart. The stems will likely be jointed, too, like those of Solomon's seal and bamboo.

Saturnine herbs have an affinity for healing the

skeletal system and the colon and can help with deep body illnesses that are difficult to get rid of or manage. Baneful herbs are powerful medicine and are used to make some of the most potent pharmaceuticals for the heart and for easing pain. They should be approached with great reverence and caution and only by experienced herbalists.

Saturn is the planet of constriction and, as such, the herbs that are under its power have constricting and diminishing effects on the body. They also help with issues that lead to such things as kidney stones and gall stones, as the energy of Saturn is associated with stones and minerals.

Saturnine herbs are powerful for binding and breaking spells, for spells meant to transform or end things. If you are looking for herbs to help seal a spell and keep it safe from manipulation, Saturn herbs are a good place to start.

* * *

These attributions are not hard and fast, though they do act as a good guideline. A plant may also partake of more than one astrological association. Yarrow, for instance, is a Mercury plant based on its morphology, but it is also sacred to Venus (one of its common names is Aphrodite's Eyebrows), so it has an affinity for both. Mullein is tall and spreading (Jupiterian), but soft to the touch (Venusian) and its leaves are used as a respiratory aid (Mercurial). Because this can become a little confusing, it is best to become familiar with the energies of the plants rather than relying on a codex of attributes made by someone else. I will leave the creation of a codex to each reader.

ELEMENTAL ATTRIBUTIONS

Along with their various planetary resonances, each plant has a preponderance of one or more elemental energies, meaning an herb can be a water, fire, air, earth, or ether plant, or possibly a combination of two or more. It is important to remember that each plant partakes in the elemental energies just as they aprtake of all the planetary resonances, but are more or less dominant in one or another. It is also important to consider each plant individually, as one plant which has a strong water attribution, for example, may be more watery in one location and less so in another location.

In The Kabala of Numbers by Sepharial, he says something along these lines:

> "The astrologers affirm that individual character answers to a simlar analyisis [to chemical analyses], for whereas all [people] are consitituted fromt eh same cosmic forces, one has more Saturn in [them] than others, being born under teh dominance of that planet, while another has more of the nature of Mars, on account of its ascendency or elevation at [their] birth..."[5]

He is speaking of the planets and their resonances in the natal chart of an individual, but we can consider both the planetary and elemental attributions of a plant in a similar way. I suggest you take the time to get to know the plants you wish to work with, so they will be able to work with you more efficiently.

Ether

Ether is both an element on its own and the source of all the rest, like white light that, once passed through a

---

5   Sepharial, The Kabala of Numbers, (New York, NY: Samuel Weiser Inc., 1974), 2.

prism, differentiates into the visible spectrum of colors. It is called the fifth element, though it is actually the essential nature of the four classical elements combined in their most infinite potential. It is the most rarefied and subtle of the elements, the least tangible. In the world of plants, psychedelics and entheogens are considered ether herbs, as they help one to associate more easily with spirits and to turn inward toward one's own place of power. Each biological part of a plant relates to one of the elements, as well, and the part of plants related to the ether element is the seed. All of the possible manifestations of the plant lie within the seed and are passed down from one generation to the next through it.

Fire

Fire herbs will have thorns or sharp leaves, like holly and mahonia, or may be irritating to the skin (poison ivy) and often resonate most fully with Mars. They may be hot to the taste and hot to the touch. They help with digestion and circulation. Fire is the most motile element, so when you are trying to identify fire herbs try to discern whether they will help move substances through the body. They will be heat loving plants that thrive in full sun, drought tolerant, with dry, brittle parts. The stem of an herb, which drives up through the soil and reaches upward toward the sun, is the part of all plants that corresponds to the element of fire. When it comes to trees and woodier plants, the bark and wood of the plant relate to fire, as these are what fire consumes to provide our homes with heat and our circles with protection.

Air

Like the Mercurial grouping of herbs, Air element herbs tend to have hollow stems and feathery leaves and usually help with respiratory issues. They will also sometimes produce cotton (pappi), like cottonwood, milkweed, and dandelion. They may be somewhat wide and spreading, but will often have stalks that reach up toward the sky. Dry resins and herbs used in incense blends will have air attributes, as do many fragrant herbs. The plant or its flowers will often be yellow or pale and often papery, like helichrysum. Air plants can also be parasitical. The plant dodder actually grows through the aerial parts of other plants, sustaining itself on the nutrients the host brings up from the soil. The leaves of plants, the parts which play and dance in the wind, are associated with elemental air and are the parts of plants most often dried and turned into ritual incense.

Water

Sometimes taking on a vaginal shape, water herbs have an affinity for sexual health, the kidneys, and the blood, often having a purifying effect on those organs. They are usually leafy, green, and nutritious, like chard and kale, and often prefer growing near water, like hemlock (a plant which strongly partakes of the air element, too). Water plants can be juicy, like aloe and purslane, storing water inside of their leaves. Cactuses are a combination of water and fire and represent the marriage of opposites. Water element plants also bear the largest, tastiest fruits. Water relates to the flower and fruit of each plant and flowers added to a ritual bath will amplify the power of the bath itself.

Earth

Earth element plants have deep roots and will have large, downward drooping leaves. They are usually used to ease ailments of the liver and colon, but also help to heal the bones, ligaments, and tendons. The flowers may be densely clustered or grow close to the ground. The root vegetables are mostly earth element plants, as are herbs that smell deep and musky, such as vetiver and spikenard, or woody, like spruce, cedar, and yerba mansa. The part of all plants related to earth is the root, which are excellent additions to any earth altar or earth centered spell.

* * *

I have listed a few herbs in Appendix B and given you some very brief notes on their possible uses, which does not take the place, in any way, of spending time with the plants yourself. Grow them, visit them in the wild, get to know their spirits, and experience what a relationship with them can be like. Your experience is paramount, as your magic is so vastly and wonderfully unique to you, including the way herbs will work in your spell craft. Take classes, read books, and stay curious about the viridis mundi, taking every opportunity to adventure through the multiverse with your herbal allies.

THAUMATURGY

Though the word "thaumaturgy" may seem a little funny it simply translates as "wonder working". Issac Bonewitz, a neo-Druid and theologist, defines it as "...using magic to actually change things in the physical world", which is exactly what witches do: Magic!

Merriam-Webster defines magic as "The use of means (such as charms and spells) believed to have supernatural power over natural forces", though the etic definitions of authors of dictionaries and the emic ones of practitioners hardly ever coincide. Most outside observers consider the practice of witchcraft and witchcraft a quaint primitivism, while witches and practitioners think of it as an art that allows a person the opportunity to be a more active participant in Creation, particularly in their own life.

One of the most influential working definitions of magic is that of Aleister Crowley who said, "Magick (sic) is the Science and Art of causing Change to occur in conformity with Will"[1], with later definitions being variations of this idea. One of my favorites is from Lisa Chamberlain who says, "...magic is the art of consciously participating in the co-creative forces of the Universe, by directing the energies of nature to cause desired changes in one's life."[2]

Training the consciousness and preparing the spirit for taking part in the weaving of the world is the very basis of le arte mystical and the spells we use are part of our

---

1   One of Aleister Crowley's most famous quotes, it first appeared in his book Magic in Theory and Practice in 1929.

2   Lisa Chamberlain, "A Wiccan Guide to Magick: What is Magic? And What is Magick?", Wicca Living, https://wiccaliving.com/what-is-magic/, accessed January 17, 2020.

training. Casting them helps the witch learn not only how to work with the energies of spirits and to develop their own power, but also fortifies the soul, organizes the mind, and aligns one's essence to the windings and workings of the via tortuosa. True witchcraft is experienced and only through working magic and performing spells can a person become fully a witch.

Within the seed of thaumaturgy are all the charms, incantations, enchantments, and hexes we use as witches to manipulate our reality. A spell (the over-arching category of magical workings) may be a simple written charm, a string of knots, a fabric pouch filled with hair and herbs, an incantation said over a candle lit with intention, etc. There is an infinite amount of possibilities when it comes to spellcraft with the only limitation being one's imagination.

It is important to note that one operative style can be used for both beneficium and maleficium. Witches work with the full spectrum of magic, preferring to walk the crooked path between the worlds of healing and harming. Starhawk said, "Beware of organizations that proclaim their devotion to the light without embracing, bowing to the dark; for when they idealize half the world they must devalue the rest"[3]. The world of the witch is neither all light nor all dark, not black and white, but a constantly shifting interplay of emotions and myriad colors that require our honesty and conviction to work with.

On the twilight path the witch has no more compunction against hexing than they do toward healing. Throughout the history of witchcraft and magic worldwide we see a slew of charms and magical items meant to bring malady to a target, such things as poppets stuck with needles, placed in vinegar, or nailed into a tiny coffin, strings of feathers and bones tied into knots, or charms made of crossed sticks left on the doorstep of an enemy. There are also thousands of

---

3   Starhawk, Dreaming the Dark: Magic, Sex, and Politics, (Boston: Beacon Press, 1988), 21.

charms meant to protect a person from maleficium, many more than any other kind of spell, which is proof enough that maleficium has been amply used.

We must learn to think about our actions, though, and decide whether the act of hexing is ethical in each unique situation. Doreen Valiente, who wrote the Wiccan Rede of "an' it harm none, do what ye will", said that if you are a witch with the power to stop a person from doing harm against others, it is a moral imperative to do so. Helping people through beneficium is well and good, even essential, but being "red of tooth and claw" is a part of who we are. There is no shame in using your fangs.

No matter if the spell is meant as beneficium or maleficium, many magical traditions tend to have at least two commonalities at their core; an associative aspect and a venerative one. The associative aspect is described by the Law of Sympathy and Imitation and the Law of Contagion. The first Law states that when two things are alike in appearance or essence, they can influence each other; the idea that "like affects like". If a thing can imitate the target of your magic closely enough it will create a sympathetic link to the target and thus become a stand-in for that target. The second Law states that if a thing has had close contact with another, they continue to have a link and that a magical action performed on one part of the pair will influence the second part from a distance.

One of the most perfect examples of the two in action is the poppet, which is made to look like the person the witch is targeting and then linked to that person's energy through "personal effects", things like hair, mucus, blood, dirt from a foot print, a picture of the target, or even the person's name written on paper. Because it imitates and is "infected" by the energy of the target it essentially becomes the target and any magic worked on the item, either to heal or harm, will be worked on the target itself. This isn't the way all magic works, of course, but for most of the spells in the witch's arsenal this description does well enough.

The venerative part of folk magic comes from its roots in animistic belief and in the belief in spirits of land and place, including the ability of a witch to contact the dead and speak to the ancestors. These beings are considered quite helpful and can be contacted in a multitude of ways, from simply saying "hello" to complicated rituals meant to bring their virtus, their spiritual power, into your spell craft. Jim Baker in The Cunning Man's Handbook says, "Unlike modern science, which limits itself to technological processes, magic [has] sought to utilize both matter and spiritual virtus in its quest for results". It is important for the witch not only to know what components a spell requires and how to perform it, but also to build relationship with spirits, both great and small, so that they are more willing to help with various tasks and lend us their strength. Magic is real, wild, and often unpredictable. We must grow and deveop our power in order to control it better, but power in magic is through relationship between spirits. Remember, however, that power is never the goal, only a tool.

Because imagination is the only limitation on your craft, a spell does not have to follow a particular formula to be effective. They often involve clearing and claiming sacred space, which can be more or less complicated depending on the witch's taste. They may include invocations of the elements and the ancestors along with whichever spirit presences are desired, or a ritual for gathering in energy and riling the participants in the rite into a frenzy. A witch may choose to use tools, symbolic items to represent various aspects of the working, and offerings to share with those who come to help (either physical or spiritual). The spell can involve magical actions to be taken before and after the rite is performed, with some spells taking over a year to complete. The movement of the planets and the luminaries, the time of year, the day and the hour thereof can all be considered in an effort to make sure that the spell is at peak potency. Some spells will work no matter the timing, though some cultures have strict guidelines for preferable days of the week, times of day, or phases of the moon. Some spells will require no preparation and can be done on the fly. It really is entirely up to the witch.

The best way to learn how to do spells is to perform them, though a useful way of learning how to make an effective one is to take the spells you like the best from authors you respect and break them down into their component steps, trying to figure out the reasoning behind them. In magic, intention is paramount and having a clear understanding and a concise intention for your spellwork is the best way to achieve an outcome close to the one your desire. I have devised the following categories to help in clarifying exactly what your intention is with a spell and understanding the spell a bit more deeply. I trust you will find them useful and inspiring to your own creativity.

MALEFICIUM

Coming from the same root as the word "malicious", maleficium is the type of magic meant to be aggressive, to injure, trap, or confound an opponent. It is the kind of magic some may choose to call "black", though we must remember that all magic is one and comes from the same place, which is neither good nor bad. The Source of magic is Chaos, the ineffable power that existed before the differentiation of opposites. For me it is the outpouring energy from the Heart of Witchcraft, which beats in the skeletal chest of the Ancient of Ancients, also known as Death. Our power as witches is primal and cannot be stuffed into such simplistic groups as "black" and "white", for nothing is ever merely black and white. It existed long before contemporary morality and will exist long after that the last of us passes beyond the bounds of Lethe.

It becomes clear, then, that the spells used to harm can be used to heal and vice versa. Performing malicious spell work will not cause bad things to happen to you, just as performing beneficial spells will not make good things happen to you; magic does not keep a tally of "good" and "bad" deeds to determine whether a witch needs reward or punishment for their actions. In my experience there is little truth in the "Rule of Three"[4], which is a furtherance of the Western misunderstanding of karma.

Most Westerners tend to oversimplify the idea of karma, thinking of it as a cosmic tit-for-tat system of justice. This is not so. Our karma is really a collection of habits that lead us into acting out the same patterns lifetime after lifetime, a system of reward and punishment. For witches I suppose our karma is to be witches (thank the Old Ones). There is no good, there is no bad; there is only the Work, which

---

4   The "Rule of Three" is the Wiccan idea that what you put out through magic comes back to you three times more powerfully.

evolves as it must on our journey into the "frightful forest", wherein grows the Twilit Grove along the Twisted Path.

A book with great insight and erudition recently written on this subject is called Of Blood and Bones: Working With Shadow Magick and the Dark Moon, by Kate Freuler. If you are still cagey about using maleficium after reading through this chapter, I highly suggest reading Freuler's book, as it is a very excellent and in depth analysis of baneful magic.

CURSES

Curses, from the Latin cursus, which translates as "course" and is best understood as the course of fate, are long lasting spells that become an integral part of the target's being in some fundamental way. They are often subtle, sometimes cruel, but never done lightly and without a sacrifice to the one who uses the curse, though sometimes they are brought onto a person by their actions and not by the hand of another. Within this category are three types of curse. Generational curses are meant to affect the fate of an entire blood line and are inheritable. Miring curses leave the target stuck in a situation, place, time, activity, or thought pattern. Finally, tutelary curses aren't really meant to harm the target, but to teach a lesson, though the lesson may be a hard one.

A curse is not only long lasting but is also adaptable, tending to moderate its own work. They are often maledictions, spells that are only spoken declarations of malintent, though other types of curse may be "built" using spell components. These latter kind will use jars, boxes, personal affects, "disgusting" things like urine and pond slime, and poking, slicing, painful things to sympathetically infect the target with the intent of the curse. These are then burned, buried, or put in hard to reach places, so that they are not likely to be tampered with. Depending on the severity and intent behind the curse, the witch may choose to build a "back door" into the spell, giving it a manufactured weakness or a condition that the cursed person must fulfill before the curse is broken. There are other ways to break curses, of course, which we will go over with beneficium later in this chapter.

Coffing Curse

This is a form of curse I call a "death" curse. It is meant to permanently and irrevocably destroy the power of an enemy. For this you will need a poppet of some kind, made of wax, clay, wood, fabric, porcelain, or whatever you choose to make it with, and then link it to your target with personal effects such as clothing or nail clippings, or with a photo of the target marked five times with their name. You will also need a small box that will fit your poppet, preferably one shaped like a coffin (any box will work, but the coffin shape has a particular energy to it), and thirteen iron nails.

On the first full moon of the year make your poppet and forge the link between it and your target. Put your nails in a jar of sacred oil made with olive oil infused with charcoal and tobacco leaf (or whatever your local nightshade might be). Every day between the full moon and the following new moon, I sing a variation on the first few lines of the "Hearse Song".

"Don't ever laugh as the hearse goes by,
for you are now the next to die.
I'll wrap you in a big white sheet
and put you six feet under me.
I'll put you in a wooden box and
cover you over with dirt and rocks.
For thirteen moons, with thirteen nails,
this curse of mine shall never fail."

On the night of the new moon, tie your poppet up

196

with black string or ribbon, saying "I bind you and your power for all time, past, present, and future, across all dimensions and in all aspects and facets of all reality. In the name of the Old Ones and by their power, you are bound. So it is." You will then place your poppet in the coffin box and hammer in the first of your iron nails in the upper left corner of the coffin lid and sing the next verse of the Hearse Song:

"The worms crawl in, the worms crawl out,
the worms play pinochle on your snout.
They eat your eyes and eat your nose
and you begin to decompose.
A big green worm with rolling eyes
crawls in your stomach and out your sides.
Your insides rot and turn to grease
and pus pours out like cottage cheese.
One more nail is hammered through,
The last shall be the end of you."

Each new moon you will sing the same verse and place another nail in the coffin lid. On the thirteenth new moon you will hammer the final nail in and sing a final verse:

"One year passed the song began
And now your end comes by my hand.
One last nail to seal the curse
Never now to be reversed.
In the coffin you shall lay,
Your eyes fall in, your teeth decay,
And that's the end of a perfect day."

Now take the coffin and bury it in a place of power or in a graveyard. To seal the spell hammer three more iron nails into the ground above the coffin and say with each nail, "By fire and earth I seal the curse. In the Old Ones' name. So it is." Then do your best to forget the spell ever happened, allowing your target to languish in the arms of your curse for all time. I've also done a coffining in less than a year, which is okay. Just do what you can in the time allotted and trust yourself, your spirits, and the strength of your spell.

Wolf Moon Curse

On the night of the Wolf Moon, the first full moon occurring in January, tie the personal effects of the target to a thin piece of meat and hang it from a tree. As the meat desiccates the power and strength of the target will become weaker and weaker and they will begin to feel hollow, void, and eternally hungry. This curse is cruel but effective and can also be used to break the power of someone trying to use magic against you. It is a version of older traditional spells as used by European witches.

To make the curse more lasting place the dried meat in a jar and place it in a cabinet or stream somewhere. Of course, the meat does not always desiccate, but may rot and putrefy signifying that either the spell is transforming the magic of your attacker, or that they are using their power against yours. Do some divination to determine which and proceed accordingly.

HEXES

Hexes are meant to effect one person for a prescribed length of time and are typically easier to break than a curse. The word comes from the German hexe, meaning "witch", a word which descends from the Old High German hag-zussa, which means "magic spell". These are derivations of an earlier Proto-Germanic word, haga, meaning "hedge, boundary at the woods", which also gave rise to haegtessa, or "hedge-rider". In witchcraft lore the spirit is sent forth "across the hedge" and there the witch brings blight to crops, disease to cattle, and torment to humanity in spectral form.

The etymology of the word "hex" does not necessitate malicious magic, rather referring to any spell at all. The differentiation between curses and hexes is somewhat arbitrary, but the word "hex" has come to be more associated with maleficium and it is in that sense I tend to use the word. Just like curses, hexes fall into various categories; comminution (breaking), fettering (binding), and excruciation (torment). Comminution can be used to break a person's power or will, where fettering prevents them from being able to aggress against you, use their power, or binds them to your will in some way. Fettering spells also include manipulative love spells and any other spell that is meant to control another person by magical means. Excruciation spells are meant for causing pain and are spells where poppets are often employed.

Fettering by Poppet Magic

Poppet magic is one of the most recognizable uses of witchcraft. The poppet is a doll, an effigy, made with clay, wax, wood, cloth…anything that makes sense for the particular spell the witch wishes to cast. My favorite material to make a poppet out of is leather, which approximates skin. Then I fill it with powdered beef jerky, bone, and sand (the earth from which the first humans are made in many cultures), which creates a fairly perfect simulacrum. Another integral part of the poppet is a personal effect of the spell's target, something which can be as mundane as their name or photo. I have a poppet I use for distance healing that is made with an open mouth into which I can slip a piece of paper labelled with my client's name, date of birth, and location, thus creating the necessary sympathetic link.

There are several ways to fetter another person by using a poppet. Use black or red embroidery thread to bind the hands and feet of the poppet and tie these together behind the back of the doll with a loop around its neck to form a hog tie, thus limiting the ways in which the target can move. The Ancient Greek version of poppets that were used specifically to bind were called kollosoi and were often made with wax or clay. The doll was molded in a bound position (with its feet and hands behind its back) and metal or wooden pins or thorns were stuck through the eyes, genitals, heart, and other vital parts to bind the pleasure or mobility of the target. A poppet can also be made and nailed to a plank of wood in a crucifixion style to bind the target from doing you harm or progressing with a particular course of action.

Comminution of Power

Breaking the power of someone who is using their power against you is a large part of the folk lore concerning witchcraft. The ways to do so are varied and creative, so I'll only describe a few to inspire you to find your own way.

If you can get a piece of the person's clothing or a more personal effect, like a used tissue, you can boil it in a pot of water and your own urine. As the liquid evaporates from the pot, so does the power of the witch. Another way is to make a poppet of the person whose power you wish to break and burn it, then scatter the ashes in a stream or river. The power of moving water to break the power of a thing or for protection is old magic and is one of our most powerful tools. Making relationship with one's local waters is a highly sacred and satisfying part of a witch's work.

Other versions of comminution spells include drawing an effigy of the person whose power you wish to break and firing an enchanted bullet at it, whipping the effigy to shreds with a bundle of thorns, or ripping it into seven pieces and burying each one in a different place along with an iron nail.

The main aspect of a comminution is to destroy a sympathetically linked simulacrum of your target. Whichever way a witch chooses to do that is entirely up to the witch. It is most effective to either bury and coffin[5] the simulacrum

---

5   This is different from the Coffining Curse and is more a final step in a spell to protect it and make sure it goes off well. When we "bury and coffin" a thing

or burn it and wash the ashes away after your spell is done, but there are as many options for ending it as there are witches who cast comminutions.

Wedging Spells

This is another type of poppet magic and is a spell to wedge something into the mind of a target, something that niggles at the edges of every thought. Whatever it is, whisper it one at a time to thirteen meal worms, living or dead, and place them into the head of your poppet. While the poppet's head is being sewn up sing, "I'll sing you one, O/ Green grow the rushes, O/ What is your one, O?/ One is one and all alone/ And evermore shall be so." Put the poppet in a cabinet, bury it somewhere near your target's house, or, best of all, put it in their bedroom where the poppet can whisper your message to them all night.

There are countless spells in countless spell books that are meant to make a person fall in love with the caster, a type of wedging spell I call OBSESSION spells. These, along with healing magic, are some of the oldest works of witchcraft in the world. One of the oldest ways to cause an obsession in a person is to bathe a poppet or representation of the target in menstrual blood or sexual fluid, some people going so far as to get these fluids on the target's actual body somehow. If you choose to use a poppet either sprinkle it over or stuff it with dill leaf and sing, "Lavender's green, dilly dilly, lavender's blue/ You must love me, dilly dilly, 'cause I love you/ Lavender's blue, dilly dilly, lavender's green/ Hear only my song, dilly dilly,/ think only of me."

Another I've heard of is to take the heart of a turtle dove (I'm sure a chicken heart from the grocery store would suffice) and put it in a poke with the photo or name of the person you desire pinned to the organ itself. Sew into the heart a magnet and every day upon waking and going to bed,

---

it means to bury it and drive three nails into the ground over the coffin as a sign that the spell is done, protected, and potent.

speak the name of your obsession and pleasure yourself. Inherent in sex and masturbation is a deep power to give life, even to spells, though it goes underutilized in the world of modern witches.

There are also honey pot spells to make a person "sweet" on you. Write the name of the person you want to either fall in love with you or be nicer to you on the back of their photo and put it inside of a jar with chamomile, rose petals, and juniper berries (you only need a pinch of each). Pour honey over everything inside the jar wile singing any love songs that come to mind. I find that while I'm making love sachets, pokes, or oils for clients I always find myself singing love songs to my charms. Keep singing as you put the lid on the jar and shake it vigorously. Put an iron nail through the lid to keep unwanted influences away from your charm and then light a red candle on top of it, so that the wax from the candle will run over the lid and seal it. Once the candle has burned all the way down, keep the jar away in a cabinet or drawer somewhere.

To escalate and protect your magic you can sew the jar into a cow heart and cover it over in a cardboard box with borax and cornmeal (make sure the heart is completely covered by the borax/cornmeal mixture) and let it sit for about a month, thus mummifying the jar inside the heart and eternalizing your charm.

A final example is one I have used to great effect to attract a person to a friend of mine. She asked me to create a charm that would bring a particular man into her life and I felt obliged to do so after doing a bit of divination to see if it would work. The charm consisted of two poppets made of matchstick worry dolls, each named after one of the people it was meant to bring together. They were stabbed through the heart with a pearl headed pin and tied together with red string. These were placed in a glass ornament with rose buds, coriander, soil from both of their footprints, and a pinch of flour, then sealed with wax. The charm was told exactly what was to be done and then was placed out of sight in a closet in her bedroom. The charm worked, as they are currently married and have two children. The funny thing is that she completely forgot about the charm, found it years later, and thought someone was trying to curse her and her family (which in a way was true). I never rectified her fear, as I thought it better to let happily married dogs lie.

Bottling Hex

Gather together a jar, a poppet with personal effects from the target or a photo with the target's name written on it, and whichever sharp, burning, or disgusting ingredients you'd like to use in your spell. Place the items together in the jar and shake it vigorously daily for thirteen days. Then the jar will be taken to a stream or river and buried in the middle of the current, thus protecting it from counter magic, or placed in a protected cabinet. The jar is sort of another form of poppet, another vessel for the spirit of your target, through which you have power over them and can heal, harm, protect, or bring misfortune to that person. The term "I'll put you in a jar" refers to this type of hex and is a threat of using one's own power to take the power of another.

JINXES

On the "lighter" side of maleficium is the jinx, which is usually a "trick" of some kind (from the Latin *tricae*, "a tangle of difficulties"). A magical trick is more like a trap than a prank, though, and jinxes are actually quite dangerous. In this category I include the Evil Eye (sometimes called *envidia* or *mal ojo*), which is a kind of maleficium laid on a person with a jealous or malicious glance, which in turn effects the person by bringing them "bad luck". Really this is an entanglement of energies that "twists the person up" and makes it difficult to proceed in the way that person may desire to, perhaps even making the person very sick. Over time and throughout many cultures people have worn amulets of protection against the Evil Eye, such as blue eyes made of glass (mati or nazar), small mirrors, buck eyes decorated with red thread or yarn and pictures of saints, or winged phalluses called fascinum. They do not always work, of course. One of the only ways to treat a case of the Evil Eye is to have the person who cast it touch the person who it has been cast upon, which is the reason that in many cultures it is customary to touch the head of babies to protect them from one's own glance.

Jinxing is often done without full intent and knowledge, especially by naturally gifted people or beginner witches, who lay the trick before they even know what is happening. This may lead a rude customer to trip on the way out of the store, or a stubborn co-worker to fall ill before an important interview, or a friend to get a giant zit right on the tip of his nose before a big date. They are not necessarily as well thought out as a hex, nor as long lasting as a curse; you jumble a person up until they stumble out of your way, which has its own dangers. The tangle can get worse over time and may lead to unintended, serious accidents, sometimes lethally so. Because it is mixed up and exacerbated by the choices the target makes a jinx can be unpredictable and the tangle can sometimes get caught up with the practitioner's own path.

Another aspect of jinxes is that they are often "laid" in the path of a target. Spell components are placed in a bottle or a poke and laid under the steps in front of the target's house, or placed somewhere near the target, such as under their car, hidden in the seams of a jacket, or hidden in a cabinet in their house. Sometimes the spell is laid somewhere along their path, like in the hallway at work or school, possibly along a trail they often jog down. A jinx is often set like a trap and the target is meant to fall into it.

Left Foot Jinx

For this you will need an enchanted hammer and nail and the left footprint of the target on a soft medium (such as dirt). Take the nail and hammer it into the footprint, then walk counter-clockwise around it as you sing, "A-tisket a-tasket/ A green and yellow basket/ You wrote a letter to your mom/ And on the way you dropped it,/ you dropped it, you dropped it,/ And on the way you dropped it./ A little boy, he picked it up/ And put it in his pocket./ You sent a letter to your love,/ you carried water in your glove,/ And by the way you dropped it, you did so, it is so./ I have a little dog that says bow-wow!/ I have a little cat that says meow-meow!/ Shan't bite you, shan't bite you,/ shall bite you./ You dropt it, you dropt it,/ And by the way you lost it." This jinx is meant to keep the target from being able to proceed and to keep them circling in place, confused and exhausted. You can choose to nail a green and yellow ribbon into the ground with your jinx, thus weakening your targets immunity as well.

Borrowed Power

This is another simple one found in the folk lore of witchcraft. It is said that if a witch is to borrow something from a person, even a neighborly cup of sugar, they can cast a spell against them and their loved ones. If a person goes through the work to break a hex and someone comes to them shortly thereafter to borrow an item, that person may be the witch who cast the hex in the first place. The witch may also steal an item from the target in order to create the sympathetic link required to work her magic.

I once was asked by an elderly woman to clear her apartment because she was hearing noises and seeing things floating above her bed. She said she suspected brujeria, as her neighbor was an avowed bruja. I went and used a pendulum to work my way through the house, like I had been taught to do, and I left a small spirit trap in a place I had felt a somewhat malevolent energy. She thanked me and asked me to put my name and number in her address book (NEVER DO THAT!), which I obliged to, then I left. On the way home I started having fluttery feelings all over my body and I started experiencing invasive thoughts I had never had before, hearing my name whispered behind me, clenching and cramping in my gut, and then that night I had my first panic attack of many.

It took me a while to figure out what happened, but after a few weeks I was able to discover that the elderly woman I had thought I was going to help had actually been laying a trap that I had blundered into. I hadn't been able to find my pendulum since the apartment clearing and I had reached out to the old woman asking after it, but she denied ever seeing it, going so far as to say she hadn't even seen me with it in her apartment (which isn't possible because she was following me around as I used it in every room). During a cleansing ceremony I did for myself and a session of hedge riding it became clear that she was the one who had laid a jinx for me and that she wasn't working alone. I did a bigger, deeper cleansing and broke my bonds to her, her coven, and anything that I had left in her apartment, including the spirit trap, my pendulum, and my name in her book. I felt a huge weight lift from my spirit and I was finally able to calm down and sleep through the night.

The next day she came into the store I was working in and said she needed me to come back to her apartment as the noises had come back. I told her I was no longer doing house cleansings and that she would have to find someone else. She insisted that I was the only one she trusted and that she needed my help desperately, but I refused again and she dejectedly left. A couple of days passed and she came into the store again, this time with a man who exuded a great deal of power. She asked me for my help to clear her apartment and impressed on me that she was in dire straits, that things had gotten much worse. Her friend stared at me the entire time, but I stood my ground and told her no. They left and never came back.

Every now and again for a few months afterward I would feel her reach out with her magic and try to use it against me, stealing energy and trying to break my spirit, but eventually I learned to subvert and break all of her attacks and have been jinx free for years now. This is a cautionary tale and I include it so that those reading my words may learn from my mistakes.

Firstly, do not be cocky in your magic; be careful. Secondly, never sign your name in another person's address book, but have them write it for themselves (this includes address books on phones). Thirdly, make sure that you have everything with you after spellwork is done, that nothing is missing; if it is, clear your connections to that thing immediately. You can always create another connection if you find the object again. Clear the object first, as another witch can lay an enchantment or jinx on it and leave it as a trap to bind you into their spell.

To clear yourself of the connection to an object or to clear the object itself imagine the thing very clearly in your mind and a ball of fire surrounding it, burning off any energy that may have a connection with you. What I say along with the visualization is, "I clear this object and myself of any connections, magical, energetic, emotional, mental, spiritual, and of any other kind. These connections are now cleared for all time, past, present, and future in all aspects and facets of every reality throughout every dimension in, out, and surrounding the multiverse. By the authority of the Old Ones, the Sacred Death, and my own power, so it is." Then clear any thought of the object or spell from your mind. If you think of it later do the clearing spell again.

Powder Traps

Laying powders is an old way of putting a jinx on a person and there are lots of powders a witch can make. As with so much of what we do, your imagination is your only true limitation. There are, of course, some traditional powders for hexing, for getting people to move, for obsession spells, "bad luck", rage, entrapment, and so much besides. What is important to know about them is that they must be sprinkled on the food your target is going to eat, or in their path (next to their doorstep, along the trail they jog, their driveway, etc.), in their bed, or perhaps in their jacket before they put it on. You have to get the powder on your target somehow, so that the link between that person and the spell is created. You could also brazenly blow it in their face, but you might be arrested. These are usually laid like sneaky little traps.

A spell in my repertoire is to take a tumbleweed of some kind, the pricklier the better, and put the photo or name of your target in the tumbleweed. Sprinkle it over with cayenne pepper, black pepper, olive oil, and urine, then set it alight. Once the tumbleweed is entirely burnt away simply take the ash and sprinkle it in front of the target's house. They will feel the need to move away and, if they do not heed that call, their luck will turn worse and worse until they go.

You can also lay these powder traps for spirits. Lay them around the point at which you summon a spirit (around your triangle of arte, spirit vessel, etc.), or in a room in which you are doing an exorcism. One of the more common examples of this type of magic is laying salt to protect against malicious spirits, or to trap spirits within a small area that can be more easily exorcised (especially when summoning troublesome house spirits or disincarnate entities).

Spirit Snares

Much like any other kind of snare, these are a type of jinx meant to trap unwary spirits instead of unwary people. They can be made of metal and made very intricately, or they can be a couple of sticks tied together with yarn. I have made them with bottles, old jars, sticks, yarn, embroidery thread...really anything I could lay hands to when I needed a snare. A famous type of snare almost everyone has assuredly seen is the Native American "dream catcher" and one that almost everyone has assuredly made, at least in elementary school, is a God's Eye, or Ojos de Dios (the two popsicle sticks wound round with yarn that teachers make students give their parents for Christmas). Little do they know they are making a powerful tool for witchcraft.

Other snares are made with bottles or jars, traditionally made of colored glass. These are filled with things like seeds, salt, sand, rice, or other small items along with tangled string, nails, thorns, etc., and images of lines and circles. The idea is that spirits get caught in the tangles or try to travel a straight line and become confused when they encounter a circle, or they have to count the grains of salt before they can leave the trap. Of course, this does not work for all spirits, some of them being quite crafty, but it is very effective for some of the less powerful, yet very troublesome, spirits that can cause havoc in the home or office.

We are constantly surrounded by spirits, though they are mostly innocuous energies that are not very cognizant of our existence. Some of them are like parasites, however, and feed on our energy, or their presence throws off our ability to heal, think, or do daily activities. Some of them are aware of us, but prefer to avoid populated areas, where others like to be of service to humans and will congregate in or near cities. Other spirits will sometimes find themselves in populated areas and make a home there.

At the school I used to teach for there is a spirit of a variety I have only seen high up in the mountains in our area, what I have come to call "brownies". It lives in our clinic building and moves things like keys and wallets, slams doors, and erupts out of shadows, startling our staff every now and again. If we leave it a toy or two, these incidents cease. It seems happy in our space and will even help us find

209

things, but it definitely is far from home. This type of spirit can be caught in a snare, though it may take a while for it to get caught in the trap. Other spirits will not fall for a snare and will need to be summoned or lead into a trap, such as the more powerful spirits that are difficult to command, persuade, or befriend.

Spirits will also be drawn to places of either natural or constructed power, things like stone circles or altars, churches, waterfalls, groves of trees, and even malls (lots of energy is expended in those places, let's be honest). Wearing spirit snares in situations like this is an option, items such as rings and necklaces enchanted for that purpose, things like spirit bottles and God's Eyes sewn into the hem of clothing or under patches, or shirts and jackets embroidered with snares. Braided hair, a hat decorated with snares and charms, or whatever else you can imagine are also useful. Sometimes spirits will be drawn to your spellcraft, potentially muddling things up or draining energy from your workings and, if you're prone to that problem, you need to ward your working space more thoroughly than the average practitioner and set snares around your sacred space at all times.

Glamoury

Though they are not as portrayed in fictional works, glamours are a real and potent form of magic. Technically a hex, they are meant to manipulate the perception of another person to persuade them into believing whatever you want them to. That said, they are much more subtle than putting on the face of another person, changing the color of your hair, or making someone believe they are eating worms instead of pasta. A glamour is more about accentuating and obscuring certain details about a situation, thing, person, idea, etc.; telling a lie very well rather than changing anything. Also, everyone isn't equally susceptible to them. The keener the person is, the more capable of sensing magic they are, the harder they are to trick.

A glamour is more like magical make up than a transformation, something to make you seem a bit more charming, your ideas a skosh more alluring, or to make you so disinteresting as to be basically invisible. You may be using one in your daily life without knowing it. Perhaps you feel like no one ever notices you, or that you tend to be very persuasive with cashiers without really trying to, or it is very easy to make people laugh when you're not really being funny. It may be a well-placed giggle, or a sexy, matte red lipstick, or...it could be a bit of magic.

Glamoury is not an easy art to master, though. It requires good timing, the ability to play to your strengths and obscure your weaknesses (or vice versa), to switch on an aura of sensuality, compassion, charisma, or power instantaneously and project it into the energetic makeup of another person, and the ability to deeply believe a thing is true with clear conviction and powerful desire while also remembering that the truth is simultaneously not as you are making it to be. It requires the witch to think clearly and forcefully with two minds at once without giving control to either, which can feel a little maddening and draining.

Spells to glamour yourself include enchanting your lipstick on a Friday in the hour of the Moon to give you a seductive flare, creating your own perfume using herbs, essential oils, gems, and charms for a more alluring aura, or enchanting jewelry to make yourself appear more charming, powerful, or courageous. Carry with you a small jar with a pearl, a rose, and a chicken heart covered in honey and sealed with red or pink wax to appear more youthful. Cut a piece of rabbit fur and mark it with the sigil of Mercury in the hour of Venus on a Monday and sew it into your clothes to make your words seem stronger and more convincing. There are lots of ways to cast a glamour, but I think your time is better spent actually becoming as you'd like others to see you rather than learning to manipulate people into believing that you're something other than you are.

BENEFICIUM

On the other side of the spectrum is beneficium; bestowals, blessings, and unsnarling. This type of magic could be called "white magic", though all magic tends to blend and become grey by the time all is said and done. As we've said, the terms "white" and "black" are unnecessarily reductionistic. Beneficium, though, is the category where we find the remedies to malicious witchcraft (though these may still cause harm to the original user of malefic magic, so are not considered "harm none" spells, either), healing magic, and the rendering of boons for clear mindedness, creativity, self-love, better dreams, indomitability in battle, etc. This type of magic is meant to bring the pieces together, to protect and amplify rather than diminish the target.

BESTOWALS

A bestowal is like a divine gift, a powerful spell that enhances the life and powers of another person. Just as with curses there are generational bestowals, though they are much rarer. An example can be found in the tale "The Three Golden Hairs of the Old Man Vesvede", an old Slavic fairy tale:

> *"At midnight he heard noises in the house, and looking through a crack in the flooring he saw the charcoal-burner asleep, his wife almost in a faint, and by the side of the newly-born babe three old women dressed in white, each holding a lighted taper in her hand, and all talking together. Now these were the three Soudiché or Fates, you must know.*
>
> *The first said, "On this boy I bestow the gift of confronting great dangers."*
>
> *The second said, "I bestow the power of happily*

escaping all these dangers, and of living to a good old age."

The third said, "I bestow upon him for wife the princess born at the selfsame hour as he, and daughter of the very king sleeping above in the loft."

At these words the lights went out and silence reigned around.

The gifts bestowed by the Fates on the main character of the story, Plavacek, made it possible for him to marry the daughter of the king and accrue great wealth; they changed his fate. Another more "real-world" example is a ceremony such as a knighting, during which the power of the nobility is bestowed on a person and thereafter their family, generation after generation. Though these spells are basically the opposite of curses they cannot undo curses by themselves and are often given to strengthen a person in the process of breaking a curse or as a reward for some great deed.

As with curses, bestowals are often said out loud and require a great deal of faith and power to bring into manifestation. They can also be built or bound into an object that is then gifted to a person, something like an enchanted ring, dagger, amulet, etc. Part of the magic in this type of enchantment is to bring out of the object its true name, or to give it a suitable one, such as "Excalibur" or "Glamdring". It may take a matter of years for an enchanted item to reveal its name to you or to accept the name it is given, but as the relationship between the item and the user grows deeper and wiser, so the magic and its potency will be more fully revealed. It is an interesting quirk of these spells that the enchanter may not always fully understand or know the power that is invested in the items by the spirit of the object, the enchanter, and whichever other spirits may play a part in its transformation. There is some modicum of control, but in many ways, magic is chaos, so there is no truly complete understanding of the works we do, especially large scale, long-lasting ones.

BLESSINGS

While bestowals are rather large and rare, blessings are fairly common. They can be as simple as well wishes, like "May the wind be always at your back" and things of that nature, or spells for attracting fortune, strength, fertility and so much more, all of which comprise the most common category of blessing; the boon.

When you go to a witch looking for love, luck, strength, etc. you are asking for a boon, a helpful spell that will make your life a little easier. Coadunation is a form of blessing that helps to put a person back together, especially after magical comminution or to bring pieces of a fractured spirit back into alignment and union with the person. Emancipation helps to break fettering spells and free people from bindings and stagnant patterns of energy. Another form of blessing is Delectation, the use of magic to bring pleasure to a person and to relieve pain.

Unlike hexes and curses, which are done against the will of a person (which is the very nature of such spells), blessings and other forms of magical healing often require the cooperation and conscious work of the person in question. It is far easier to break a thing than to mend it, after all. The next few examples are, again, just a few to get your creative juices flowing.

Abracadabra Charm

One of the oldest known charms in the world, the ABRACADABRA Charm has been used to heal, curse, and protect people for thousands of years. It is first found in the 2nd century CE in the works of Serenus Sammonicus, physician to emperor Caracalla, and is described in his work Liber Medicinalis as a cure for malaria. Its true origin and mean-

214

ing, however, is lost to the ages. It can be used to great effect in the diminishment of things, such as fear, angst, malicious forces, and illness. Writing the word in the shape of a triangle (see image) on a piece of paper and wearing it on one's person will help to end or diminish negative circumstances, so long as the person using the charm is also doing the necessary work (seeing a therapist, a doctor, etc.). Magic is a tool that works alongside many others and can help to solve problems, but hardly ever does so on its own. One could also write it on a large enough candle and, as the candle burns downward to the final "A" at the triangle's apex, the magic will help a solution to the present problem become apparent. To help with nightmares write the charm down on paper and sleep with it under your pillow, then, when the nightmares have abated, burn the charm.

```
A B R A C A D A B R A
A B R A C A D A B R
A B R A C A D A B
A B R A C A D A
A B R A C A D
A B R A C A
A B R A C
A B R A
A B R
A B
A
```

DIAGRAM 8
How to draw out the ABRACADABRA Charm.

215

Quilting Charm

This is a coadunation charm meant to help bring something broken together again. It cannot return the spirit, relationship, or what have you to its older state, but can bring it into union in a new way. By doing the work of discovering which parts of a thing are broken (take for instance someone who is working with early childhood traumas) one can name at least some of the parts that need to come together in order to be more effectively healed. Once you have two or more pieces you would like to work with, write about them on separate pieces of cloth and stitch them together (like magical surgery), and keep the resulting "quilt" in a special place of power on an appropriate altar space, or some other sacred area. As more pieces are revealed, stitch them onto the existing creation until you feel that the piece is finished. Then, using an embroidery hoop or something like it, quilt magical patterns across the fabric, tying everything together with symbols of healing, communion, unity, and strength. Keep the finished charm in its own place of honor, whatever that is for you.

Pins and a Candle

Another old world working, this requires a candle and a number of pins (however many it takes for your spell to feel complete, though I find three is a good number). This is a rendition of something like the ABRACADABRA Charm, as both can be classed as "diminishment charms" or "countdown charms". Enchant the candle by anointing it with an appropriate oil or other fluid (sexual fluids, spit, snot, urine, and menstrual blood can be powerful tools in charms like this), then marking it with the name of your illness, aggressor, or other thing to be diminished, and any other important target of your working. Bless the pins in fire and smoke, then stick them through the candle wax starting at the top and progressing toward the base of the candle (put the candle in a holder beforehand, so you know where to stop for fire-safe-

216

ty's sake). Light the candle and instruct it that as it burns down and the pins fall, so your target will sympathetically diminish. Watch how the pins fall and use this as a form of divination, which will take practice. Are they buried in wax? Do they stick head or tip down? Did they completely fall out of the wax, or get caught in it? Did they fall out and cross, lie parallel, or create some shape together? Pay attention to your gut, your heart, and your thoughts and then make your divinations.

Plant Charm

My mother taught me this type of charm when my brothers were born. She took each placenta and buried it beneath a tree she bought especially for her spell, then tended the trees. As the tree flourished my brothers were also meant to. We lived in a sometimes harsh mountain environment in a spiritually charged valley, though, so the trees actually died shortly after they were planted. My brothers are both fine, so I know that the spell doesn't necessarily kill the target, but I have heard of other people using this spell to heal illnesses and addictions by bleeding into the soil under a sapling and tending the tree as it grows. It can also be used to make strong covenants by burying a symbol of the covenant or copies of the paperwork under the sapling, or all parties urinating, bleeding, spitting or in some other way adding themselves to the soil that feeds the tree (perhaps with photos or fingerprints on paper) and then helping the tree to remain strong. You can also use other plants to do this. I am certain an aloe would do as well as an oak.

Planting wishes in the garden is an option, by writing your wishes on a stone and leaving it amongst your plant allies, or by whispering it to the seeds you sew. Ashes from burnt offerings and spell components can be used to add power to the soil, too. Just spread the ashes around the base of your plants (make sure nothing toxic was burned, of course) to nourish your plants and they will transform the ashes into

217

strength for themselves and for you. Other old world plant charms include tying clouties (also spelled clooties), loosely tied cloth or natural fiber ribbon, to the branches of sacred trees, which will get your prayer or wish off the ground and to the spirits who can help. Making wishes on coins or other bits of metal (preferably silver) and driving them into the wood of fallen trees is also an old world plant charm.

Poppet Healing

Healing with a poppet is quite a lot like harming with one. By creating a simulacrum and linking it sympathetically with the personal effects of the person to be healed the witch can use charm work, herbal medicine, and energy work over a distance or for a protracted period of time. By taking the person's personal effects and wrapping them in a simple square of cloth with healing herbs or herbs of protection you effectively make a poke and a poppet all in one. The herbs and whatever spells you perform on the poke poppet will influence the target.

I like to use porcelain dolls, which can be found in thrift stores for very little money and make a dramatic addition to poppetry. Most of them are made with fabric bodies that can be opened and into which you can stuff herbs, personal effects, and spell components and it is surprisingly easy to find dolls that resemble your target. A very useful addition to your healing poppet is a copy of the target's natal chart, which describes the basic essence of the person and can guide the witch during the healing work nearly as well as if that person were bodily there.

If you make your own poppet you can tie prayer ribbons into the doll, then keep the doll around or burn it as appropriate. Each ribbon ought to be one particular wish for the person, one spell, so that they don't start interacting in strange and cluttered ways. Also try to keep the prayers moving in one direction so as not to confuse the poppet and your magic. You can also use knot magic in your poppet by tying the energies of healing spells and spirits into the poppet or tying the energies of illness up (tie the knot over the part of the body your target complains about) so they have a harder time spreading or causing trouble. Cover your poppet in flour and salt to protect and strengthen your client during illness or during strenuous times in that person's life. Simply keep the poppet in a box with the flour and salt mixture and lightly shake it every day and whisper encouraging things to it.

Giving weapons to poppets is always fun. Little gifts of whips, scourges, magic wands, daggers, cudgels, brooms, knotted cord, or whatever else you think your poppet may need can help them do their job more effectively. The poppets are often appreciative for whatever you give them, though sometimes you may choose to give them the actual illness that you are trying to treat in your client with a spell called a transference charm. Like treats like, as they say, and to give a poppet the sickness can syphon the illness away from the person and into the doll, which can then be destroyed, cleansed, or transformed in some way. Say your client comes to you with warts. Sew a poppet and, wherever the warts are on your client, sew little beads that represent the growths and to begin transitioning the warts to your poppet.

UNSNARLING

Unsnarling is used to break jinxes and the methods for doing so are eclectic and often unique. Divination is required in most instances to discover the appropriate methods of removal, or, more accurately, of untwisting the client. The methods vary from a bath with a tea made of specific herbs, fumigations with smoke, or being brushed down with a chicken (yes, an actual chicken). Again, transference charms, can be used to take the jinx off of one person and pass it to another, which is a bit unethical. Another for the removal of warts, for instance, is taking a bean and rubbing it counter-clockwise around the wart, one bean per wart. These beans are placed in a bag, which is thrown into a busy thouroughfare. The person who picks it up will also pick up the warts.

Another simple method of untangling a client is to brush their hair with a specially enchanted comb while singing the nursery rhyme "London Bridge is Falling Down". Hair is a strongly magical part of many traditional cultures and is often a large part of fairy tales and myth. The great strength and invulnerability of the Biblical hero Samson are bound to his hair and, in the Hans Christian Anderson story "The Little Mermaid", the protagnoist's sisters trade their hair to the Sea Witch for the dagger that could kill the prince and set their sister free. In Norse mythology, the goddess Sif had gloriously long, blonde hair that was stolen by Loki, which spurred not only the creation of a golden headpiece for Sif but Odin's spear, Gungnir, and Thor's hammer, Mjolnir.

Cultures the world over have taboos and traditions concerning hair, often linking it to the spirit or to extrasensory perception. Some cultures have strictures against ever cutting their hair, while others shave it all off as a sign of the detachment from the material world. Some have taboos about people ever being allowed to touch another person's hair, where others seek out head pats and have braiding parties. People wear their hair differently when they are sad or happy, celebrating or grieving, at peace or at war. For witches, hair is one of our most powerful and versatile tools. It is linked intrinsically to the person who grew it, to their past, their hopes and fears, their health, their inner reserves of power. Hair is often used to lay a jinx, so being able to unsnarl the jinx with the hair of the person suffering the effects of the jinx makes (magical) sense.

Thrashing shadows is another option for unsnarling a client. Take the person outside on a Thursday or Saturday when the sun is at its highest. Take a besom, whip, or scourge and violently whip the persons shadow with plenty of swearing and rage-filled growling and howling. Boiling the clients urine and pouring it on the ground to be thrashed is a variation on shadow whipping. The idea here is that the witch who laid the jinx on the client is still linked to the magic and can be harmed through that link, their power broken, by the magic of another person. It is basically to boil the witch with the urine and then pour them out into the mud.

Tidying up the house is one of the simplest ways to unsnarl a person. Sometimes the jinx is accidentally laid on oneself, so to tidy the house and clear out stagnant, trapped energies can really turn things around. While you are cleaning up, open all the windows and doors that you can so energy, magic, and spirits can flow as easily as possible and use suffumigations to get stuck things unstuck. Sweep the floors, making sure to sweep toward the doors, then make a tea with herbs like azafran, fenugreek, sage, usnea, and agrimony and wash the floors, door and window frames, and all the mirrors in the house (do not forget the mirrors!). Thank the spirits of the land your home is on, the spirits of the house itself, the ancestors and spirits who watch over and work with you, and lay a blessing on your home, which should effectively unsnarl you.

APOTROPAIC MAGIC

Another type of beneficium that could be considered a type of blessing, but I feel deserves its own category, is apotropaic magic, protective magic meant to ward off harmful influences or cause them to abate. These include charms like "evil eye" amulets, statues of protective gods and spirits, and various hand gestures and sayings. Apotropaic magic may also be tied into talismans, which are meant to amplify and draw power to the wearer.

The evil eye is a type of jinx which is usually accidental. It is passed through envious gazes and backhanded compliments but can just as easily be given without any malicious intention. One of the cures for (or sometimes causes of) "evil eye" is for the person who cast it to touch the person who caught it, which has led to the tradition of touching the head of babies in cultures throughout the world, just to be safe. Nearly everyone has seen the blue glass mati or nazar, the "evil eye" amulets found in the Middle East and the Mediterranean that are commonly seen as wall ornaments, beads, and sometimes on the tail of planes. Those are also a type of apotropaic charm.

Another popular Arabic amulet is the hamsa, or "Hand of Fatima", a depiction of an open right hand with an eye in the palm. Here in the southwest we have ojo de venado, or buck eye amulets, meant to ward off evil influence from envy, or envidia. In Rome people would hang or wear fascinum, an erect phallus with wings and sometimes an erect phallus of its own sported between legs with eagle taloned feet, which may in turn have held erect phalluses. Some also had tails that ended in¬—you guessed it— an erect phallus! Throughout history and all over the globe, the belief in an ability to "cast an evil glance" and cause misfortune to others has been prevalent and, no matter which culture you look at, there will be plenty of apotropaic charms to protect oneself from said misfortune.

People also carry images of different spirits, gods, or symbolic representations of their faith to protect them from harm. Think of Christians wearing crosses around their necks (or bedazzled on back pockets and hoodies, or inside of a fish on the back of their truck), or Catholics in the Southwest who wear imagery of La Virgen de Guadalupe as a form of spiritual protection, or pagans of various ilks wearing pentacles over every available surface of their body.

In Ancient Mesopotamia people would carry around amulets that were carved to look like Pazuzu, the king of the evil wind demons, who was thought to be the biggest, baddest spirit around and who would frighten off any other evil spirits wanting to cause trouble. In Ancient Egypt amulets of the "Eye of Horus" and the "Eye of Ra" were worn to protect against misfortune, and in Ancient Greece Gorgons could be found carved into the temple walls to protect them and the people there to worship. Gargoyles crouched among the towers of cathedrals are also apotropaic in this way. There are too many examples to recount, but this type of magic is prolific no matter where you look.

When I was little I was told that rapidly tapping the tip of your thumb against the tip of every other finger, back and forth repetitively, would ward of negative energy, which I do to this day every time I get "weird vibes". Manu fica, or "fig hand", is a gesture found throughout Europe, Southeast Asia, and the Mediterranean meant to ward off the evil eye and the spirits of the dead. The gesture is made by placing the thumb between the index and middle finger (or the middle and ring finger) and making a fist.

Images of open hands, like the motion Americans think of as a sign for "stop", have been used throughout the ages to protect people from harm, as has the "devil's horns" gesture, where one holds aloft the index and pinky finger and brings the other three fingers forward like a snout (as seen at most heavy metal concerts). The Sign of Benediction, the index and middle finger held up together with the rest curled into the palm as seen in portrayals of many saints and especially those of Jesus Christ, is a protective sign, as is the "peace" sign, where the index and middle finger are held up and apart. Apotropaic hand magic is simple and effective, lending to their longevity, making them a part of the folk ways of protecting oneself from malicious magic the world over.

CURSE BREAKING

The last thing to talk about here is the breaking of curses and hexes. It isn't always as simple as doing a spell backwards, or taking a salt bath, burning a reversing candle, or standing under full moonlight. The ways to break curses are as multitudinous as the curses themselves and are often somewhat complicated, so I will not be giving any "tried and true" recipes here. It is important to divine for the appropriate method of curse breaking, using a couple of systems (like getting a second opinion) before proceeding. Sometimes a thing that breaks one curse only makes a different curse worse.

I've heard of cases where a curse was broken by a guided meditation, or by drinking basil and pepper tea three times a day for a week, but also where a person had to fill her shoes with beans and wear them while she walked seven times around a church. Sometimes boiling the victim's clothes in water or milk will break a curse, or burying a jar of urine from everyone in the house in ashes will do the trick, or various more bloody options may be required. Again, the ways to break curses can be strange, so practice your divination skills and trust your ability, then proceed with caution, respect, and deep intention.

* * *

Spell craft is the method we use in coercing the world to shift in accordance to our Will and, however we choose to go about it, all ways are acceptable so long as we are willing to accept the consequences of our actions. We must also be willing to do the work required to perform the spells properly and with intentionality, to clarify our Will and truly know what it is we desire from our work. Thaumaturgy is the last of the six seeds because it is through the development of the other five that we become ready to enter the space necessary for spell casting: a respectful, focused, clear, and connected mindset of intentionality.

DANCING IN SHADOWS
Concluding Remarks

We come to the fork in the Crooked Path where we must part ways. Hopefully, through reading this book and playing with the concepts presented in it, you feel more fully a part of the craft, ready to step intentionally into your life as a witch. It is my desire that my words have helped to feed the Cunning Fire in you, empower your spirit, and make the work less daunting and more exciting. Please remember, though, that witchcraft is work and we must practice and experience the craft, not just buy and read books about it.

Witchcraft is a living, breathing, growing entity all on its own and we are asking to take part in its life, in its power. We are asking ourselves to be up to the task, as well, holding ourselves responsible for our growth as well as the growth of our Twilit Grove. As the Grove grows, more and more is revealed to us, more light is poured out between the leaves to show us other hidden things, but with that light comes the shadow.

The greater our knowledge and the greater our power, the greater our responsibility to ourselves and our community. The greater our responsibility to the spirits, to the ancestors, to the Earth, the greater our responsibility to ourselves. We must learn to dance with the shadows, for we are Devils and we do not shy away from darkness, but look to learn from it, to love it, to play with it.

Ours is a wild power, hard to constrain, and it has a strong desire to go wither-a-wither it wants. Through our dedication to our Art, through growing the Grove by tending to the six seed practices I have described, the witch can learn to dance with grace and intentionality instead of wild abandon (though that sometimes has its place, as well). As any gardener knows, tending to plants sometimes requires pruning and fertilizing, weeding and containing, sewing and reaping, especially if we are to have the most beautiful garden possible, one that bears much fruit.

I encourage you to look beyond this book and really explore the works on witchcraft that are available. Utilize online resources, book borrowing co-ops, social media groups, and reach out to other members in the community. You may decide you don't like being part of the community very much, but it is better to experience that than to deny the possibility of liking it from the get-go. Do your own research, do your own work, become your own witch.

Utilize what you learned in this book to become more discerning. That's what the development of the seeds is all about; honing your craft so that you can better recognize hokum from Truth. The seeds help to develop your intuition, to hone your psyche, to magnetize your spirit toward that which is inline with your highest good, with what will help you grow and prosper in you craft. When the seeds have grown into tall, strong trees, the wind will blow through the leaves of the Twilit Grove and guide you authentically along the via tortuosa, where we walk together garbed in our full power.

Though we must part, we remain connected by the Heart of Witchcraft; we share blood. Now that you are on the path, you will never again be alone. Everywhere you go, there we are, a siblinghood of empowered witches that long for your success, your happiness, and your sovereignty. Look into the shadow and you will see familiar faces; reach out to the moonlight, and you will feel us reaching back; walk with courage, for we walk with you in the Twilit places.

To say, "I am a witch," is to say that you are backed and bolstered by a strong lineage that bows to no one. It is an act of revolution. If you are dedicating yourself to these practices and growing in skill, you will also grow in confidence, independence, and compassion. You will see the places where our systems are broken and need healing, where we can best use our power. What use is having power, in growing your craft, if you don't use it to help the people who need it?

Our world is over-run with people who seek to hoard as much power as possible, who want to be part of a small elite holding all the cards while pretending to deal them out in a game stacked fully in their own favor. Stop playing that game. Take your power back and use it revolutionarily to live in love, to empower each other, to increase our power together. There is nothing stopping us; we are witches, raw power given form. What is our purpose, if not to protect those who have yet to claim their own power? What is our skill, if not to guide the return of power to the people?

Gather the fruits of your craft and share them. Teach the new generation about the power of witchcraft, teach older generations about it, and let it nourish everyone. Witchcraft, again, is not about hoarding power for yourself alone, but for each individual, each unique spirit, to gather to itself its own power so that the world can become stronger, better connected, and can usher in a new age of empowered being.

As a witch, you are a guide though the Twilight, through the in-between places. It is a heavy responsibility, but one we must shoulder to aid the Earth and our people in their healing. We must experience our lives genuinely, authentically, and without apology so that others can see that living fully, dancing with shadows and devils, is nothing to fear, but something to embrace. Be you; there is only one, and that one is an essential inspiration!

May we meet in the Twilight,

Az ze.

DEVILS
IN THE DETAILS

- A Brief History of -
Witchcraft

T he following is an abbreviated history of the veins of magic I have been most influenced by through the teachings of my grandparents and my own study. These include the occultism of the late 19th and early 20th centuries, Theosophy, the philosophy of G. I. Gurdjieff, Qabalah, the work of Aleister Crowley, the Masons, the Rosicrucians, and the New Age, Goddess, and Witchcraft movements. Rather than an exhaustive history of magic and witchcraft and the various influences of its evolution (I am not a trained historian and it would take volumes and volumes to do the subject justice), think of this as a brief history of my own influences and why this book is currently in your hands.

* * *

Some of the deepest roots of the word "witch" come from the PIE word *weik-* , which is the root of words having to do with ancestors and home as well as shaping, bending, binding, conquering, and in other ways using the will to shape things[1]. The witch is the one who knows how to bend and shape the world, to tap into a deep vein of energy and utilize it to alter the fabric of reality. Though it has come to have negative connotations, it remains, at its heart, a word associated with power, sensuality, and rebelliousness.

In regard to her own reasoning for calling herself a witch, Laurie Cabot has said, "To me the word witch is a delicious word filled with the most ancient memories that go back to our earliest ancestors, who lived close to natural cycles and understood and appreciated the power and energy that we share with the cosmos. The word Witch can stir these

---

1 Douglas Harper, "*weik- (2)," Online Etymology Dictionary, https://www. etymonline.com/word/*weik- (accessed January 17, 2020).

memories and feelings even in the most skeptical minds."[2] I think it is the desire to "live deliciously" that may explain in part why people have begun to reclaim the word. Our society wants nothing but fuzzy feelings of obedience, light, and comfort with a denial of our basically animal nature. Calling oneself a "witch" feels like reaching out to grasp the power in the warm belly of Chaos, to experience the hidden, sensuous world in the dark, at the edge of the woods and the border of the mind. It feels like a denial of the fear of the beast in the world's soul and a revelry in the pure, astringent tang of the beast's reality.

Of course, that isn't what most people think of when they hear the word "witch." For most of modern history, witchcraft, if not all magic, has been defined as "a class of inappropriate sacred rituals, which were excluded from normative Christian practice"[3]. Accordingly, people have felt a need for a defender against this outsider kind of magic, a righteous protector who knows the tricks of the witches and can perform "miracles". These are the medicine people, the cunning folk[4] who protect their villages from malicious magic. Keep in mind that this goes all the way back to the pre-Christian world; the witch, by whatever name they were called in a given culture, was considered the adversary of the medicine person of that culture.

The witch and the cunning person have used very similar, basically indistinguishable, methods, but one has been acknowledged as wicked and the other helpful. Once a culture's habitus[5] begins to shift, however, those who were

---

2   Laurie Cabot and Tom Cowan, The Power of the Witch: The Earth, the Moon, and the Magical Path to Enlightenment (New York: Delta Publishing, 1990).

3   Sophie Page, "Medieval Magic," in The Oxford Illustrated History of Witchcraft and Magic, ed. Owen Davies (Oxford: Oxford University Press, 2017), 29

4   The term "cunning folk" is technically British, but I use it as a stand in for the many names given to medicine people, wise ones, and healers over the globe.

5   "A range of beliefs so embedded in the culture that it is both omnipresent

once considered medicine people, powerful helpers on the side of the prevailing gods, would be considered strange, uncomfortable, cultural hold-overs that would then be suspected of working on the side of the "devils", the old gods who were no longer considered "good"; they would become witches or devils themselves. According to the official servants of whichever gods are in vogue at any given time, anyone working with spiritual powers that are not deemed orthodox is a danger to the people.

There is a difference, however, between the official definition of what constitutes malevolent witchcraft and the popular definition. The common person, even after the habitus starts to shift and the laws begin to change, may continue going to confer with the cunning person because their magic and medicine had been effective in the past. They know how to deal with spiritual issues that the prevailing clergy and the physicians may not know how to handle. Even after they are considered "witches" from an official standpoint, the general populace may still consider them to be a useful part of the community. Over time, as the older generations pass away and the current habitus takes firm hold of the subconscious and secret drives of the youth, the people who practice the old ways of conjure and curing will become more and more the outsider, the uncanny, the witch.

The history of magic, however, is a wild tangle of fact and fiction stretching back through time to the earliest culture we have verifiable proof of, that of European Early Modern Humans (or EEMH, who previously have been called Cro-Magnon[6]), about 40,000-10,000 years ago. What

---

and cognitively invisible, and which every individual unconsciously adopts to one extent or another." Jim Baker, The Cunning Man's Handbook: The Practice of English Folk Magic, 1550-1900 (London: Avalonia, 2014), Kindle Edition, 317-318.

6   K. Kris Hirst, "Why Don't We Call Them 'Cro-Magnon' Anymore?" ThoughtCo., https://www.thoughtco.com/we-dont-call-them-cro-magnon-170738 (accessed January 17, 2020).

those people believed is hard to determine, but we do know that they made jewelry (possibly ceremonial or symbolic), made fine tools, and had burial rituals. The presence of ceremony around death may be evidence they had animistic beliefs and a reverence for the earth, though we cannot say for certain. There are also several "Venus" figurines associated with EEMH and the Upper Paleolithic period, including the Venus of Holhe Fels, the earliest undisputed representation of a human being dating back approximately 40,000 years[7].

It is important to note that Anatomically Modern Humans evolved about 200,000 years ago in Africa and likely had civilizations as well, but there is no evidence of what they might have been like. There is a definite Eurocentrism in contemporary anthropology and we need to make sure that we turn from that and recognize that our early African ancestors were equally advanced and thoroughly evolved as their European descendants.

Throughout early human history we find multiple works of art, such as earthen vessels, statuary, jewelry, cave images, and figurines, which seem to display the basic tenets of Sympathy, or the magic of correlations. In the Caverne des Trois Freres in France there is an image called "The Sorcerer," an obvious depiction of a penis-having human dancing in the skin of a horned animal. This is one of the earliest depictions of what seems like ritual garb, or possibly a representation of therianthropy (shape shifting)[8]. There are other images that depict successful hunts, animals with spears in their side, animals gathered in large numbers, and what seem to be sorcerous ritual scenes, which may be early forms of

---

7   The Editors of Encyclopaedia Britannica, "Cro-Magnon: Prehistoric Human,"Encyclopaedia Britannica, https://www.britannica.com/topic/Cro-Magnon (accessed January 17, 2020)

8   Gary Zabel, "Therianthropes, Shamans, and Sorcerers," Philosophy 281: Philosophy of Magic, Witchcraft, and the Occult, http://www.faculty.umb.edu/gary_zabel/Courses/Phil%20281/Philosophy%20of%20Magic/My%20Documents/Therianthropes.htm

sympathetic hunting magic aimed at bringing abundance to those early peoples. Doreen Valiente, the mother of modern witchcraft, said, "The depths of a cave were man's first sanctuary. In deep, silent, inaccessible places, away from the surroundings of their everyday life, the Stone Age hunters worshipped and practiced magic."[9]

The views of authors such as Charles Leland, Margaret Murray, and Marija Gimbutas lead to the Witch-Cult Hypothesis and the Goddess Movement, concepts which state that pre-historic cultures were peaceful, egalitarian, matriarchal, and goddess-centered and that the witch hunts of Medieval and Early Modern Europe were calculated attempts by the Church to destroy the pre-Christian, pagan religion. This view has largely been rejected by the archaeological community. Evidence suggests, rather, that early cultures were not female dominated and that early peoples were likely egalitarian hunter/gatherers with somewhat advanced cultural practices involving animism, sympathetic magical practices, herbal medicine, and talismanic magic. There are, of course, many matrilineal and matrifocal societies, but the idea that early societies were female-dominant in the way that the toxically patriarchal societies of today are male-dominant is not based in fact[10].

In some places, the animism of our ancestors evolved and became part of more complicated systems of belief involving large pantheons and specific rituals and magical practices, many of which began to replace the worship of ancestors to with the arbitration of a priest or priestess. The first records we have of a religion like this are those of the peoples of Mesopotamia, who believed the earth is flat, floating in a great abyss with Heaven above, and that everything is surrounded by a boundless sea, out of which the

---

9 Doreen Valiente, An ABC of Witchcraft Past and Present 2nd ed. (London: Robert Hale, 1984).

10 Cynthia Eller, The Myth of Matriarchal Prehistory: Why An Invented Past Will Not Give Women a Future (Boston: Beacon Press, 2000).

entire universe was born. In Sumer, the word for universe was an-ki, the names of the Sky Father and the Earth Mother, whose children were the Anunnaki. The most powerful of the Anunnaki were Enlil, the sky god, and Inanna, the goddess of fertility, irrigation, beauty, love, and war.

Remember that in basically every civilization throughout human history there have been magical practices accepted by the religious authorities that are performed to counter the non-sanctioned magic practiced by "witches." Even in Mesopotamia there were sanctions against certain "pagan" practices, or what later Europe would name witchcraft. The people who used such magic were called kassapu (male) and kassaptu (female)[11]. Mesopotamia had people called asipu, or exorcists, who quieted spirits enraged by the magic of the kassapu/aptu[12]. There were also other roles played by both men and women to protect against malicious magic, though the practices deemed malicious were likely akin to the ancestral practices which had been dismissed by the society in power. What we see in much of this palliative and apotropaic magic are reflections of the magic the "witch" must also have been using, like making a clay figure of the target, piercing it with metal pokers, and burning it in a fire to destroy the malefactor's power (a ritual called malqu)[13].

The Egyptians, another polytheistic society, brought magic to a new height. The priesthood could calculate the movements of stars with incredible accuracy, there were libraries devoted to the interpretation of dreams, and vendors who carved the icons of deities in which the gods could

---

11   Peter Maxwell-Stuart, "Magic in the Ancient World," in The Oxford Illustrated History of Witchcraft and Magic, ed. Owen Davies (Oxford: Oxford University Press, 2017), 3.

12   Ibid., 3.

13   Ibid., 3.

dwell, allowing the peasantry to bring the gods home[14]. It is the religious structure of the Egyptians (along with the Greco-Roman cultures) that influenced the most famous mystery cult in modern European history, the Order of the Golden Dawn, which itself influenced most modern ceremonial magic, occultism, theosophy, and witchcraft[15].

In Egypt the people believed in a ubiquitous energy of magic called heka, a force that could be harnessed by anyone and allowed the gods to have their powers. It was personified in the deity Heka, god of magic and medicine, who was believed to be the most primordial of all things and that from which all creation comes[16]. The official magicians in Egypt were called "chief lector-priests," but we can also assume any number of lay magic users throughout the kingdoms[17]. There were practices against the malicious magic of witches, too, which were very similar to those of the Mesopotamians. Both cultures believed in the Evil Eye, a concept which exists the world over. The wadjet, or protective eye, now called the Eye of Horus, was used as an amulet to ward off the power of any witch casting an evil glance on an unsuspecting person[18].

Protective, or apotropaic, magic, can be found not only in the Ancient Middle East and Ancient Egypt, but throughout time and all over the world. In the Roman Empire there was an amulet called a fascinum, which was a statuette of a large, erect penis with wings and sometimes a

---

14   Ibid., 6.

15   New World Encyclopedia, "Hermetic Order of the Golden Dawn," New World Encyclopedia, https://www.newworldencyclopedia.org/entry/ Hermetic_Order_of_the_Golden_Dawn (accessed April 17, 2020).

16   Joshua J. Mark, "Heka," Ancient History Encyclopedia, https://www.ancient.eu/Heka/ (accessed April 17, 2020).

17   Maxwell-Stuart, "Magic in the Ancient World," 6.

18   Ibid., 8.

large, erect penis of its own. The god Fascinus was the embodiment of the divine phallus, a symbol of fertility and virility and a protector against evil magic. The fascinum amulet was used to deflect invidia, the Roman concept of the evil eye, and malicious witchcraft. The term fascination means "to have an irresistible and unseen influence over another", which comes from the Latin fascinare, meaning "to bewitch, especially through the eyes or tongue". Phallic fascination is part of cultures the world over from the Egyptian gods Min, Ptah, and Osiris to the Kokopelli of the Pueblo peoples, to the Greek god Pan and the priapic wand of Dionysos, to the Shiva Lingha, the representation of the god Shiva's penis[19].

Ancient civilizations had not only magical safe guards against malicious magic, but also severe punishments for those who were found guilty of maleficium, the practice of "evil" magic. In 4th Century Greece, a woman named Theoris of Lemnos was prosecuted for casting incantations and using poisons. She was what is called a pharmakis, a word most often translated as "witch," though it is more accurately a person who uses herbs and magic to cure and kill. Theoris was executed along with her family[20].

Burning alive, drawing and quartering, and feeding a person to the beasts (among many others) were all possible deaths for anyone convicted of performing black magic to kill, particularly poisoning and necromancy. Practicing the arts did not always result in capital punishments for magic users. Death sentences were reserved for people who had killed or caused grievous harm to others, whether through magic or not[21].

Magic, particularly popular magic, plays a role in all civilizations. If you've ever picked up a lucky penny,

---

19 Ibid., 23.

20 Derek Collins, "The Trial of Theoris of Lemnos: A 4th Century Witch or Folk Healer?" Western Folklore 59, no. ¾ (2000): 251–278. JSTOR.

21 Maxwell-Stuart. "Magic in the Ancient World", 22.

knocked on wood, worn your lucky underwear, or broken a wish bone on Thanksgiving, you've practiced modern day versions of very old magic. The belief in the power of magic is part of our subconscious life, built into our very nature. Witches, even the village cunning folk, have always been feared, reviled, and denigrated by the prevailing culture. There has never been a "golden age" of witchcraft. What we see as our halcyon days were the heights of the prevalent religion in any given time and, when those civilizations were conquered or subsumed by another, the old religious practices became superstitions and folk beliefs, if not total taboos, and termed "witchcraft".

The greatest conquest of a new religious ideology over another was, of course, Christianity. Pagans and Christians have a long history together. In Pagan Rome it was routine to torture Christians, to place them in pits with lions, crucify them, or in some other way torture them to death. Persecution was not universal, just as witch hunts were not universal, and these punishments were not meted out specifically against Christians, but to any person considered criminal. Christians had some periods of respite from persecution, notably when the emperor Gallienus overturned the anti-Christian laws of his father, Emperor Valerian, in 260 CE and, though Christianity was not made an official religion, worship of the Christian God was tolerated[22].

For nearly forty years there was freedom of worship, until 303 CE when the Emperor Diocletian and the junior co-emperor Galerius took power and instituted a series of edicts ordering the destruction of churches, ecclesiastical property, and the burning of Christian texts, a period called the "Great Persecution"[23]. The types of tortures and punish-

---

22   Koji Toyota, "On the 'Edict of Toleration' of the Emperor Gallienus," Journal of Classical Studies 28 (March 26, 1980): 88-98, doi: 10.20578/jclst.28.0_88.

23   G. E. M. De Ste. Croix, "Aspects of the 'Great' Persecution," The Harvard Theological Review 47, no. 2 (April 1954): 75–113. JSTOR, https://www.jstor.org/stable/1508458 (accessed January 17, 2020).

ments Christians were sentenced to depended on the decisions of provincial governors and there were also periods when imprisoned clergy were given the opportunity to regain their freedom if they renounced Christianity and made sacrifice to the Roman gods.

Then, in 305 CE, Constantine became emperor in the Western Roman Empire, and gained control of the East (defeating the Emperors Maxentius and Licinius) in 324. He was the first emperor to convert to Christianity and he moved the capital of Rome to Byzantium (which he renamed Constantinople, after himself), and, though his official law was toleration of both old and new gods, he began to phase out the iconography of the old religion, replacing it with that of Christianity. He called the Counsel of Nicea, which determined that God and Christ are equally eternal and divine, and determined which gospels would be considered canon and which apocryphal. Constantine is also credited with creating the Christogram. In 380, Emperor Theodosius I made Christianity the state religion of the Roman Empire[24] [25].

In the Early days of the Church, pagans and Christians got along nicely in many regions and the people began to convert to its tenets not by force, but by choice. As pagans began to join the faith many of their beliefs were also transferred in, especially holidays and symbols that were already common in their regions, but were adapted to Christian ideology. The Midsummer holiday, Litha, celebrated on June 24th with bonfires and harvest dances, became the Feast Day of John the Baptist, helping to enmesh the pagan celebrations with those of the Christians. Many of the holidays of the Church are of pagan origin, including Christmas (Yule), Easter (Ostara), Halloween (Samhain), and Candlemas (Im-

---

24 Dr Sophie Lunn-Rockliffe, "Christianity and the Roman Empire," BBC History, http://www.bbc.co.uk/history/ancient/romans/christianityromanempire_article_01.shtml (accessed April 22, 2020).

25 Donald L. Wasson, "Constantine I," Ancient History Encyclopedia, https://www.ancient.eu/Constantine_I/ (accessed April 22, 2020).

bolc)[26]. This process of assimilation made the transition easier for both sides.

Constantine's son, Constantine II, was completely intolerant of the old religion, though, pronouncing that temples should be destroyed and people caught offering to the old gods should be put to death. The persecutions escalated from there throughout the Roman Empire and many of the old religious sites were either sacked and destroyed or repurposed for Christian worship[27].

A pattern in the Christianization of any culture is that it happened in large, urban areas first and slowly leaked into more rural areas, which is why the lore of the old religions still exists in the practices of many country folk. In a city it is easier to institute and control religious doctrine, while the country remains wild and untamed, a place for the old gods to compromise with the new, culminating in a folk magic that uses herbs and animal parts, but all while reciting Christian prayers. From the 4th century onward the Christianization of Europe carried on at a steady pace, undergoing various schisms and reformations.

The Middle Ages of Europe began after the fall of the Roman Empire in 476 and lasted through the 15th century. During much of this thousand-year period, as in antiquity, acts of magic were not necessarily severely punished. In 511, the Salic Law punished magic users with various fines, though sometimes the sentence would be a lifetime of slavery. There were capital punishments, as well, but it was not the norm. In fact, it was the aim of the church to quell belief in any supernatural power beside God's and they were just as likely to punish the accuser as the accused. The Lombard Code of 643 states "Let nobody presume to kill a foreign serving maid or female slave as a witch, for it is not possible,

---

26   www.daily.jstor.org/how-irish-holidays-blend-catholic-and-pagan   traditions/

27   Craig Morley, "Constantius II", Ancient History Encyclopedia, http://www.ancient.eu/Constantius_II/ (accessed April 22, 2020).

nor ought to be believed by Christian minds," a view in line with the writings of St. Augustine[28].

The Canon Episcopi of 900 CE also follows this logic and states:

> "It is also not to be omitted that some unconstrained women, perverted by Satan, seduced by illusions and phantasms of demons, believe and openly profess that, in the dead of night, they ride upon certain beasts with the pagan goddess Diana.... But it were well if they alone perished in their infidelity and did not draw so many others into the pit of their faithlessness. For an innumerable multitude, deceived by this false opinion, believe this to be true and, so believing, wander from the right faith and relapse into pagan errors when they think that there is any divinity or power except the one God."[29]

The document describes all witchcraft, though not all magic, as Devil-worship and lunacy. The Devil exists, but humans cannot partake in his supernatural powers; he only leads them away from the "true faith".

It becomes clear that the aim of the Church in the early centuries of its existence was to avoid bloodshed and that the official stance on witchcraft was its non-existence. The true enemy, according to the church, were heretics, those who either fought against the orthodoxy of Rome or ignored it, though it was rare that even they were put to death. Torture was largely outlawed by the Church, but things were

---

28   World Heritage Encyclopedia, "Eurpoean Witchcraft," Project Gutenberg Self-Publishing Press, http://www.self.gutenberg.org/articles/eng/European_Witchcraft (accessed April 22, 2020).

29   Occult World, "Canon Episcopi," Occult World, https://occult-world.com/witch-glossary/canon-episcopi/(accessed April 22, 2020).

shifting in the Empire[30].

A new group of heretics, the Cathars and the Waldensians, began to proliferate in Northern Italy and Southern France, then throughout Western Europe, from the 12th to 14th centuries. The Cathars were a sect of Christianity with Gnostic and Zoroastrian leanings, believing there to be two gods; a good God of the New Testament, father of Christ, and an evil god of the Old Testament, father of Satan. This theistic dualism was unacceptable to the Church and the doctrines of the Cathars were labelled not only heretical, but dangerous[31].

The Waldensians were an ascetic group of monks who preached the scriptures to the laity (for free, which the Church considered scandalous). They denied the importance of the Sacraments and the existence of purgatory and believed that a person could confess to anyone, not just the priesthood. They sought, after a fashion, to decentralize power from the church and give it into the hands of the people, which, at least in the eyes of Pope Lucius III, was as good as ecclesiastical treason, for which he excommunicated every Waldensian in 1184 at the Synod of Verona[32].

It was largely the tensions between the Church and these heretical groups that led to the establishment of the Inquisition, first as a group of bishops sent to France in the late 12th century and later as a full-on judicial assaulting branch of the Church in 1232 under the auspice of Pope Gregory. The Inquisitors, those meant to find and punish "heretics", were often overzealous, sometimes burning at the stake even those who had confessed to heresy. They were also wont to

---

30 Kevin Knight, "Witchcraft," New Advent Catholic Encyclopedia, http://www.newadvent.org/cathen/15674a.htm (accessed April 22, 2020).

31 Kevin Knight, "Cathari," New Advent Catholic Encyclopedia, http://www.newadvent.org/cathen/03435a.htm (accessed April 22, 2020).

32 Kevin Knight, "Waldenses," New Advent Catholic Encyclopedia, http://www.newadvent.org/cathen/15527b.htm (accessed April 22, 2020).

using extreme forms of torture to extricate confessions. It was particularly brutal in Spain under the rulership of Ferdinand and Isabella who used the Inquisition as a tool to rid Spain of conversos, Jews who had converted to Christianity, who many of the powerful families of Spain viewed with suspicion and disdain. In France the Inquisition routed the Knights Templar (under the direction of King Philip IV, who owed the organization a great deal of money) between 1307 and 1314, and burned Joan of Arc alive at the stake in 1412 when she was only nineteen years old.

The tense socio-political-religious atmosphere in Europe at this time was beginning to fray the nerves of those in power and fears began to mount throughout the kingdoms, even into England where the Inquisition had never taken hold. The idea that there were possibly mislead, rebellious groups trying to decentralize power, educate the masses, and tell them that they had any form of sovereignty was dangerous and reeked of revolution.

Though the draconian abuses of power by the Inquisition were viewed with horror, the many confessions across so much land had made it clear that dangerous people touched by the Devil and his demons had infiltrated society. There were clergy who disagreed with the stance taken in the Canon Epsicopi and its ilk, most famously the Dominican known as Thomas Aquinas. In the 13th century he wrote of the realness of witchcraft and the ability of a person to make an unwitting pact with the Devil through heresy.

Throughout the history of persecutions against witches and heretics the idea that a human can make a pact with the Devil (or a demon, or even a Holy Guardian Angel) is a popular and integral concept. Figures like Theophilus of Adana, Faustus, Pope Sylvester II, and Urbain Grandier (among many others) were said to have made "Deals with the Devil", all of them either learned men or clergy. By the 15th century there was a huge amount of literature, influenced by writers such as Aquinas, which stressed the reality of demons who had dealings with people, including sexual acts (think Lilith and the nocturnal emission).

Using Thomas Aquinas as a springboard for their ideas, other clergy members and religious thinkers began to conjecture that, through a pact with the Devil, a human being may be able to gain true supernatural power, like the powers that for centuries the Church had denied were possible. If this were true, then perhaps heretics made pacts to become witches and carry forth these supernatural powers against true Christians.

In the 1430's Johannes Nider wrote several tracts, including one called the Formicarius, which detailed the malicious work of peasant witches. He also wrote about the weakness of women and their proclivity toward demonic temptation[33]. Throughout European history women had been denigrated and considered weak of mind and moral, so it wasn't a difficult task to convince people that, if anyone were to be tricked into making a pact with Satan, it would be a woman, not a man of letters.

Yet, much of what we know of High Magic (le Haute Magie, or "learned magic") during the middle ages comes from the works of the clergy and other learned men, as they were literate while the commoners were usually not. In the late 11th century through the 13th, after the Crusades, books by Islamic and Jewish authors on alchemy, astrology, herbalism, and topics such as Hermetics and Kabbalah were made available for the first time in Western Europe and were being transcribed into Latin in great numbers[34].

The medical works of Ali ibn Abbas al-Majusi and the political philosophies of Ibn Rushd (Averroes) were

---

33 James Sharpe, "The Demonologists", in The Oxford Illustrated History of Witchcraft and Magic, ed. Owen Davies, (Oxford: Oxford University Press, 2017), 74.

34 Sophie Page, "Medieval Magic", in The Oxford Illustrated History of Witchcraft and Magic, ed. Owen Davies (Oxford: Oxford University Press, 2017), 31-36.

among them, along with a slew of medical texts from Muslim scholars from the 8th century to the 11th. One of the best known and most prolific of the Arabic authors to be translated into Latin was Abu Ali ibn Sina (also called Avicenna), a polymath who wrote on topics of medicine, chemistry, mathematics, astronomy, astrology, musical theory, and philosophy. Most of the authors had been influenced to an extent by Plato, Aristotle, and the Neoplatonists, with Avicenna being one of the most successful at adapting the antique philosophers to the Islamic scholastic theology. Because of the common ground of Plato and Aristotle, the ideas from these texts were better understandable to European scholars and were not treated with too much fear by Church officials[35].

In the 15th century the philosophers Marsilio Ficino and Giovanni Pico della Mirandola independently came to the idea that there is a hidden, ancient wisdom that could be found in the Hermetic philosophies (Ficino) and in the Kabbalah (Pico). For both, the "True Faith" within Christianity, the "ancient theology" as Ficino called it, was to be found in these and various other systems of mysticism, but also in the many books translated from Arabic mentioned above. Inspired by the Neoplatonic philosophers of the 3rd-6th centuries, both believed that at the root of things, all spiritualities (indeed, all things in general) derive from one source called "The One" or "The Good" which they attributed to the Christian God, making their philosophies both perennial and Christ-centered.

Both Ficino and Pico thought that magic was the key to opening the pathway to a mystical union with God, a practical method for attainment of the immortal soul's true goal, making them the first influential Christian thinkers to bring magic into an understanding not only of their faith, but of God. Their work was the very foundation upon which later magicians would build, including Agrippa von Nettesheim,

---

35   Ibid., 31-36

whose Three Books on Occult Philosophy would clarify the magical practices dreamed of especially by Pico. All of this was made possible by the translation of those great works of magic and philosophy from the Muslim countries invaded during the Crusades[36] [37].

During this time magic was classified into two main groups: Natural Magic, the study of the occult properties of things like plants and stones, and Image Magic, a practice considered by many learned men to be "demonic" as it called on spirits to imbue talismans and amulets with power. The former type was considered more acceptable than the latter (though not by much) because its aim was to discover the secrets of Nature (i.e. God), such as how "the sheep divines the wolf as a predator", how to use plants to heal, and find lost objects. Through various academic means, particularly the study of alchemy, the natural magicians hoped to pierce the veil between this world and the Divine to discover how best to know God's Will.

Image Magic was considered evil because it put the sorcerer in contact with spirits and the dead (basically necomancy) and sought to give a person luck or love through magical means. These men were also looking for the secrets of Nature, but sought to wrestle them straight from the demon's mouth, so to speak. Through complicated and in-depth cermonial ritual they sought power over spirits and the dead to gain access to arcane knowledge[38]. These magicians were laregely clergymen who went against the will of the Church, summoning spirits into magical circles and

---

36   Brian Copenhaver, "Giovanni Pico Della Mirandola," Stanford Encyclopedia of Philosophy, https://plato.stanford.edu/entries/pico-della-mirandola/ (accessed April 22, 2020).

37   Christopher S. Celenza, "Marsilio Ficino," Stanford Encyclopedia of Philosophy, https://plato.stanford.edu/entries/ficino/ (accessed April 22, 2020).

38   Page. "Medieval Magic," 32-33.

forcing them through magic to do their will (like Faust to Mephistopheles), though usually for a steeper price than the magician might have wanted to pay (like Mephistopheles to Faust)[39].

The reasoning for their actions was thus: If Christ taught the Apostles to command demons, what sin could there be in these magicians doing the same? Today, this type of magic is exemplified most popularly in a later work, The Lesser Key of Solomon, also called the Lemegeton, a book aimed at controlling and commanding infernal spirits (and contacting angels) in the fashion of Solomon the King. Authorship of the five books contained in the work (Ars Goetia, Ars Theurgia-Goetia, Ars Paulina, Ars Almadel, and Ars Notoria) was attributed to Solomon himself, though it was likely compiled from various grimoires in the 16th-17th centuries[40].

Not quite in the vein of Natural Magic, but not quite considered demonic either, was the magic known as Theurgy, a type of conjuring magic that aimed at summoning angels to explain the universe and reveal secrets. The Ars Notoria, mentioned above, and the Liber Razielis (originally Sefer Raziel HaMalakh), a book of universal secrets said to have been dictated to Adam by the Archangel Raziel, are such magical texts. Books like these were viewed with suspicion, if not outright loathing.

One of the more famous and influential of these books on today's witchcraft was The Book of Abra Melin the Mage, written by Abraham of Wurzburg in the 15th century and translated by Samuel Liddell MacGregor Mathers in the 20th century. This grimoire revolves around the operation of the "Knowledge and Conversation of the Holy Guardian

---

39 Ibid., 44-55

40 Joseph H. Peterson, "The Lesser Key of Solomon," Esoteric Archives, http://www.esotericarchives.com/solomon/lemegeton.htm (accessed April 22, 2020).

Angel", requiring an extremely long process of meditations and exercises meant to achieve a revelatory experience of magical secrets and powers[41]. The concepts and practices described in it were later performed and developed by Aleister Crowley[42]. These magics, though abhorred by the Church, were viewed with less suspicion than the type of magic done by peasant witches. After all, the grimoires taught these men of learning how to command devils and speak with angels, while the witch was in league with Satan himself.

It was also during this period that the Roman Catholic Church was beginning to see the dawning of a reformation movement. The tide started rising with the teachings of Arnold of Bresica in the 1130s and the Waldensians in the 1170s, and followed through to the work of "the Morning Star of the Reformation", John Wycliffe, who believed that the gospel should be available to all people in the common language. In 1332 he translated the Vulgate Bible (the Latin version held to be holy by the Roman Church) into vernacular English. Later, in 1526, William Tyndale printed the first complete English copies of the Bible and disseminated them amongst the common people at an affordable price, something made possible by the invention of the printing press by Johannes Gutenberg in 1440.

The movement culminated in Protestantism, which is said to have started in 1517 with the 95 Theses of Martin Luther, hammered into the doors of All Saints Church with a "nail in the coffin" of the Catholic Church's theocracy. The tenets of Protestantism are similar to those of the Waldensians in that there is a denial of the power of the sacraments, tithes, and indulgences, a leaning toward asceticism, and the dissemination of the Gospel to the laity. They also had a dark side, though. They preached that the Devil was real and pres-

---

41 S.L. MacGregor Mathers, "The Book of the Sacred Magic of Abramelin the Mage," Internet Sacred Text Archive, https://www.sacred-texts.com/grim/abr/index.htm (accessed April 22, 2020).

42 Doreen Valiente, The Rebirth of Witchcraft, (London: Robert Hale, 2008).

ent, that demons stalked the world looking for souls to send to Hell, that salvation was a hair's breadth from damnation, that God was more often in a punishing mood than a beatific one, and that some humans chose to fight alongside the Devil as his warriors in the guise of witches. It was this thinking and fear mongering that would make the world ripe for the witch trials of the 15th-17th centuries.

In 1486, Heinrich Kramer (sometimes Heinrich Institoris, a Latinized version of his name), a Dominican Inquisitor from Germany, wrote a book that would change the fate of witchcraft forever. The Malleus Maleficarum, "the Hammer [Against] the Witches", was a treatise on inquisitorial methods for sussing out witches from among the peasantry, particularly among women. It details not only what witches do and are capable of through the most heinous of magics, but also ways for the "witch hunter" to find witches and methods of torture one could utilize to extract a "confession"[43].

Though the Catholic Church and various important clergy and judges disagreed with the draconian nature of the book, the appalling Malleus was second only to the Bible in popularity until the mid-1600's and went through multiple printings (again, thanks to the bitter-sweet invention of the Gutenberg press).

Over the intervening centuries many books were written on how to find witches and what to do with them once found, such as the works of a French judge named Pierre de Lancre. Many of his ideas were influenced by earlier myths told about Jews and early Christians in Rome, though he also focused on the popular folklore of witches, particularly the idea of the Sabbat (a word which makes it clear that the lore of witches and the prejudices against the Jewish people were conflated). This was said to be a sort of sacreligious party at which witches made pacts with the Devil by sleeping with

---

43   Sharpe, "Demonologists", 76-77.

him, kissing his anus during a mass orgy, or by sacrificing and eating babies. Pierre de Lancre also popularized the idea that a witch would obtain a mark on her body as a sign of her Sabbatical pact[44].

The witches mark could be anything, from a mole to a genital wart, a birthmark to a scar, so it could be found on anyone. The tradition of the "witch hunter" or "witch pricker" was born of a need to discover these various physical attributes on the body of an accused witch. The hunter would use long needles to poke the entire body, looking for a point where the accused could feel no pain or didn't bleed. Of course, after hours of being pricked, the body stops sending signals of pain, so this "mark" could be found every time. If that failed, any mole or freckle would do to make an accusation stick. It was also said that witches could not recite the Lord's Prayer in full (which was common among the illiterate peasantry) and that they were often in the company of "familiar spirits", demons in the shape of pets[45]. Another popular test for witches was "swimming", tossing a bound person into a body of water to see if they would float, a sure sign that the water rejected them as they rejected the waters of Baptism. If they drowned, the people could feel safe in the knowledge that the accused was with their Lord[46].

Remember that these witch trials were taking place in ecclesiastical courts in rural areas, where the power of the judges was limited, especially because witchcraft was not yet a felony charge. There were many and disparate definitions of witchcraft, various punishments from fees to death, depending on whether a person was harmed through magic or not. The higher courts would often refuse to witness

---

44   Ibid., 74-96.

45   Rita Voltmer, "The Witch Trials", in The Oxford Illustrated History of Witchcraft and Magic, ed. Owen Davies (Oxford: Oxford University Press, 2017), 116-118.

46   Ibid., 112

witchcraft cases or would dismiss them, leading to local decisions on the matter (sometimes through mob justice). It wasn't until the establishment of the Witchcraft Acts by the Tudors of England that witchcraft became a felony charge worthy of capital punishment in the courts of common law[47].

The world was on the edge of madness when the Anglican Reformation of England in 1532 tipped it into chaos. Henry VIII, wanting to divorce Catherine of Aragon but without successful permission from Pope Clement VII. He instead divorced all of England from Rome, thereby establishing the Protestant Church of England with Henry at its head, giving him the authority to allow his own divorce. The whole schism was really a sort of temper tantrum and, though he had denounced Papal authority, Henry never really denounced Catholicism. Much of the ceremonial and ecclesiastical life of the Church of England stayed the same as before the Anglican Reformation, though the separation allowed for the formation of new laws that no longer needed Rome's sanction. One of those was the Witchcraft Act of 1542, which defined witchcraft as "using invocations or other specifically magical acts to hurt someone, get money, or behave badly towards Christianity" and defined any act that even resembled witchcraft as a felony. This meant that "being a witch—whether or not specific harm was caused to another person—was enough to get you executed" and your property seized[48].

After Henry VIII's death a series of successions occurred. A dizzying back-and-forth of the passage and repeal of laws left the English people in a wretchedly confused state. New tortures were instated for heretics, both Protes-

---

47   Dries Vanysacker, "Review," Church History and Religious Culture 90, no. 4 (2010): 697–699, JSTOR, http://www.jstor.org/stable/23922534 (accessed January 17, 2020).

48   Kat Eschner, "England's Witch Trials Were Lawful," Smithsonian Magazine, https://www.smithsonianmag.com/smart-news/englands-witch-trials-were-lawful-180964514/ (accessed April 22, 2020).

tant and Catholic, that caused much bloodshed and suffering. Jason Louv describes the spirit of the age well with these words:

"Rather than a singular Church, there were now many. Rather than one world, there were now two [the Americas]. Rather than the inherited knowledge of the Gospels and the ancients, science would soon come to show that nearly everything Western man assumed to be true was likely not. And rather than existing at the center of the cosmos, mankind was now relegated to orbiting the sun [Copernican heliocentrism]. If it seemed like the end of the world, that's because it was—the final and definitive death of the Middle Ages, and the beginning of the modern world to come."[49]

Henry's successor, Edward VI, only nine years old when he was crowned, was the first English monarch to be raised Protestant and did everything in his power to further reform the Church of England and concretize the official religion as Anglicanism. One of his first measures was to repeal the Witchcraft Act of his father, returning the laws to their previous vagueness. His reign was short, as he died of lung disease at the age of fifteen. Edward and his advisory council, attempting to prevent the repeal of his religious decrees by avoiding the succession of his half-sisters, Mary and Elizabeth Tudor, chose instead his distant cousin, Lady Jane Grey, as his successor (a position backed by the Duke of Northumberland). Her reign lasted nine days (earning her the title "The Nine Days' Queen") before Mary Tudor deposed her and claimed the throne. Jane was soon beheaded, as was the Duke of Northumberland, for high treason.

Mary I, also known as "Bloody Mary" and the sub-

---

49   Louv, John Dee, 11.

ject of the darker-than-you-think nursery rhyme "Mary, Mary, Quite Contrary," was a staunch Catholic. She did what she could to re-reform the Church and return as much to Catholicism as was within her power. Her reign of five years was a bloody, vengeful affair, during which she killed nearly 300 religious protestors and married Philip, King of Spain, to concretize an allyship between her realm and a Catholic powerhouse. She died in 1558, probably of uterine cancer, and was succeeded, finally, by Elizabeth I, Queen of England and Ireland, who again reformed the Church of England toward Protestantism.

Later, Elizabeth I enacted the Witchcraft Act of 1563, called "An Act Against Conjuarations, Enchantments, and Witchcrafts", which defined witchcraft similarly to the earlier law of 1542, but gave less grave punishments for first offenses. Capital punishment was instituted for second offenses and for those who murdered through sorcerous means, making hers a much less harsh version than the Act of 1542[50]. Historical documents make it clear that Elizabeth I used various methods of torture, but not to find witches. Catholics, religious dissenters, and those convicted or suspected of heresy and treason were her targets. Witchcraft, again made a felony, but not defined as heresy, was something to be dealt with in secular courts, having little to do with ecclesiastical law.

Though she reinstated the Witchcraft Act and was suspicious of magic, Elizabeth was actually very interested in Hermetic philosophy and alchemy, and, for a time, found diversion and good council in the company of one of the greatest thinkers of the Elizabethan era, John Dee. Together, they changed the face of the world forever.

Up to this point there was no British Empire (a phrase coined by Dee) and England was still an island nation with no outlying lands under its rule. That would change with

---

50   Vanysacker, "Review," 697.

Dee's help. John Louv says, "Dee created the plan for global Protestant victory over the Church—a world-wide Empire of Angels, with Elizabeth I, not the pope, as its spiritual and political head"[51]. Dee, who was a scientist as well as a magician, thought of himself as Merlin and Elizabeth as Arthur in a Renaissance "Age of Legends", which he hoped would end in the Apocalypse. He believed the end of the world would bring about the Second Coming of Christ and scour the lands clean of sin, making the way for the dawning of a fully Christian world, at peace with its Savior at the helm[52].

He saw the path to the realization of his vision in Elizabeth and the conquest of the New World. His works on navigation during this time were a sort of British Westward Expansion philosophy. With his knowledge of navigation, mathematics, cartography, and natural philosophy he made the maritime British Empire a possibility. Without Dee the British Fleet and the British Colonies would not have existed, for better or worse.

Dee's ideas were a fulcrum for change in the occult world, as well. His lineage is based in the works of Giovanni Pico della Mirandola, considered the first Cabalist (Christian Kabbalah), the operative magic of Cornelius Agrippa and Johannes Trithemius, the medical and astrological writings of Parcelsus, the angelology and spiritual hierarchies of Pseudo-Dionysus, along with extensive reading into Hermeticism, Neoplatonism, theology, and the sciences. This combination of disciplines was essential to his work. All of the Christian teachings that informed him made it clear to Dee that, through operative magic, human beings could discover the prisca theologia (the ancient faith) and learn not only how to climb the hierarchy of being[53], but alter and ma-

---

51   Louv, John Dee, 34

52   Ibid., 70

53   The scala naturae, or Ladder of Being, is the concept of hierarchical creation from minerals all the way up to God.

nipulate nature itself through scientific means. His aim was really to reverse the fallen nature of humankind, thus returning the race to its perfected, Edenic state[54].

His method he called "archemastery", which was inspired by the philosophy of Abu Yusuf al-Kindi, a Muslim Hermeticist. In his work On the Stellar Rays, al-Kindi explains that it is an effect of light emitted by planets and stars that moves mankind, an emanationist theory steeped in Neoplatonism and the natural philosophy of the East. The book also explains that these rays can be manipulated through magical means to alter destiny. Dee ran with this idea and combined it with his studies of optics and mathematics to create a fully scientific method, not only of magic, but of astral physics that could harness and utilize invisible, natural forces through the use of crystals and mirrors to truly effect the real and present world. For Dee, light was the key to the secrets of the universe and the Apocalypse.

Dee's system, indeed most of his philosophy, hinged on his work with Cabala, which itself deals with the ten sephirot, or vessels that contain the light of God as it emanates from its mysterious source. In his Monas Hieroglyphica, Dee describes a glyph of his own devising in twenty-four aphorisms. The symbol represents the entirety of Cabalistic thought and the symbolism found in Kabbalah proper. It is through such works that the later Qabalah of occultists like Dion Fortune, Aleister Crowley, and many others was able to come to fruition. Dee died in 1609 in relative obscurity and poverty at his estate in Mortlake, the location of his immense library (at one point holding about 4,000 volumes on science and the occult).

Elizabeth I died six years prior in 1603 and her successor, James VI of Scotland and I of England and Ireland, came to the throne, thus uniting all three kingdoms under one monarch. His mother was Mary, Queen of Scots, who

---

54   Ibid., 62-71

Elizabeth had beheaded for high treason in 1587, an obvious sore spot for James. He was a unique monarch in that he was not only a king but a lay demonologist, even writing a book in 1597 called Daemonologie, a treatise on witches and their allyship with the Devil. Likely the most paranoid monarch of the House of Tudor, he enacted a law in 1604 called "An Act against Conjuration, Witchcraft and dealing with evil and wicked spirits" (sic), or the Jacobean Act. It stripped the 1563 Act of the more lenient penalties for first time offenders and made all witchcraft and associations with witches a capital felony. The Act also defined witches as "…creatures of the Devil, workers of arcane arts who traffick with Satan"[55]. It was really an expansion of the Scottish Witchcraft Act of 1563, merely broadening the scope of what defines witchcraft to include anything that even looked like magic.

The events that spurred his paranoia surrounding witches started in 1589 when his new bride, Anne of Denmark, set sail to Scotland after a proxy wedding in Copenhagen, but had to dock in Norway after her ship was almost lost during a series of storms at sea. James sailed in large retinue to meet her there, and they were formally married in Oslo. In the Spring of 1590, he and Anne sailed back to Edinburgh, though the journey home was again beset by terrible storms. A woman in Denmark, Anne Koldings, upon having been questioned and tortured for suspected witchcraft, described a ritual aimed at killing the King and his new Queen and named the other women who had taken part, one of which was the wife of the Mayor of Copenhagen. As a result of these trials fourteen women were burned at the stake.

Until 1590, witchcraft was something James didn't seem to worry overmuch about, as it could be handled by less-

---

55   John Newton. "Introduction: Witchcraft; Witch Codes; Witch Act". Witchcaft and the Act of of 1604. Edited by John Newton and Jo Bath. (Koninklijke Brill NV. Leiden: 2008). https://www.scribd.com/document/347524628/SMRT-131-Witchcraft-and-the-Act-of-1604-pdf, 27 (accessed April 17th 2020)

er courts and wasn't worth his time. Witchcraft in Scotland during his childhood was considered widespread. Witches there were believed to mainly traffick with fairies and the dead after making pacts made with the Devil, as illustrated by the trials of Janet Boyman in 1572 and Elizabeth Dunlop in 1576. After his personal run-in with maleficium, however, his views shifted and he decided to take a very personal interest in the activity of witches. The trials in Denmark implicated several supposed witches in Scotland, including some higher officials and nobles, so, upon arriving home, James began his own series of Scottish witch prosecutions in an event known as the North Berwick Trials[56].

Among those accused was the first cousin of the king and possible ringleader of the witches, Francis Stewart, Fifth Earl of Bothwell. His father, James Hepburn, had been the lead suspect in the death of King James's father, Henry Stuart. Besides the apparent animosity James held toward Francis, other accused people indicated him as well. Among these was Gillis Duncan, a servant from Trenant. Under torture, she accused upwards of seventy other people, men and women, of being part of the plot against King James. One of those accused by Duncan was Agnes Sampson, a well-known cunning woman and widow with several children, who was stripped, shaved and examined for a witches mark, then tortured with a witches bridle while James watched. She finally confessed and said that she had attended sabbaths with over 200 other people, including Gillis Duncan and another prominent citizen, a school master named Doctor Fian. He was subjected to several extreme tortures before confession and being burned at the stake in 1591.

King James had a pamphlet printed in London in that year titled Newes from Scotland - declaring the damnable life and death of Dr. Fian, a notable sorcerer[57], which de-

---

56   Ibid., 34

57   A copy of the 1591 pamphlet was included in King James's Daemonologie

scribed the events leading up to and during the trials. The pamphlet painted witches as holding backwards versions of Presbyterian services (much like the Catholic idea of a "black mass") with the Devil presiding as minister and the witches taking his infernal sacraments. The pamphlet described the witches as "the reprobate, chosen by God for destruction." According to Calvinist teachings, which James had been raised with in Scotland, God predestines and permits everything, even such "evil" acts as witchcraft, and decides who will be saved and who damned. The way James portrayed it, witches were divinely chosen punching bags, "the vessels of God's wrath."[58]

Also in 1597, as part of what was called the Great Witch Hunt (of which this was only one of five in Scotland), another series of trials was sparked by the confessions of Margaret Aitken, also called the Great Witch of Balwearie. Attempting to save her own life, she said that she could determine other witches by a mark in their eyes only she could detect. Officials took her from town to town to discover witches and she implicated around 200 other people, mostly women, before her accusations were discovered to be imposture. Many of the accused had already been tortured and executed, though others who were still in custody when Aitken confessed to lying were eventually set free. Aitken herself was burned at the stake as a witch.[59]

Though the trial records are largely incomplete and true numbers cannot be known, estimates for the number of accused witches in Scotland from the beginning of James VI reign to the end of the witch trials is about 4,000 men and women with about 200 of those sentenced to execution.

---

of 1597.

58 Newton, John. "Introduction", 13

59 Thomas Wright, A History of Scotland (London: London Print. and Pub., 1852), 329.

Seventy-five percent of those executed were women.[60]

Under the umbrella of the Witchcraft Act of 1604, the most notorious of the witch hunters, Matthew Hopkins, who called himself "The Witch-Finder General", sent about 300 people (mostly women) to their deaths in East Anglia from 1644-45, more than all other witch hunters in the previous 160 years. Why was he so prolific? He charged a good deal of money to find witches, so it was in his best interest to find as many as possible and he used heinous sorts of torture to do so, including thumb screws, water boarding, starvation, sleep deprivation, and swimming. He was also a proponent of witch pricking, for which he used a special tool he called a "jabber", a sharp spike set into a handle. He would switch out real jabbers for ones that had a retractable spike, so the accused would feel nothing and Hopkins could claim he'd found the mark. He died in 1647, likely of tuberculosis[61].

Though there can be no accurate tally of the number of executions of alleged witches during the Early Modern witch trials, an estimated total in Europe and the Colonies (including the Salem Witch Trials, which claimed 20 lives between 1692-93) claimed about 40,000-60,000 lives, mostly women and mostly in the Holy Roman Empire (about 15,000)[62]. With the advent of the Age of Enlightenmentt the witch trial period met its slow "end"[63]. The last recorded execution for witchcraft in the British Isles was that of Janet Horne in 1727, an old woman from Dornoch, Scotland. Her daughter had a congenital condition that affected her hands

---

60   The University of Edinburgh, "The Survey of Scottish Witchcraft," Scottish History, https://www.shca.ed.ac.uk/Research/witches/introduction.html (accessed April 22, 2020).

61   John S. Morrill, "Matthew Hopkins: English Witch-Hunter," Encyclopaedia Britannica, https://www.britannica.com/biography/Matthew-Hopkins (accessed April 22, 2020).

62   Voltmer, "Witch Trials", 101-104

63   Sharpe, "Demonologists", 88-96

and feet, which people thought had been caused by Janet turning her daughter into a horse, shodding her, and riding her through the countryside. Tales like that mixed with Janet's general eccentricity and undoubted dementia led to her being stripped, tarred, strapped to a barrel, rolled through the streets, and then burned alive. Her daughter was thankfully able to escape[64] [65].

In 1735, the Parliament of Britain repealed the "Act against Conjuration, Witchcraft, and dealing with evil and wicked spirits"(sic), (under which law Janet Horne was put to death)[66] and replaced it with the 1735 Witchcraft Act. Witchcraft was now redefined as a crime and an act of fraud with persons pretending to or deluded into thinking they could consort with demons. Even to suggest that people could possess supernatural power was made illegal and punishable by imprisonment. Owen Davies says of the Act, "The fight was now not against the evil of witchcraft, but, instead, against the evil influence which such 'ignorant' and 'superstitious delusions' had on the minds of the uneducated masses."[67]

In his book The Cunning Man's Handbook: The Practice of English Folk Magic 1550-1900, Jim Baker says one of the official perspectives on the matter was "One of the Devil's ploys was to play on peoples' desperation, fears,

---

64   National Library of Scotland, "'Janet Horne' by Edwin Morgan," Source and activity 6, https://www.nls.uk/learning-zone/literature-and-language/themes-in-focus/witches/source-6 (accessed April 22, 2020).

65   eill, W. N. "The Last Execution for Witchcraft in Scotland, 1722." The Scottish Historical Review, vol. 20, no. 79, 1923, pp. 218–221. JSTOR, www.jstor.org/stable/25519547. Accessed 18 Jan. 2020.

66   Parliament, "The Statutes of the Realm. Printed by Command of His Majesty King George the Third. In Pursuance of an Address of the House of Commons of Great Britain," in Original Records and Authentic Manuscripts, Volume Four, Part Two (Buffalo: William S. Hein & Co., Inc., 1993): 1,028–1,029. https://www.encyclopediavirginia.org/_An_Acte_against_Conjuration_Witchcrafte_and_dealing_with_evill_and_wicked_Spirits_1604 (accessed April 22, 2020).

67   Owen Davies, Witchcraft, Magic and Culture 1736-1951 (Manchester: Manchester University Press, 1990), 1–2.

desires, hatreds and greed to lure them into sin through the temptation of using magic, either through witchcraft or sorcery"[68]. Of course, the belief in the power of the Devil didn't diminish, especially amongst the religious. Now the belief was that those who believed they had supernatural power were just the the Devil's hapless dupes, tricked into selling their soul in exchange, not for power, but for nothing at all.

It was these shifting ideas in politics and religion along with a populace sick of being ground beneath the boot-heel of the Church (and a constellation of other factors) that led to the Age of Enlightenment, the period between the late 17th to the early 19th century. It was a time of liberal thinking, dominated by reason and empiricism, that aimed at social and scientific progress, toleration, and a separation of church and state. The movement was largely centralized in France with thinkers like Fracois-Marie Arouet (better known as Voltaire), Jean-Jacques Rousseau, Denis Diderot, Charles Louis de Secondat (Baron of Montesquieu), among other political and economic philosophers, artists, poets, and intellectual powerhouses that seemed to proliferate during the time. New ways of thinking about sociopolitical imbalances led to an undermining of religious and monarchical authority, culminating in the French Revolution and the public beheading of much of the French aristocracy.

A strong mental energy pulsed through the people of Europe and the Americas and there was a great sense of liberation and freedom that lead to multiple revolutions (including not only the American Revolution, but also the Haitian Revolution, the largest and most successful slave rebellion in history). In the wake of the Enlightenment there was an interesting reaction in certain intellectual circles that led to the period at the end of the 19th century called the French Occult Revival, which stimulated the great interest in esotericism that fueled the development of the secret lodges,

---

68   Jim Baker, The Cunning Man's Handbook: The Practice of English Folk Magic, 1550-1900 (London: Avalonia, 2014), Kindle Edition, 362-363.

fraternities, and various works that have led to witchcraft as we have it today.

The major players in this revival were thinkers perturbed and disillusioned with the Catholic church, with religious thought as it had been for centuries, and with the social instability of the past decades. They also had trouble with the hardline materialism and empiricism of Enlightenment thought and the general secularization that had begun to pervade European culture. They did not want to be divorced from their faith, but felt it needed a good sprucing up and a return to its "true" roots in the occult and esoteric works of antiquity and the Middle Ages. Remember that most of the magical and ritual thinking found in European grimoires was researched, practiced, and recorded by men of faith and learning, and it was to these works that the Occult Revivalists turned. They looked to find a pure, uncontaminated, ancient doctrine, an enduring occult tradition that could unify the world under the banner of Truth[69].

Among the most influential people of the time (in the evolution of esotericism) was the scientist Franz Mesmer. He certainly didn't consider himself an occultist, though, but rather a man of science. A doctor from Germany, Mesmer is best known for his "discovery" of what he called "magnetic fluid" and "animal magnetism". For Mesmer, this fluid was an invisible, ever-present, all-permeating thing that could be controlled via "animal magnetism", an energetic force possessed by vegetables, animals, and humans. By training and learning to work with this force, the physician could work wondrous cures on his patients with the mere laying on of hands or even through concentration alone.

By the force of "animal magnetism" a person could remove obstacles and blockages that corrupted the balanced

---

69   Katie Anderson, "The Occult Revival in Nineteenth Century France," Academia, https://www.academia.edu/1371245/The_Occult_Revival_in_Nineteenth_Century_France (accessed April 22, 2020).

flow of the patient's fluid, thus correcting disease and sus-
ceptibility to illness. This smacks of the occult and the practices of witchcraft, but Mesmer was never interested in esotericism as such. He was a man of science and very much
in vogue with the zeitgeist of the Enlightenment, though his
ideas did strike home with occult oriented people[70]. Mesmer
was also very influential in the field of complementary and
alternative medicine and modalities such as Reiki, Polari-
ty Therapy, Core Synchronism, Cranial Sacral Therapy, and
other modalities like them, all of which owe something to
his philosophy and his work[71].

Mention of Franz Mesmer often coincides with an
earlier thinker, Emanuel Swedenborg, the Swedish philoso-
pher, mystic, and theologian who wrote about his visions of
the afterlife and the immortality of the soul[72]. Swedenborg
reported that, during trance state, he had seen that there are
a number not only of Hells, but Heavens, and that the spirits (presumably of the dead) can be contacted and used as
messengers between this world and the others. He warned
against the practice, but it proved too enticing, especially
with the help of Franz Mesmer's techniques of producing
trance states in which people reported seeing or hearing entities (which came to be called mesmerism). Swedenborg's
ideas on what happens after death in conjunction with the
work of Mesmer were uniquely suited to pave the way for
another of the more influential schools of thought during the
late 19th to 20th centuries: Spiritualism.

The Spiritualists' practice was to make contact with

---

70   The Editors of Encyclopaedia, "Franz Anton Mesmer," Encyclopaedia Britannica, https://www.britannica.com/biography/Franz-Anton-Mesmer (accessed
April 22, 2020).

71   John S. Haller, Swedenborg, Mesmer, and the Mind/Body Connection: The
Roots of Complementary Medicine (Swedenborg Studies) (West Chester, PA:
Swedenborg Foundation Publishers, 2010).

72   He also thought he had been appointed by Jesus Christ to reform Christianity. Yet another mystic trying to renew Christ's message!

the dead through séances. Spiritualists listened to taps in the walls and floors and other ambient sounds, and used automatic writing and spirit boards to communicate with spririts. The practice lent itself to a great deal of chicanery and the whole movement lost credibility over time. Harry Houdini, the world-renowned magician, spent the latter part of his life debunking and falsifying spiritualist mediums[73]. Spiritualism is still practiced and is actually enjoying a bit of a renaissance, as the proliferation of planchette shaped jewelry and hand-made spirit boards for sale online attests to. Seances and Ouija have become part of the practice of necromancy still in use by witches today, though many people warn against them, as the dangers include possible inducement of psychosis and possession. The appeal of direct contact with spirits and developing the power of mediumship is still alluring to many of us, though.

One of the most famous magicians of the Enlightenment period and the French Occult Revival and a definite detractor of Spiritualism (though he once had ties with the movement) was Eliphas Levi, born Alphonse Louis Constant in 1810. His work had a deep impact on the Order of the Golden Dawn and Alesiter Crowley (who believed himself to be the reincarnation of Levi). Much of Levi's motivation and the impetus for his work is summed up in the first sentence of his 1855 book Dogme et Rituel de la Haute Magie:

"Behind the veil of all the hieratic and mystical allegories of ancient doctrines, behind the darkness and strange ordeals of all initiations, under the seal of all sacred writings, in the ruins of Nineveh or Thebes, on the crumbling stones of old temples and on the blackened visage of the Assyrian or Egyptian sphinx, in the monstrous or marvellous paintings

---

73   The Great Harry Houdini, "Houdini and the Supernatural," Houdini: His Life and His Art, https://www.thegreatharryhoudini.com/occult.html (accessed April 22, 2020).

which interpret to the faithful of India the inspired pages of the Vedas, in the cryptic emblems of our old books on alchemy, in the ceremonies practiced at reception by all secret societies, there are found indications of a doctrine which is everywhere the same and everywhere carefully concealed"[74].

Levi can be considered a bridge between the materialistic rationalism that was in vogue at the time and the sometimes irrational worlds of spirit and magic. His philosophy was one that did not seek to disregard scientific inquiry and discovery, but also did not disregard something just because it could not be rationally described. He used science and rational discourse in his research on kabbalah, mysticism, ritual magic, tarot, and other occult systems, attempting through scientific method to discover the "secret doctrine" he was searching for. He considered occultism to be the true Catholicism and the religion of true socialism, denouncing much of what the average Catholic or Christian (or Socialist, for that matter) believed as contaminated and untrue.

To avoid as much trouble as possible, his public views on things sometimes teeter-tottered and his overall ideology is somewhat confusing because of that. He had a strong love for the knowledge of Kabbalists, Gnostics, and other esoteric thinkers, but a strong distaste for their traditions, which he viewed as successions of corrupted failures. His work was meant to purify and birth these mysteries anew as a universal system of "Truth"[75]. He is also one of the occultists responsible for bringing the tarot into the repertoire of magicians and one of the first people to assign the Hebrew

---

74 Eliphas Levi, The Doctrine and Ritual of High Magic: A New Translation, trans. John Michael Greer and Mark Anthony Mikituk, (New York: TarcherPerigee Publishing, 2017).

75 Julian Strube, "The "Baphomet" of Eliphas Levi: Its Meaning and Historical Context", in Correspondences 4 (2016): 37-79.

letters to the Major Arcana. Levi was the first artist to draw the famous Baphomet image now so closely ingrained with witchcraft, Satanism, and esotericism in general[76].

This image is the synthesis of all of Levi's work in one pictographic representation, the "icon of his 'true' doctrine"[77] and is not meant to be Satanic in the slightest (no matter what Anton Szandor LaVey may want us to think). Instead, think of the Baphomet as the symbol of opposites in unity, of the bestial and the divine in harmony, of the masculine and the feminine brought together in a new synthesis, but also as a symbol of the magnetistic principles of occult practice, positive and negative, destruction and creation, all under the Will of the magician, the adept, the purveyor of the "true" faith. For Levi, this Baphomet is a symbol of the Astral Light, the force governing the principles of magical operations, that which lies beyond opposites and fallibilities[78]. Perhaps lending to the perceptions of the Baphomet as an anti-Christian symbol are the rare-yet-present mentions of Lucifer and Satan as "positive and negative instruments" of the astral light in his work, though Levi denied the actual existence of either[79].

In 1875, the year Levi died, the Theosophical Movement, which aimed at coaxing the West to turn to India for spiritual enlightenment, was founded by another important mystic, the infamous Helena Petrovna Blavatsky. Influenced by both Levi and Mesmer, she was interested in finding a synthesis of science and spirit to discern "Truth" through magic and trance and is one of the most famous spiritualists. Writing at a time when science and the idea of evolution were pushing people further and further from theological

---

76   Levi, Doctrine, trans. Greer, xii-xxxii.

77   Strube. "The Baphomet", 40

78   Ibid., 37-79

79   Ibid., 72

study, she felt that her particular system of Occultism would prove the perfect religious antidote for the spiritual ills of a society in crisis[80]. As such, she provided a new philosophy meant to synthesize the magic of nature with the science of the new age, or as Mark Bevir explains in "The West Turns Eastward: Madame Blavatsky and the Transformation of the Occult Tradition":

"Blavatsky believed only in natural magic. In accord with the assumptions of her own age, she wanted to defend magic on natural and scientific grounds, not on supernatural or dogmatic grounds such as that of the Bible as divine revelation. Thus, she denied that occult science transgressed the law."[81]

Her work sought to show how the divine principles of the universe were not antithetical to new ideas such as evolution, but rather manifested through such natural processes as part of an intrinsic, spiritual process of purification back toward divinity. She was also a forward-thinking feminist, believing women should be emancipated and that the idea of subservience to anyone or anything other than one's self and one's own spiritual evolution was anathema to the "True Religion". She in general disregarded gender as a triviality and basically as a falsity, believing that souls would reincarnate in more masculine or more feminine bodies repeatedly until reaching a synthesis between the two as a "Divine Androgyne", something she consciously tried to manifest within her own life.

Like Levi, she denied the existence of Satan/Lucifer/ the Devil as actual entities external from the mind, rather considering them as a dark counterbalance to "God", who,

---

80   Mark Bevir, "The West Turns Eastward: Madame Blavatsky and the Transformation of the Occult Tradition," Journal of the American Academy of Religion 62, no. 3 (Autumn 1994): 747-767.

81   Ibid., 754

for Blavatsky, was merely the light counterpoint within the mind. Both are required for spiritual evolution to take place, for without one or the other "we would be no more than animals". In fact, Blavatsky considered Lucifer as a sort of hero, who emancipated Eve from the Garden in the guise of the Serpent. She also thought the Serpent was Jehovah, though, and in the case of both Lucifer and Jehovah, the Devil and Christ, they were merely two sides of the same thing: the mind[82].

She was considered a charlatan and a con-artist by many, but still held séances that were aimed at getting in touch with Ascended Masters, high level adepts of magic and spiritual enlightenment in the East, who would propel letters about the secrets of the universe through windows or cause rose petals to fall from the ceiling for the believers present[83]. Though her understanding of Hinduism and Eastern Philosophy were largely cherry-picked versions that built an almost completely fabricated version of that religion, her ideas remain powerful today. She wrote two enormous treaties on spirituality, Isis Unveiled and The Secret Doctrine, which have both been influential on the evolution of witchcraft, though Blavatsky herself warned against the practice and would have disliked much of what is found in this book!

Many of her ideas and those propounded by the Theosophical Society, if not precisely anti-Christian, were certainly not Christ centered and claimed all religions were missing the point in many ways. The motto of the Society is "There is No Religion Higher Than Truth". In fact, the Theo-

---

82 Per Faxneld, "Blavatsky the Satanist: Luciferianism in Theosophy, and its Feminist Implications," Temenos - Nordic Journal of Comparative Religion 48 (January 2013): 203-230, doi: 10.33356/temenos.7512.

83 J. Barton Scott, "The Unmasking of a 19th Century Occult Imposter,"Atlas Obscura, https://www.atlasobscura.com/articles/the-unmasking-of-the-19th-centurys-seance-queen (accessed April 22, 2020).

sophical Society's standpoint was one that denied a personal God completely, rather favoring an impersonal, eternal principle that works through natural law which the many gods that propagate the world's faiths merely represent facets of, including Christ. She also denied the immortality of individual souls, but considered all souls as part of one larger, impersonal Universal Soul that reincarnated itself repeatedly[84]. Blavatsky could be considered a pantheistic monist, for she believed to her very core in the maxim, "Out of One, Many."

Not all of Blavatsky's students agreed with her, though. One of the most famous students of Theosophy (though she quickly fell out with the group) who has been an important character in the history of witchcraft is the mystic known as Dion Fortune (born Violet Firth). In 1919 she also became part of a splinter group of the Hermetic Order of the Golden Dawn, Alpha et Omega, run by Moina Mathers. While she was still involved with both institutions she founded her own order called the Christian Mystic Lodge of the Theosophical Society, which would later become the Society of the Inner Light that still operates today. Fortune considered herself Christian and felt it was best to coax people (especially Europeans) toward, not away from, a kind of Christian Mysticism, specifically one taught to her, she said, by the Master Jesus Himself.

She used her own group as a platform for doing just that. She expressed issues with some of the tenets put forward by Blavatsky and her peers, especially their focus on Indian philosophies and the anti-British Raj sentiment that circulated within the Society.

She is one of the most famous mediums of the "Ascended Masters", a school of thought geared at contacting highly developed, multi-dimensional, spiritual beings (both human and non-human) who are considered to govern and guide the universe and proliferate their teachings through

---

84   Bevir, "West Turns Eastward", 759-60.

mediumistic channeling. It was actually her developing skills as an astral traveler and the work given to her by the Masters that led to her dismissal from the A+O by Moina Mathers. Her writings are important because of her influential ideas in occultism, especially those found in her books The Mystical Qabalah and Psychic Self-Defense. The former sets forward a clear system and practical use for the Qabalah of the occultists, helping the reader to better understand the more nuanced and obfuscated aspects inherent in it. The latter is a useful guide for those who are interested in working with magic and astral travel and who have an interest in exorcism.

Operative during the early years of the Theosophical society was another mystic inspired by the philosophy and religions of the East, George Ivanovich Gurdjieff, one of the most influential spiritual teachers in my own life. He said that there were usually three ways to work practically toward spiritual realization: The way of the body (the fakir's path), the way of emotions (the monk's path), and the way of the mind (the yogi's path). He argued that following any one of these would lead to imbalanced spiritual evolution and could not lead to true enlightenment. Instead, there is a fourth way that can synthesize all three of the others to lead much more quickly and efficiently to development of the soul[85]. The body, the emotions, and the mind are all centers that process different kinds of energy and, if one is to develop one at the cost of the others, that person cannot fully harmonize all of the energies necessary to the development of the soul.

Gurdjieff believed that most people are not truly awake and that the average state called "wakefulness" is actually just another form of sleep. He thought that self-remembering, putting oneself in uncomfortable situations, hard work and arduous labor, and undergoing periodic "shocks" are essential to staying present and awake so that

---

85 Gurdjieff believed people are not born with a soul, but must create one through "The work" of self-development.

one can continuously work on oneself. He developed a series of spiritual movements inspired by the sacred dances of the dervishes and wrote a canon of music that was meant to help guide the student toward self-mastery. His system is an active one, never really allowing the student to do any one activity for too long, so that there is always the opportunity for confronting the self. He believed that there are many "I's" with contradicting desires and habits that make up the "personality" of each person, which itself is merely the programming each of us unconsciously runs throughout the day.

Gurdjieff's system, however, does not preclude anything, so there is no need to leave society or follow a particular diet (he was a bit on the hedonistic side, especially when it came to food and strong drink), so long as the person acts on their desires from a unified state of consciousness and from a place of real choice. It is also not a philosophy that works toward being other or greater than oneself, as other systems tend to be. The Fourth Way is a series of self-engineered experiences that allow one to be fully and utterly present in any moment as a unified whole, totally free and sovereign, and able to harness and direct one's own energy and power at will toward any pursuit. It is simply a system aimed at living fully. According to Michael de Salzmann, the son of some of Gurdjieff's best-known students, "The change in oneself through the Gurdjieff work is not to transform oneself into something else. It is to become what one is."[86]

This history, no matter how brief, would not be complete without mentioning one of Gurdjieff's least favorite people, the Beast 666, "The Wickedest Man in the World", the notorious Aleister Crowley. Enigmatic, self-aggrandizing, and narcissistic, he was a masterful poet, a mountaineer,

---

86   Margaret Croydon, "Getting in Touch with Gurdjieff," The New York Times, https://www.nytimes.com/1979/07/29/archives/getting-in-touch-with-gurd-jieff.html (accessed April 22, 2020).

artist, psychonaut, libertine, and a powerful magician. Crowley has not only become one of the most notorious and misunderstood titans of occultism today, but an enduring icon of the "cultural exile" reveling in rebellion. In his lifetime he garnered little respect from the world at large and had few followers, mostly members of the Ordo Templi Orientis and his own groups, the Argentum Astrum and the Abbey of Thelema.

He entered the O.T.O. in 1910 and was its head by 1925. During that time, he worked to remove much of the O.T.O.'s Masonic influences in favor of his own Thelema and his own flair. His magic was theatrical and often hyper-sexualized, his lifestyle was deeply decadent, but his devotion to the occult and the dissemination of Thelema were strong driving forces in his life that kept him focused on his chosen purpose. His work with the Kabbalah and ritual magic, alchemy and astrology, his revisionist version of tarot in the Book of Thoth, not to mention the motto of his work- "Do what thou wilt shall be the whole of the law. Love is the law, Love under Will"- have left indelible marks on the world of witchcraft. He died of chronic bronchitis, destitute and relatively obscure, in 1947[87] [88].

A person of note that unforunately remains obscure, but was certainly influential on Crowley's philosophy and magic, is Paschal Beverley Randolph, the African American doctor and magician. He founded the Fraternitas Rosae Crucis in 1958 in California, which still stands as the oldest Rosicrucian organization in the United States. The Ordo Templi Orientis and The Hermetic Brotherhood of Luxor drew heavily on Randolph's magico-sexual ideas, though it

---

87 The Editors of Encyclopaedia Britannica, "Aleister Crowley: British Occultist," Encyclopaedia Britannica, https://www.britannica.com/biography/Aleister-Crowley (accessed April 22, 2020).

88 Hymenaeus Beta XII°, "Aleister Crowley," United States Grand Lodge Ordo Templi Orientis, https://oto-usa.org/thelema/crowley/ (accessed April 22, 2020).

remains unclear whether he was a member of the HB of L. or the O.T.O.

His association with the Rosicrucian order and his work with seership, ceremonial and sex magic, and his understanding of Love and Will were highly influential not only on Crowley and his organizations, but the occult world in general[89]. His philosophy can be distilled down to this quote: "LOVE LIETH AT THE FOUNDATION (of all that is); and Love is convertibly passion; enthusiasm; affection; heat; fire; soul God."[90] He was also an avid advocate for sexual liberation and birth control, the emancipation of women, the abolition of slavery, voting rights, evolutionary theory, and the rights of all people to use their Will to create their world. In fact, without his work, witchcraft, the occult, and the world at large would look very different today.

In 1947, near the end of his life, Crowley initiated arguably the most important person to contemporary witchcraft into the O.T.O; Gerald B. Gardner, the "Father of Modern Witchcraft", a man without whom this book would likely not have been written. Though he was a sickly child, his life was adventurous, taking him back and forth from England to more exotic locales, though the majority of the experiences that would lead him further into witchcraft happened in the New Forest and Bricket Wood in Southern Britain. His lifelong interest in the occult and esotericism led Gardner to join a couple of Masonic Lodges, to work for a Rosicrucian Order/theatrical group, and to become part of the Folk-Lore Society in London where he met the people who would initiate him into an existing group of witches called the New

---

89 T Allen Greenfied, "Paschal Beverly Randolph: Sexual Magick in the 19th Century," United States Grand Lodge Ordo Templi Orientis, https://oto-usa.org/usgl/lion-eagle/paschal-beverly-randolph/ (accessed April 22, 2020).

90 Pascal B. Randolph, Eulis, affectional alchemy: the history of love: its wondrous magic, chemistry, rules, laws, moods, modes and rationale. Being the third revelation of soul and sex and a reply to "Why is man immortal?" Internet Archive, http://archive.org/stream/eulisaffectional00rand/eulisaffectional00rand_djvu.txt (accessed January 22, 2020).

Forest Coven in 1939.

Though Gardner thought that the coven was a vestige of a pre-Christian cult, research shows that the coven was established in the 1930s, inspired by local folk traditions and the work of Margaret Murray. The most famous reported working by the New Forest coven is called "Operation Cone of Power", which was a magical working meant to deter Hitler from crossing the sea and invading England, which he never did.

Gardner eventually became the head of the O.T.O in Europe, which he quickly grew tired of and, in 1951, left the order to Frederic Mellinger in order to focus on his own work, the burgeoning religion of Wicca. He had acquired a small cottage and had it moved piece by piece to a new location near Bricket Wood. This became the hub of the Wiccan movement, which Gardner still called Gardnerianism. It wasn't until 1952-3 when he met and initiated Doreen Valiente, the "Mother of Modern Witchcraft", that things really started moving. She acted as Gardner's High Priestess and helped to formulate much of the Book of Shadows used in Wiccan covens, helping to remove direct quotes from Crowley's work and the work of Eliphas Levi and helped Gardner to formulate his prose into rhyme[91]. Though they later parted ways over Gardner's need for the limelight and blatant disregard for the privacy of the Craft, she never lost her love for him. She is one of the greatest scholars within early witchcraft culture, a sober yet humorous observer of events, and an honest and authentic human being all around.

Well before their split, Valiente helped Gardner publish Witchcraft Today in 1954. This was only possible because, in 1951, the British government had repealed the Witchcraft Act of 1735 and replaced it with the "Fraudulent Mediums Act" after the sensational trial of a medium named Helen Duncan in 1944. The Act states that it is illegal to

---

91   Valiente, The Rebirth of Witchcraft.

fraudulently claim supernatural ability to gain money, but did not outlaw witchcraft or possibly true claims of supernatural ability. With the repeal of the Witchcraft Act, Gardner could publish his book without fear of censure. From there it was only a matter of time before the movement took hold and spread like wildfire.

Offshoots of Wicca that have gained large followings are the Alexandrian Wicca of Alex Sanders (the self-professed "King of the Witches) and the Reclaiming Tradition of Starhawk, which is an environmental and social justice activist group based on nature and goddess worship. It has been largely influenced by the Feri tradition of Victor and Cora Anderson and the feminist, Dianic witchcraft of Z. Budapest. Today there are a huge number of covens, all of whom have different ways of doing things, but all of whom can trace their lineage back to Gerald Gardner and Wicca.

In the 1960s, Robert Cochrane founded Traditional Witchcraft, which he said was taught to him by his grandmother. The truth seems to be that he based much of his practice on Wicca and mixed it with more "shamanic" ways of thinking and practice, historical research, folklore and mythology, and his own inventiveness. According to Valiente (who joined his Clan of Tubal Cain for a time), though he may not have been part of a centuries old lineage of witchcraft, he was certainly a beautiful thinker and poet with a true genius for symbolic and artistic ritual that truly moved the spirits.

Traditional Witchcraft (or Trad Craft) has gained in popularity since Cochrane's day, though it can be confusing, especially if you are not versed in the history of witchcraft and how it has come down to us in its current forms. The idea behind the movement is no longer that its practices are part of an unbroken lineage of magic passed down from antiquity (there is no such thing and anyone who tries to convince you of such is lying), but rather that there is real power in the magic of old world and regional folk lore, though it may be hidden beneath a fine Christian glaze. It tends to turn toward more earthy "low magic", like the practices of kitchen and hedge witchery, using everyday objects to make magic and finding magic in everyday tasks. Traditional Witchcraft may be delineated by the work of authors like Robert Cochrane, Andrew Chumbley, Gemma Gary, Shani Oates, Daniel Schulke, Sybil Leek, Evan John Jones, Robin Artisson, Lee Morgan, and many others.

When people think of witchcraft the initial thought that arises is that all practitioners are Wiccan. This is not true. There are many different types of witch, all of whom descend from a multitude of lineages, not all of which are Gardnerian or Alexandrian. In my opinion all modern Craft still owes quite a lot to Gerald Gardner and Doreen Valiente. Without their work and advocacy witchcraft could not have grown in the way that it has since 1954. One of the most important things to remember about any kind of witchcraft is that all of it is based in history, folk lore, and the intuitive imagination of the practitioner. There are no modern traditions that go back further than the 1950s with the founding of the first Gardnerian coven. The majority of what you will encounter in the field of magic is the work of individuals or groups who are working through their own experiments and answering their own questions, discovering their desires, and developing their own power. A given tradition may work for you, it may not. Magic is uniquely personal, so don't feel bad if you don't know everything there is to know about another person's path.

Practitioners of witchcraft are often avid readers of fairytales, mythology, anthropology, ethnology, history, and science. The aim is to synthesize our research with our own beliefs and the beliefs of our region into both magic and medicine which help modern people with age old problems. One of the primary characteristics of modern witchcraft is a return to the lore of one's own ancestral tradition as a starting place to find our own unique magic. Much of the work done in witchcraft today is from England and other parts of Europe, but there is also powerful work being done here in the USA.

So, what does the walk of the witch look like? In our system of witchcraft we tend to be inspired by and take cues from the mythology of witchcraft from the Early Modern Period, folk practices of our bioregion (the Southwestern United States), ancestral practices from rural England and Scotland, what kernels of truth can be found in witchcraft confessions, occultism and Qabalah as practiced by those magicians and witches mentioned in the above history, my own family's practices, and by looking to the historical and sacred core of what the church and other prevailing religious bodies have termed "demonic". We are reclaiming the words "witch", "demon", and "devil" and taking our power back to understand what it truly means to be filled by cunning fire.

A GATHERING OF DEVILS

- A Few Descriptions of Our Herbal Allies -

Rife in the witchcraft community is talk about fairies, but I think it is best to remember that these "fairies" are none other than the viridis genii we spoke of earlier in this book. These spirits are also the same as the "devils" of folk lore and the "small gods", our witchly kin. When you are working with these spirits, remember that they deserve the same respect and understanding we give to our loved ones and that they are powerful, potent allies that need to be dealt with carefully and wisely.

HERBS ON THE POISON PATH

Atropa belladonna— Also known as deadly nightshade, this is one of the best known of the baneful (poisonous) herbs. The flowers are five-lobed bells of dark purple or maroon that become black berries famed for their lethality and medicinal fortitude. It is used for heart disorders and has a history in beauty products (the name belladonna means "Beautiful woman"). Too much will lead to heart failure. Magically it is used to help summon spirits, blessing the tools of necromancy, for commanding spirits, for severing ties, and for transformative magic.

Datura stramonium- Thorn apple, Devil's testicle, Devil's trumpet, and moonflower are all alternative names for this beautiful plant. The leaves are large and sometimes a bit fuzzy, smelling of rancid peanut-butter when rubbed. The flowers are large, fragrant white trumpets that aim up toward the moon as if playing an infernal nocturne for the firmament. Datura is a very effective pain reliever and can be used

283

for respiratory disorders and nausea.

This sacred plant is also known as Toloache, "bowed head", a reference to the high regard in which it is held. It has been used by medicine people in the Southwest, Mexico, and South America as a vision inducing plant. This ought to be avoided by anyone without experience, though, as many people have ended up in a padded room after playing with a spirit which is far to powerful for playful experimentation. A strong magical ally, datura can be used to heal generational issues and in the breaking of curses.

Hyoscyamus niger— Black henbane, also known as skunk cabbage and pig bean, is a powerful soporific (sleep inducer). It is purported to be an ingredient in hebanon, made famous as the poison poured in the ear of the king in the Shakespearean play Hamlet. The flowers of this plant are yellow with deep purple veination and the leaves are large and covered in fur. The whole plant, including the seeds, are used as medicine as well as poison. A useful pain reliever, it is also used as an aphrodisiac and as a sleep aid. Magically it is linked to the Underworld, particularly the goddess Persephone, and can be used in necromantic rituals to draw spirits near, or to put angry spirits to rest.

Mandragora officinarum— Probably the most famous of the magical herbs, the mandrake has a long and interesting history. It is said that the mandrake is part human, grown from the bodily fluids of a hanged man. If one pulls the root from the ground, it will let out a shrill shriek that will cause an agonizing death. Therefore, it is suggested that the magician or witch dig around the root to loosen it, then tie one end of a rope to the root and one to the neck of a hungry dog before throwing a piece of meat. The dog will do the dirty work and take the consequences for you.

This is, of course, wrong. The mandrake, though its root is oddly human-looking, does not grow from blood and urine, but from a seed, as most plants do. It will not scream when dug up, but, if you get enough juice on your bare skin, it can cause hallucination and possible death, so be careful if you choose to work with this plant. It was widely used in Ancient Greece through the Middle Ages for its pain reliving properties, as an aphrodisiac, and as a sleep and dream aid. It may be the plant moly, which is the plant that protected Odysseus from the spells of Circe.

Magically it is one of the strongest plants I can think of. It can be used to alter one's very fate, manipulating probability in the favor of the witch (at least for a time), and can be used for commanding spirits, protection from maleficium, and amplification of magical power to a great degree. Mandrake roots are also carved in the shape of a human, a charm called the alraun, that is said to bring good luck, good health, and great fortune to those who possess it and take care of it. They require regular offerings, or feedings, and ought to be treated as a benefactor would be. Otherwise the consequences could be dire.

Nicotiana rustica— The tobacco plant is highly sacred and in some cultures is revered as a god. One of the teachers I have been lucky enough to be trained by is a Medicine Woman, a true Curandera. Her husband is a Medicine Man from Peru who uses the tobacco plant in all of his healings and blessings (he calls it sheri). They think of it as an ancestor and guide rather than "just a plant". They taught me to use it for healing, both physically and spiritually, and it has become one of my most important teachers.

Tobacco has gotten a bad rap because of "Big Tobacco", though, in moderation and when used in reverence, it is not tobacco itself that causes disease, but the copious amounts of carcinogenic chemicals found in commercial tobacco. The huge furry leaves have a sticky resin that makes a deliciously thick smoke, and the trumpet shaped flowers vary in color from white, to yellow, to green, to pink. No matter which one you work with, all the species are valuable guides.

Tobacco is used remedially for a number of reasons including toothache, headache, canker sores, anxiety, and stomach upset. It can also be used for a variety of skin disorders and as an antibacterial application in cases of infected wounds. It has been a powerful ally for millennia and it is only since the advent of commercial cigarettes that it has become a problem. I use it in spellwork and healing, as well as for suffumigatiing clients with the smoke to get a better reading on their energy and to make travelling through their Lower Astral easier. I can then remove harmful energies and protect the person from spiritual and magical attack. There is no more powerful plant than tobacco for blessing and healing, in my opinion.

Aconitum napellus— Also called Wolfsbane, this tall banewort has fallen out of use in recent years because it is one of the more dangerous plants one could choose to make relationship with. Just getting the juices on your bare skin can be enough to stop your heart in a very short amount of time, so extremely diligent caution is required, if not total abstinence form its use. Farmers at one point would dig the root and stick their arrows in its juice to poison the wolves that bothered their flocks, thus earning it its pseudonym. Powerfully tied to the rites of Hekate, it can be used to bless the ritual tools of the witch, especially those meant for command of spirits, such as the knife, any tools of necromancy, or any tool dedicated to working with Hekate. It can also be used to bless an area and keep out all unwanted spirits.

Actea rubra and alba— Baneberry, as it is commonly called, can be found in shady woods and, though it is toxic, the leaves of the plant can be used as an analog to black cohosh. The white species (alba) is called doll's eyes, because the berry is waxy white with a black spot right at the end of

286

the fruit, making it look like a googly eye. Magically, this is a plant to be used in malicious love spells that are meant to manipulate and control, but can also be used to ease broken hearts when made into a phylactery and worn near the breast.

Conium maculatum— Oh, baneful hemlock that claimed dear Socrates! This is a plant that needs to be very well understood before one works with it and only under the guidance of an experienced wortcunner. Hemlock poisoning leads to slow paralysis that begins in the limbs, making them heavy and leaden, before ending in respiratory paralysis and conscious suffocation without control of one's body. It has been recorded as one of the traditional herbs used in the unguenta lamiarum, though I have never added it to any of mine and they work just fine. Even though it is lethal in extremely small doses, hemlock has been used to ease the pain of arthritis and cramps, for the gums of teething children, and for illnesses like bronchitis and whooping cough. There are far safer options, though, and they should be used instead.

Digitalis spp.— Foxglove and Fairy Mitten are two of this herb's nicknames, though I've also heard Dead Man's Mouth as it is believed that one can hear the voices of the dead through the snout shaped flowers. The flowers come in a variety of colors, always with dark spots inside the mouth. These are said to be made by the feet of fairies as they dance the night away and this plant is incredibly sacred to the fair folk. They will viciously attack anyone who meddles with them, as all Digitalis belong to them.

Digitalis has a long history of use for heart conditions, though I would suggest avoiding it as even a small amount can kill via an ironic heart attack. Its magical uses are various, often having to do with compelling the fae or other spirits to stay away from a place, for amplifying one's power (by wearing the flowers on the fingertips), and for necromantic rites. It can also be used for luck in love and gambling, though the results are sporadic at best.

Papver somniferum— The sleeping poppy, sacred to Morpheus, the lord of dreams, and the source of the insidious substance opium. This plant has a very long history of use as a soporific and pain reliever and is often included in herbal anesthetics. Though the spirit of this plant has been abused and taken advantage of by those wishing for an opium high, it still serves a powerful purpose in alleviating stress, anxiety, cramps, and muscle tension, and for alleviating gastric distress caused by overly tight smooth muscle.

Its magical uses are in a similar vein. The smoke from the leaf and flower can be used to still the rage of spirits and can help the witch to vision and hedgeride. It can also be used to still passions, bind enemies, and cause a person's magic to wane.

Thermopsis montana—Also called golden banner and golden pea, this mountain native can be used as a replacement for blue cohosh, helping to indicate Braxton Hicks contractions and to relive heaviness in the pelvis during menses. As a pea family plant, though, it does concentrate solanine and is considered toxic, particularly its seeds.

The seed pods grow in upright bunches all clustered together and, when dried, they make an excellent rattle. The golden color of the flowers links this plant to Jupiter, though its overall structure is related to Ares, making it an excellent plant to use for quick money spells.

Turbina corymbose— This is a member of the morning glory family and is a woody vine with large white to purple flowers. The seeds are small and round, which the Nahuatl name, ololiuqui (round thing), refers to. The vine itself is called snake plant (coaxihuitl). It is used to get rid of bruising and with pain in the digestive tract, but it is most often used as a sacred inebriant. The effects, when present, are similar to the effect of Psilocybe.

Bannisteriopsis caapi— Also called yage, this is a thick vine from the South American jungle, this is one of the constituents in the preparation known as ayahuasca, though the indigenous peoples for whom the medicine is sacred prefer the name Natem. This is the ingredient that provides the MAOI that inhibits the degradation of DMT so that it can enter the cells of the brain. The vine itself is considered a Master Teacher and is held in great sacredness, It is said to proffer telepathic power on those who make relationship with it.

Psychotria viridis— A perennial shrub called chacruna ("to mix") in Nahuatl, this is the DMT containing part of the Natem preparation. A common traditional use for the plant is to squeeze fresh juice from the leaves and put drops in the eyes of someone suffering from migraines, or for clarity of inner vision. The preparation of Natem is a purgative medicine, meant to aid in the exorcism of "contamination" and spirits that may cause illness, so the medicine person will wander about with a rattle and tobacco smoke to help purge and purify those spirits. The vomiting and diarrhea associated with the ceremony is considered a physical manifestation of this more spiritual effect.

FUNGI ON THE POISON PATH

Amanita muscaria— The fly agaric mushroom is one of the most highly represented fungi in folk art, with its plump, red cap covered in white speckles. It is an important staple of the diet of Northern peoples in the boreal forests of Europe and is said to have a delightful nutty flavor that most people find quite agreeable. The active constituents, muscimol and ibotenic acid, must be boiled out before eating the mushrooms, though. This beautiful and curious fungus is also associated with celebrations of the mid-Winter holiday and may be the inspiration for the outfit Santa Claus wears.

The mushroom brings a sense of heavy-headedness and clarity along with euphoria, a gentle calm. Because of the ibotenic acid the mushroom can cause nausea and lead to vomiting, though, like with Natem, the experience is related as a cleansing experience, rather than purely terrible.

Psiloscybe cubensis— Magic mushrooms, or hongitos, are one of the best known entheogenic substances in the modern world. They have recently been studied for their beneficial effects on depression and cluster migraines. In the 1960's, Maria Sabina, the Sacredotista do los Hongos Magicos who lived in Southern Mexico, brought the mushrooms to fame by treating celebrities such as Bob Dylan, Mick Jagger, and John Lennon through her veladas, or healing rituals. These mushroom spirits are story tellers, helping the person who takes them to understand their own story and how to better express and embrace their authentic power.

A COVEN OF HERBS

Anethum graveolens— Dill is not only good for pickles and tzatziki sauce, it is a handy digestive aid, helping with gas and stomachache, and has powerful effect against staphylo-coccus and saccharomyces bacteria. It is an air element plant with Mercury as its ruler and is one of the most used herbs for love charms. It helps to smooth things over, even energies out, so it is especially useful during difficult retrogrades or during meetings with difficult coworkers. Making a powder with dill seed, fenugreek, and calendula flower will make an excellent prosperity spell you can sprinkle through your house or business.

Calendula officinalis— The flower of this plant looks like a big, gold coin and it is used in prosperity and money-draw magic. It is also a useful aid in spells meant to make people kinder toward you (honey pot charms), as it exudes the warmth of the sun. It is this solar aspect that also makes it useful during hedgerides that take you to the Underworld, as the light of the calendula flower will help to guide you and keep you safe. Calendula is ruled by the Sun and is largely aligned to the elements of fire and water.

Coriandrum sativum— Cilantro is a common herb that is the center of a huge ambivalence; either you love it or hate it. For people who can taste the aldehydes in the plant, it will taste like soap, where for others the herb will taste fresh and delightful. Like dill, cilantro is great aid for the relieving of gas and stomachache, especially the seeds, which are marketed as coriander. Also like dill it is used for love charms most frequently, but tends more toward deeper commitments and can help to attain self-love.

Echinacea purpurea— Arguably one of the best-known herbs, echinacea is found in basically all herbal tisanes made to increase immunity and is often found in conjunction with elder in cold and flu formulas. It has been used to stave off the effects of both spider and snake venom and can help to protect the witch from maleficium, especially if one carries the root wrapped in red thread in a poke. The flower and leaf can be used to amplify magical power and clairvoyant ability, making it a useful herb for necromancy. It is also well loved by the fair folk, so having it one's garden helps to increase the population of beneficial spirits.

Eupatorium perfoliatum— Of all the herbs listed here, it is boneset that has the strongest effect against inhuman spirits that are causing a ruckus. A friend of mine was living in a home that was rife with the energies of spirits, both inhuman and disincarnate, and I told her to make a tea with boneset, then to pour it down the drains of her house and to sprinkle it all throughout and around the house. The doors all began to swing wildly and the pipes burst, but the aggressive spiritual activity ceased thereafter. Boneset has a powerful ability to reduce fever and was used to treat an illness known as "breakbone fever," thus earning its common name. It is also used in cold and flu remedies.

Mahonia repens— Also called creeping mahonia and Oregon grape, this plant grows close to the ground and sports sharp-edged leaves similar to holly. The flowers grow upright in large bundles of delicate yellow flowers that give way to delicious purple berries. It is a strong antibacterial overall, and the root is full of berberine, which gives it a yellow coloration. It is also useful in cases of giardia infestation.

Matricaria chamomilla- You are probably familiar with chamomile as part of tension tamer formulas and tisanes meant to ease stomach upset, particularly colic. It can also be used to treat menstrual cramps and may be found in formulas for cold and flu relief, as the plant is mildly antiviral. It is gentle enough to be used with children and pregnancy, but can have a powerful action for pain relief. If you or your client is allergic to ragweed, however, it can have an adverse reaction and end in hives and itchiness. Chamomile in charms is an ingredient for increase, potentizing and empowering spellwork and magical power and bringing prosperity and luck.

Potentilla repens— Also called cinquefoil and five-finger grass, this herb is used in charms for attainment. The leaves look like little, open hands and will help you to take hold of things. Conversely, it can stop others from taking things from you and from meddling in your affairs. It is also an aid for stomach trouble and makes a good bitter.

Rosa spp.— Any rose is useful in love magic and spells meant to make people softer toward you. Rose petals are an excellent addition to honey pots. It helps to amplify the powers of Venus and can be used in clearing ceremonies and glamoury. Rose is one of the best remedies for skin disorders, helping to alleviate redness and itching, but also softening skin and making it more supple. It helps to keep wounds clean and to heal, acting as a styptic as well. Rose water acts as an excellent setting spray and can relieve the appearance of fine lines, as well as relieve stress. It may help to ease over-active, painful liver disorders.

Roses can also be used for protection, particularly from unknown sources of malevolent intent. Place your photo or hair in a jar with seven thorny stems of a rose and a length of red thread and burn a black candle on top of the charm to amplify and seal it. Rose thorns can be used in love spells by sticking the thorn through the photo of your target and pricking your own finger with it, smearing your blood on the photo while thinking of smoochies with that person.

Salvia rosmarinus— Rosemary is a powerful ally in magic, not just a culinary herb. It is a great cleanser and helps to repel spirits and energies that are not beneficial to our work and remedies the negative effects of necromancy or contact with the dead, especially when used with juniper. It is an herb associated with remembrance and can help aid in memorization by wearing a spring on one's collar or by having the oil on a bit of cloth you sniff while studying.

Its ancient associations link it to Venus and fidelity magic, but it also has attributes of Mars and elemental fire, making it a great protector from unwanted attention. Some of its attributes are of the Sun and can help keep the mind clear and focused during hedgeriding and divination. The smoke can act as a repellent, or, when mixed with herbs that attract spirits, can be used to agitate them and make them aggressive. When planted in the garden it attracts beneficial spirits and when planted near the door or gate will deter thieves.

Rosemary is a strong antibacterial plant which is highly resinous. Use it to help with bronchitis and tightness in the lungs, stomach troubles, and gas. It also has a gentle effect on the emotions, helping to ease stress and anger. Rosemary also has effects in the cardiovascular system and pairs well with linden and hawthorn, so long as the person taking the combo is not already taking blood pressure medications.

Taraxacum officinale— Dente de leon, fairy clock, and piss-a-bed are all common names for the plant best known as dandelion. Though it is treated with great disrespect and as a nuisance, dandelion is one of the most sacred flowers to grow in our yards and forests. The plant has strong attributes of Mars, Jupiter, the Sun, and Saturn as well as having fairly balanced manifestations of all five elements, making it a powerful and useful ally in your magic. It is sacred to Hekate, goddess of witchcraft, and to Lucifer, Dionysos, and the Devil.

Use the root tied around with white string to protect yourself from unknown spirits or use one as a poppet by tying the name of your target to the root. Keep this type of thing in a wooden box between uses and replace the tag with each new target. A large root can also be used as a wand for necromantic rituals, or added to powder recipes used during necromancy. The leaves of the dandelion can be added to incense used during Underworld journeys and to protective smokes and spells. Line the inside of the box you keep your dandelion root poppet or your alraun in with dandelion leaves to protect it from maleficium.

Verbascum thapsis—King's candle, witches' torch, Hekate's torch, gordo lobo, and toilet paper plant are all alternative names for mullein. Another of the plants sacred to Hekate, it is useful in a variety of ways. The leaves are huge and covered in a velveteen coat of hair that makes them luxuriously soft, though they can become airborne and irritating to the lungs once the leaf is dried. The leaf is used, however, for respiratory health and lung support for people with chronic lung conditions or repetitive respiratory illnesses. It has also shown promise as an herbal anti-viral, especially in cases of mild influenza.

The flowers have five yellow petals and red-orange filaments and anthers. They can be used to infuse an oil that will help with pain relief, especially in the neck and jaw, though I have had good luck with all sorts of joint issues, especially when mixed with cottonwood bud. The flowers are also a lymphagogue and can help to move congested fluids out of the lymphatic system.

The root is best dug in the first two years of the plant's life while it is still a small rosette and before it sends up its towering stalk. It is a useful remedy for muscular spasm, particularly if the spasm is in the low back, and can be used as a remedy for incontinence.

Magically, mullein is a potent plant. It has associations with Jupiter, as seen in its size, but also to Mercury with its respiratory uses and to Saturn with the way its flowers grow. The plant is largely aligned to the element of fire and can be used as a representative of that power, particularly when the dried stalks are used to make taper candles. Dipping the dried flower stalk in tallow or some natural wax will create a kind of torch that can be used during rituals or to lead the ritual participants to the ritual space. These are called "hag tapers", but they are not the same as candles and have a fairly large flame; please use caution when burning them.

Mullein can be added to any incense for Hekate, or for those aligned to Jupiter, Saturn, or Mercury. The herb can also be added to smoking blends, especially those meant to align one's energy to the planets that rule mullein, to the element fire, or to Hekate and other chthonic deities. During hedge rides to the Underworld mullein is a particularly powerful herb to have on your person as a phylactery, in a poke, or to burn in an incense meant to protect you from the interference of spirits with less-than-savory intentions. Add both the leaf and the flower to such blends, as the flower is a symbol of the Astral Light, the permeating force that governs all magic, and the leaf is powerful aid for protection. I have also had success using mullein in place of dittany in operations that call for the rarer herb. Remember to use weeds and invasive species where possible to keep your practice local and sustainable.

Zingiber officinalis— Ginger is an herb strongly correlated with Mars and the element of fire. The flower of the plant looks like a red-hot spear growing out of pointed leaves and has all the truly Martian attributes, including spiciness and the ability to increase circulation and gut motility. It is a powerful addition to love spells, especially those that are meant to coerce and manipulate another person and will them into your bed. These spells tend to go awry, though, with codependency and angry obsession being a common result. Be cautious if you choose to use ginger in this manner and add something like Valerian root for balance, or, if things get out of hand, drown the charm in white vinegar to neutralize the spell. Using it to aid in the bedroom, however, is not so bad an idea and charms of ginger root can not only help with stamina and endurance, but with overall health. Ginger is also an herb often added to quick money spells, but the money that comes in is fast to go, so try stabilizing the spell by burying your charm, or adding in things like periwinkle to help you see things clearly and keep your head level.

TEN SOUTHWESTERN HERBS

Sphaeralcea spp.— Globemallow is one of my favorite plants and it grows everywhere in New Mexico. Considered a common weed, this plant is enormously useful. It has soft green, somewhat hirsute leaves with many orange, five-petaled flowers that produce a large amount of mucilage. As the name suggests, globemallow is related to marshmallow and is useful for the same things. The entire plant is helpful in cases of cough, painful stomach or bladder, urinary tract infection, and constipation, but is also used for skin issues and to hydrate skin and hair. It was the especially beloved plant of a famous curandera from Mexico and Texas, Doña Lupé, a healer of legendary skill. It is her relationship with this herb that gave it the name yerba de la negrita, "the herb of the little black one", because she claimed that using an infusion of copper globemallow as a rinse kept her hair black and shiny, even into advanced age.

Copper globemallow can be used in love and beauty spells, glamours, and charisma charms as well as spells meant to help balance and strengthen the energetic sexual centers. Weaving the stems together and wearing a bracelet or crown of the flowers will increase attractivity and charisma. An oxymel made with the leaves and flowers will help to alleviate the symptoms of love spells gone awry.

Ulmus pumila— One of the most reviled, yet most important, trees in the Southwest, Siberian elm is an analog for the endangered slippery elm. The seed pods, or samaras, are edible fresh or dried, and the inner bark produces a large amount of mucilage that can help with sore throats, constipation, diarrhea, and cough.

All trees are sacred, but elms hold a place of high regard. In Nordic mythology the first woman, Ulma, emerged from an elm and the wood of this tree can be used to help in manifestation work. It is also very helpful for dream magic and for making hedge tools, particularly those meant for protection, as the wood of the elm is a powerful apotropaic charm in and of itself. In England, the elm has historically been used to make coffins and has been valued by multiple cultures for making things like drums and wagon wheels, as the wood is resistant to splitting.

A touching story about an elm: New England's tallest elm, named Herbie, was 217 years old and 110 feet tall when it succumbed to Dutch elm disease and had to be felled in 2010. Its caretaker, Frank Knight, started caring for the tree in 1956 and did so every day for half his life. Two years after Herbie came down, Knight died at the age of 103 and was buried in a coffin made of Herbie's wood, which had been secretly commissioned by Knight's family.

Gutierrezia sarothrae— If you have ever stood on a mesa in the Western United States and looked out on a vast expanse of low-growing bunches of fragrant, yellow flowers you have seen snakeweed (also called snake broom, broom weed, escoba, and escoba de la vibora). It is unassuming and ubiquitous, but is a powerful ally. Just a small broom of the stems and flowers boiled in water and strained into a bath will help to ease muscle pain and soreness, arthritis, and overall achiness, and a tincture made from it will help with cough and sore throat, as well as upset stomach. It makes a great addition to herbal bitters, too.

Magically, use the flowers in suffumigations meant to cleanse energies and help with transitions, such as when moving or to cleanse the body of a loved one after death. As with many snake related herbs, this plant can be used in charms for luck and memory acuity.

Pinus edulus— Piñon pine is New Mexico's state tree and is one of the most recognizable of our native plants. It is the primary ingredient in one of the traditional remedies made here in the Southwest, trementina, which is a wonderful treatment for almost all skin disorders, drawing out splinters, and for healing cuts, burns, and bites. It also smells amazing! The fresh leaves can be chewed as a laxative, or applied as a spit poultice for wounds, and the fresh sap can be used as a sore throat aid. If you are looking to harvest more than a tiny amount of pinon sap, only take from fallen branches or from the ground, never from a living tree; the tree needs it more than you do.

Piñon sap is a magical analog for frankincense and can replace the latter in spells and ritual. It is useful in cleansings and for attracting beneficial spirits, depending on the intent of the user. Brooms made of piñon branches (again, already fallen) can be used to brush the body of a person to remove unnecessary or malicious energies. The cones, as with most conifers, are appropriate additions to fertility spells, sex magic, and altars for fertility festivals like the Vernal Equinox and Midsummer.

Fouquiera splendens— A strange looking plant, ocotillo is also called octopus cactus, though it isn't a cactus at all. It is actually a shrub that has branches that look like spiny tentacles erupting from the earth that are covered in leathery green leaves and tipped with red flowers in the Spring. The flowers of ocotillo evolved alongside hummingbirds and they are the perfect trumpet shape to fit their graceful beaks. Tinctures made from the phloem of the branches is a fantastic aid for circulation, particularly in the lower extremities, and can be used to treat conditions like benign prostatic hyperplasia, pelvic inflammatory disease, and restless leg syndrome. It is also used to treat dysmenorrhea and various types of congestion. It is a Martian and Mercurial plant and partakes strongly of elemental fire and water.

Wands and staves made from its wood are excellent for rustling up storms and calling on the winds. It is also a wood of mastery, helping to assert your will on reality and to compel spirits to come and go. Flower essence of ocotillo is helpful in facing grief and transforming it, to emerge whole and powerful from the "womb of pain" and to help move stagnant energies that cause physical pains and illness.

Atremsia tridentata— In Northern New Mexico this shrub lends its fragrance to the landscape, earning it the name Taos sage. It also goes by the moniker big sagebrush and Great Basin sagebrush. Boiling the leaves and breathing the steam thereof can help to ease congestion and headaches and to remediate coughs, and the subsequent infusion can be used as a wash for wounds, itchiness, achy muscles, or eczema. Caution must be used when taking the infusion or tincture internally, as the volatile oils found in big sagebrush can be hepatotoxic, though it has been used internally as a treatment for ulcers and colds.

One of our primary herbs for suffumigations, big sagebrush makes copious amounts of smoke with only a little bit of plant matter. It is best to find fallen branches, or plants that have been removed as part of trail maintenance, leaving the living plants alone. The smoke from the dried leaves helps to remove stagnant energy and remove unnecessary and unhealthy energetic connections, as well as helping the reluctant dead to move on. It can also be burned as an offering to beneficial spirits. It represents the moon seen in the middle of the day, the subconscious brought into manifestation through consciousness and intentionality, and is a great help in bringing dreams into reality.

Larrea tridentata— This Martian/Venusian is one of my favorite plants, chaparral, also called creosote and gobernadora. It is the plant that makes Southern New Mexico and the Sonoran Desert smell eternally like rain. The resins of this plant can be infused into an oil and used as a very effective sunscreen that smells of pop-gun smoke. It has been used for centuries to help with cold and flu, gas, cramping, and even shows some promise in the realm of cancer treatment, though, as with sagebrush, it ought to be used with caution due to potential hepatotoxicity. Externally it can be used to treat arthritis and inflammation, skin disorders, redness in the skin, and bug bites. It is also said to be an effective treatment for snake bites, but I've never put it to the test.

The fiery properties of this plant and its Martian affiliation make it a powerful protector, though think of it more as the fearsome mother who will kill to protect her children. Larrea is the matriarch of the llano, providing shade for animals in an environment with very little in the way of cool spots to rest, and is an appropriate offering for matriarchal, protector-type deities and spirits. It is a great smoke plant used in necromancy for contacting ancestors. Chaparral carried in a poke will provide some protection from misfortune and nasty surprises and helps to protect you from injustice, so carry it if ever you must go to court. If you are creating an incense for fierce support, something to use before public speaking engagements, performances, or just during hard times, chaparral is a great addition. It can also be used to help support and give strength during major transitions in your life, especially if you are losing a job, a house, or any other situation where a protective "mom hug" would make you feel better.

Juniperus spp.— Juniper is one of the most versatile plants I have ever worked with. It is good for skin disorders, aches and pains, respiratory and digestive illnesses, cold and flu, gas and bloating, restless leg syndrome, muscle spasm, and so much else! Tinctures and infusions are the most often used, but poultices and compresses are also effective. It can be used as a bitter tonic and is helpful when trying to work with stimulating the liver.

It is a Martian herb, but also has correlations to Jupiter and Mercury and, according to some authors, Saturn. It is a powerful aid in dispelling spirits, especially disincarnate entities, and helps in cases of shock caused by paranormal phenomena. Sometimes when people encounter spirits and magic, even experienced practitioners, they come away drained, depleted, sick, and dissociated from reality. Juniper smoke or an infusion of juniper berries used as a wash and then taken internally can help to alleviate those symptoms. The smoke from the dried leaves and twigs or from the resin is used to very efficiently clear and sanctify spaces for ritual work, though, as with most plants, preferentially choose to use fallen pieces and leave the tree alone. There is more than enough to go around on the ground.

Grindelia squarosa— Grindelia, called gumweed, snot-weed, and curly cup, is a very unique smelling plant found in wayside areas. It has citrus green foliage with tiny, curved teeth protruding from the receptacle of the aster-like, yellow flower. Before the flower fully blooms, the depression within the cup is filled with a sticky, white mucus that protects the delicate petals from insect predation, but is also what the wortcunner is after when gathering grindelia for medicine. It is at this stage that the plant is best gathered for its use as an expectorant and aid for relieving too much mucus in the digestive tract, for sore throats and help in healing a persistent, productive cough, and for fighting colds.

Magically the plant helps us to retain that which is ours, to help protect our assets, and also offers protection from meddling influences and those who would steal our energy. It can also be added to charms with cinquefoil leaf (five finger grass) to help attain goals and get what you want. It is a solar herb, as are many of the Asteraceae family, and has some Mercurial attributes.

Elaeagnus angustifolia— An invasive tree species, Russian olive can be a real nuisance, but also a great boon to those who know its properties. The bark, leaves, and flowers are all highly antimicrobial and can be used to help keep wounds clean or made into a water infusion for a countertop cleaner. I have friends here in Albuquerque who make an intoxicating perfume from the flowers, which have a heady, pungent fragrance that scents the Bosque (our riparian area) for a short time in the Summer.

The fruit that the tree produces is not the tastiest in the world, but the "olives" are full of phytonutrients and antioxidants and have been used to treat kidney diseases, and show promise as a future part of cancer treatments. An alcohol extraction of the fruit has also been shown as an effective anti-inflammatory agent and for decreasing pain and muscle soreness.

Russian olive has long, sharp thorns that can be used in poppet magic, especially for bindings, or that can be woven into a witch's ladder for protection or cursing someone. Boxes made of its wood are useful for hiding secret things or for storing items that need protection from the magic of others. The flowers, though their scent is fleeting, can be laid on the altar as an offering, particularly if you are asking the ancestors or other spirits for knowledge. A branch from the Russian olive makes an excellent besom and the long, slender branches can be used for spirit traps.

Bibliography

Bevir, Mark. "The West Turns Eastward: Madame Blavatsky and the Transformation of the Occult Tradition." Journal of the American Academy of Religion 62, no. 3 (Autumn, 1994): 747-767.

Beyerl, Paul. The Master Book of Herbalism. Ashland, OH: Phoenix Publishing Inc., 1984.
---. A Compendium of Herbal Magick. Ashland, OH: Phoenix Publishing Inc., 2008.

Blavatsky, Helena P. Isis Unveiled: A Master Key to the Mysteries of Ancient and Modern Science and Theology, Vol. 1 and 2. Pasadena: Theosophical University Press, 1988.
---. The Secret Doctrine: The Synthesis of Science, Religion, and Philosophy. Pasadena: The Theosophical University Press, 1999.
Boyer, Corinne. Under the Bramble Arch. Cornwall: Troy Books Publishing, 2019.

Cabot, Laurie and Tom Cowan. Power of the Witch: The Earth, the Moon, and the Magical Path to Enlightenment. New York: Bantam Doubleday Dell Publishing Group, Inc., 1990.

Case, Paul Foster. The Tarot: A Key to the Wisdom of the Ages. Richmond: Macoy Publishing Company, 1947.

Cavendish, Richard. The Black Arts. New York: G. P. Putnam's Sons, 1967.
---. The Tarot. London: Chancellor Press, 1988.

Collins, Derek. "The Trial of Theoris of Lemnos: A 4th Century Witch or Folk Healer?" Western Folklore 59, no. ¾ (2000) 251–278. JSTOR, http://www.jstor.org/stable/1500236 (accessed January 17, 2020).

Crowley, Aleister. 777 and Other Qabalistic Writings of Aleister Crowley Including Gematria and Sepher Sephiroth. Newburyport, MA: RedWheel/Weiser, LLC, 1986.

Cunningham, Scott. Magical Herbalism: The Secret Craft of the Wise. Woodbury, MN: Llewelyn Publications, 1986.

Davies, Owen. Grimoires: A History of Magic Books. Oxford: Oxford University Press, 2010.

Davis, Hubert J. The Silver Bullet and Other American Witch Stories. Middle Village, NY: Jonathan David Publishers, 1975.

De Ste. Croix, G. E. M. "Aspects of the 'Great' Persecution." The Harvard Theological Review 47, no. 2 (1954): 75–113. http://www.jstor.org/stable/1508458 (accessed January 17, 2020).

Dickerson, Cody. The Language of the Corpse: The Power of the Cadaver in Germanic and Icelandic Sorcery. Hercules, CA: Three Hands Press, 2016.

Drew, A. J. A Wiccan Formulary and Herbal. Newburyport, MA: New Page Books, 2005.

Eller, Cynthia. The Myth of Matriarchal Prehistory: Why An Invented Past Will Not Give Women a Future. Boston: Beacon Press, 2000.

Farrar, Janet and Stewart. A Witches' Bible: The Complete Witches' Handbook. Ashland, OH: Phoenix Publishing Inc., 1996.

Fenton-Smith, Paul. The Tarot Revealed: A Beginner's Guide. N.p.: Inspired Living, 2008.

Fortune, Dion. Sane Occultism. Newburyport, MA: Samuel Weiser Inc., 1977.
---. Psychic Self-Defense. Newburyport, MA: RedWheel/ Weiser, LLC, 2001.
---. Practical Occultism in Daily Life. N.p.: Ariel Press, 2011.
---. The Cosmic Doctrine. Newburyport, MA: RedWheel/ Weiser, LLC, 2000.
---. Applied Magic. Newburyport, MA: RedWheel/Weiser, LLC, 2000.

Gardback, Johannes Bjorn. Trolldom: Spells and Methods of the Norse Folk Magic Tradition. Forestville, CA: The Yronwode Institution for the Preservation and Popularization of Indigenous Ethnomagicology, 2015.

Gardner, Gerald B. The Meaning of Witchcraft. Newburyport, MA: RedWheel/Weiser, LLC, 2004.
---. Witchcraft Today. New York: Citadel Press, 2004

Garber, Allison. The Hedge Witch's Herbal Grimoire. Pittsburgh: Poison Apple Printshop and Native Apothecary, 2015.

Gary, Gemma. Traditional Witchcraft: A Cornish Book of Ways. Cornwall: Troy Books, 2015.
---. The Black Toad: West Country Witchcraft and Magic. Cornwall: Troy Books, 2011.
---. The Devil's Dozen: Thirteen Craft Rites of the Old One. Cornwall: Troy Books, 2015.

Green, James. The Herbal Medicine Maker's Handbook: A Home Manual. New York: Crossing Press, 2000.

Greene, Rosalyn. The Magic of Shapeshifting. Newburyport, MA: RedWheel/Weiser, LLC., 2000.

Haining, Peter. The Anatomy of Witchcraft. New York: Taplinger Publishing Co., 1972.

Hatsis, Thomas. The Witches' Ointment. Rochester, VT: Park Street Press, 2015.

Haller Jr., John S. Swedenborg, Mesmer, and the Mind/Body Connection: The Roots of Complementary Medicine. West Chester, PA: Swedenborg Foundation, 2010.

Hoffman, David. The Herbal Handbook: A User's Guide to Medical Herbalism. Rochester, VT: Healing Arts Press, 1988.

Horne, Roger J. Folk Witchcraft: A Guide to Lore, Land, and the Familiar Spirit for the Solitary Practitioner. N.p.:Moon Over the Mountain Press, 2019.

Howard, Michael. By Moonlight and Spirit Flight: The Praxis of the Otherworldly Journey to the Witches' Sabbath. Hercules, CA: Three Hands Press, 2019.
--- and Daniel A. Schulke (editors). The Luminous Stone: Lucifer in Western Esotericism. Hercules, CA: Three Hands

Press, 2016.

Huson, Paul. Mastering Witchcraft: A Practical Guide for Witches, Warlocks, and Covens. Bloomington: iUniverse, Inc., 2006.
---. The Devil's Picturebook: The Compleat Guide to Tarot Cards: Their Origin and Their Usage. Bloomington: iUniverse, Inc., 2003.

Hutcheson, Cory Thomas. 54 Devils: The Art and Folklore of Fortune-Telling with Playing Cards. Privately published, CreateSpace Independent Publishing Platform, 2013.

Hutton, Ronald. Triumph of the Moon. Oxford: Oxford University Press, 2019.

Jackson, Michele. Bones, Stones, and Curios: A Contemporary Method of Casting the Bones. Forestville, CA: Lucky Mojo Curio Co., 2014.

Jackson, Nigel Aldcroft. The Call of the Horned Piper. Somerset: Capall Bann Publishing, 1995.
---. Compleat Vampyre: Vampyre Shaman, Werewolves, Witchery, and the Dark Mythology of the Undead. Somerset: Capall Bann Publishing, 1997.

K, Amber. Covencraft: Witchcraft for Three or More. Llewelyn Publications, 1998.

Kaplan, Stuart R, Mary K. Greer, Elizabeth Foley O'Connor, and Melinda Boyd Parsons. Pamela Coleman Smith: The Untold Story. U. S. Games Systems Inc., 2018.
---. Tarot: Cards for Fun and Fortune Telling. U. S. Games Systems, 1997.

Kelden. The Crooked Path: An Introduction to Traditional

Witchcraft. Llewelyn Publications, 2020.

Kieckhefer, Richard. Magic in the Middle Ages. Cambridge University Press, 1995.

Kincaid, Douglas. Borax: The Jewel of Midnight. SABAX Publishing, 2017.

Lachman, Gary. Madame Blavatsky: The Mother of Modern Spirituality. Penguin Group, 2012.

Lavender, Susan, and Anna Franklin. Herb Craft: A Guide to the Shamanic and Ritual Use of Herbs. Capall Bann Publishing, 1996.

Leitch, Aaron. The Essential Enochian Grimoire: An Introduction to Angel Magick from Dr. John Dee to the Golden Dawn. Woodbury, MN: Llewelyn Publications, 2014.

Leland, Charles G. Aradia, or the Gospel of the Witches. Privately published, CreateSpace Independent Publishing Platform, 2014.

Levack, Brian P. The Witch-Hunt in Early Modern Europe. Abingdon, Oxon: Routledge, 2006.

Louv, Jason. John Dee and the Empire of Angels: Enochian Magick and the Occult Roots of the Modern World. Rochester, VT: Inner Traditions, 2018.

Maple, Eric. Superstition and the Supestitious. New York: A. S. Barnes, 1972.

Matthews, Caitlin. The Complete Lenormand Oracle Handbook: Reading the Language and Symbols of the Cards. Rochester, VT: Destiny Books, 2014.

Maurey, Eugene. Exorcism: How to Clear At a Distance a Spirit Possessed Person. Atglen, PA: Whitford Press, 1988.

Maxwell-Stuart, Peter. "Magic in the Ancient World". In The Oxford Illustrated History of Magic and Witchcraft, edited by Owen Davies. Oxford: Oxford University Press, 2017.

Moore, Michael. Medicinal Plants of the Mountain West. Santa Fe: Museum of New Mexico Press, 2003.

Morgan, Lee. A Deed Without a Name: Unearthing the Legacy of Traditional Witchcraft. N.p.: Moon Books, 2013.

Muller-Eberling, Claudia, Christian Ratsch, and Wolf-Dieter Storl. Witchcraft Medicine: Healing Arts, Shamanic Practices, and Forbidden Plants. Translated by Annabel Lee. Rochester, VT: Inner Traditions, 2003.

Murray, Margaret. The Witch Cult in Western Europe: A Study in Anthropology. Salt Lake City: Bravo Ebooks, 2009.

Nottingham, Gary St. M. Welsh Border Witchcraft: A Rendition of the Occult History of the Welsh March. London: Avalonia, 2018.

Oberon, Aaron. Southern Cunning: Folkloric Witchcraft in the American South. N.p.: Moon Books, 2019.

Orapello, Christopher and Tara-Love Maguire. Besom, Stang, and Sword: A Guide to Traditional Witchcraft, the Six-Fold Path, and the Hidden Landscape. Newburyport, MA: Weiser Books, 2018.

Ostling, Michael (editor). Fairies, Demons, and Nature Spirits: Small Gods at the Margins of Christendom. London: Palgrave Macmillan, 2018.

Ouspensky, P. D. The Fourth Way. New York: Vintage Books, 1971.

Page, Sophie. "Medieval Magic". In The Oxford Illustrated History of Magic and Witchcraft, edited by Owen Davies. Oxford: Oxford University Press, 2017.

Paul, Jim (translator). The Rune Poem: Wisdom's Fulfillment, Prophecy's Reach. San Francisco: Chronicle Books, 1996.

Paxson, Diana L. Taking Up the Runes: A Complete Guide to Using Runes in Spells, Rituals, Divination, and Magic. Newburyport, MA: RedWheel/Weiser, LLC., 2005.

Pearson, Nigel G. Wortcunning: A Folk Medicine Herbal. Cornwall: Troy Books Publishing, 2019.
---. Treading the Mill: Workings in Traditional Witchcraft. Cornwall: Troy Books, 2017.
---. Wortcunning: A Folk Magic Herbal. Cornwall: Troy Books Publishing, 2019.

Pendell, Dale. Pharmako/Poeia. Berkeley: North Atlantic Books, 2010.
---. Pharmako/Dynamis. Berkeley: North Atlantic Books, 2010.
---. Pharmako/Gnosis: Plant Teachers and the Poison Path. Berkeley: North Atlantic Books, 2010.

Pennick, Nigel. Magical Alphabets: The Secrets and Significance of Ancient Scripts Including Runes, Greek, Ogham, Hebrew, and Alchemical Alphabets. Newburyport, MA: RedWheel/ Weiser, LLC., 1992.

Popham, Sajah. Evolutionary Herbalism: Science, Spirituality, and Medicine from the Heart of Nature. Berkeley: North Atlantic Books, 2019.

Ravenwolf, Silver and Nigel Jackson. Rune Mysteries: Companion to the Witches Runes. Woodbury, MN: Llewelyn Publications, 1999.

Richmond, Nancy and Misty Murray Walkup. Appalachian Folklore, Omens, Signs, and Superstitions. Privately published, CreateSpace Independent Publishing Platform, 2011.

Sagan, Samuel. Entity Possession: Freeing the Energy Body of Negative Influences. Rochester, VT: Destiny Books, 1997.

Schulke, Daniel A. Veneficum: Magic Witchcraft, and the Poison Path. Hercules, CA: Three Hands Press, 2017.

Sharpe, James. "The Demonologists". In The Oxford Illustrated History of Magic and Witchcraft, edited by Owen Davies. Oxford: Oxford University Press, 2017.

Shirley, John. Gurdjieff: An Introduction to His Life and Ideas. New York: Jeremy P. Tarcher/Penguin, 2004.

Starhawk. The Spiral Dance: A Rebirth of the Religion of the Great Goddess. New York: HarperCollins Publishers, 1999.
---. Dreaming the Dark: Magic, Sex, and Politics. Boston: Beacon Press, 1982.
---. The Earth Path: Grounding Your Spirit in the Rhythms of Nature. New York: HarperCollins Publishers, 2005.
---. Truth or Dare: Encounters with Power, Authority, and Mystery. New York: Harper and Row Publishers, 1990.
---. The Twelve Wild Swans A Journey to the Realm of Magic, Healing, and Action. New York: HarperCollins Publishers, 2001.

---. Webs of Power: Notes from the Global Uprising. Gabriola, BC: New Society Publishers, 2003.

Storl, Wolf D. The Herbal Lore of Wise Women and Wortcunners: The Healing Power of Medicinal Plants. Berkeley: North Atlantic Books, 2012.

Thompson, C. J. S. The Mystic Mandrake. New Hyde Park, NY: University Books Inc., 1968.

Thorson, Edred. Runelore: A Handbook of Esoteric Runology. Newburyport, MA: Samuel Weiser Inc., 1987.
---. Runecaster's Handbook: The Well of Wyrd. Newburyport, MA: Samuel Weiser, Inc., 1999.
---. Northern Magic: Rune Mysteries and Shamanism. Woodbury, MN: Llewelyn Publications, 2005.
---. Futhark: A Handbook of Rune Magic. Newburyport, MA: RedWheel/Weiser, LLC., 1994.

Toyota, Koji. "On the 'Edict of Toleration' of the Emperor Gallienus." Journal of Classical Studies 28 (March 26, 1980): 88-98, doi: 10.20578/jclst.28.0_88.

Valiente, Doreen. An ABC of Witchcraft Past and Present. Phoenix Publishing Inc., 1973.
---. Natural Magic. Ramsbury, Wilts: Robert Hale/Crowood Press Ltd., 2018.
---. The Rebirth of Witchcraft. Ramsbury, Wilts: Robert Hale/Crowood Press Ltd., 2016.
---. Where Witchcraft Lives. London: The Doreen Valiente Foundation, 2014.
---. Witchcraft for Tomorrow. Ashland, OH: Phoenix Publishing Inc., 1978.
--- and Evan Jones. Witchcraft: A Tradition Renewed. Ashland, OH: Phoenix Publishing Inc., 1990.

Voltmer, Rita. "The Witch Trials". In The Oxford Illustrated History of Magic and Witchcraft, edited by Owen Davies. Oxford: Oxford University Press, 2017.

Wachter, Aidan. Six Ways: Approaches And Entries for Practical Magic. Albuquerque: Red Temple Press, 2018.

Webb, Don. Uncle Setnakt's Essential Guide to the Left Hand Path. Bastrop, TX: Lodestar, 1999.

Wilson, Colin. The War Against Sleep: The Philosophy of Gurdjieff. London: The Aquarian Press Limited, 1980.

Wood, Matthew. The Earthwise Herbal: A Compete Guide to Old World Medicinal Plants. Berkeley: North Atlantic Books, 2008.
Yronwode, Catherine. Hoodoo Herb and Root Magic: A Materia Magica of African-American Conjure and Traditional Formulary Giving the Spiritual Uses of Natural Herbs, Roots, Minerals, and Zoological Curios. Forestville, CA: The Lucky Mojo Curio Co., 2009.

Zell-Ravenheart, Oberon and Morning Glory. Creating Circles and Ceremonies: Rituals for All Seasons and Reasons. Newburyport, MA: New Page Books, 2006.

Index

A

Abel 51, 52
Adam 50, 51, 114, 250
Adonai 49, 51, 154
alchemist 21, 21–334
altar 25, 35, 36, 38, 39, 43, 54, 56, 58, 60, 65, 73, 74, 75, 104,
125, 136, 137, 140, 159, 186, 216, 303
amulet 113, 147, 213, 222, 239, 240
ancestors 9, 24, 26, 27, 35, 36, 39, 42, 64, 74, 75, 76, 110, 115,
116, 134, 135, 136, 137, 138, 139, 140, 148, 149, 159,
192, 221, 227, 233, 237, 301, 303
anchor 124
animism 37, 51, 65, 228, 246
apotropaic 221, 223
Aradia 49, 125, 312
Ark 52, 53
axis mundi 52, 56, 57
Az ze 81, 144, 171, 229

B

bale 41
banishment 36, 38, 39, 147
bell 35
beneficium 38, 56, 112, 191, 196, 212, 221
besom 36
bestowal 212
binding 142, 143, 144, 179, 199, 233
blasting rod 37, 147
Blavatsky, Helena Petrovna 269, 270, 271, 272, 307, 312
blessing 212, 214

CPSIA information can be obtained
at www.ICGtesting.com
Printed in the USA
JSHW020024240421
13919JS00006B/115